THE
WILL TO SURVIVE

To Neil and Ron, but for whom, the reader will realise,
this story would never have been completed.

THE
WILL TO SURVIVE

A PRIVATE'S VIEW AS A POW

DOUGLAS MCLAGGAN

Kangaroo Press

Cover design by Kerry Klinner.
Photos courtesy of the Australian War Memorial.
Photos by George Aspinall originally appeared in
Changi Photographer published by ABC Enterprises.

First published in 1995 by Kangaroo Press Pty Ltd
3 Whitehall Road Kenthurst NSW 2156 Australia
P.O. Box 6125 Dural Delivery Centre NSW 2158
Printed by Star Printery Pty Ltd, Erskineville 2043

ISBN 0 86417 706 2

CONTENTS

ACKNOWLEDGMENTS

To my daughters: Allwyn, for prompting me to start transcribing my diaries after fifty years. Her question of me was, 'What are the influencing factors in your life that in turn had their effect upon my life?'. And Merriss, for the correction of so many spelling mistakes and help with the first draft.

I thank Lew Crabtree for reading my original manuscript. He expressed an interest in the events and experiences related in my story beyond that of my immediate family. His suggestions for chapter headings have been adopted and are appreciated.

There is a dual appreciation for the assistance given by Kevin Rodgers. His chain of contacts led to the eventual publishers and in this regard I particularly thank Dr Hank Nelson of the Australian National University for his meticulous reading of the draft work. I also thank Kevin Rodgers for allowing me the office space for my computer, which enabled me to set up the transcription of my diaries. I am grateful to Bruce Thomson and particularly to Michael Hemsley for their valuable advice and assistance in the technical aspects of WORDSTAR 6 and so enabling me to format and edit the documentation during the preparation of the manuscript.

To René, Ceulen and his wife Marion, daughter of Pieter 't Hart, who was a Dutch mate in Changi, I record my appreciation for their encouragement and interest, which in turn led to the submitting of a Dutch translation to potential publishers in Holland.

I have made every effort to locate and gain permission from the copyright holder of every element used in this production. Any clearance neglected is due to my inability to locate the copyright holder and forgiveness is requested.

Douglas McLaggan
November 1994

In my diary I used imperial measurements, with a few exceptions. The following table of conversion gives their metric equivalents:

1 inch (in) = 2.5 cm
1 foot (12 in) = 30.5 cm
1 yard (3 feet) = 91.5 cm
1 mile = 1.6 km
1 ounce (oz) = 28.3 g
1 pound (lb; 16 oz) = 454 g
1 stone (14 lb) = 6.4 kg
1 hundredweight (112 lb) = 50.8 kg

FOREWORD

It is not easy to get to know Doug McLaggan. He is a modest self-effacing man who does not readily talk about himself. He is a very private person, though one with a twinkle in his eye and a ready laugh, who can quite easily disappear in a crowd. I have known him for some years and very gradually, from the confines of the consulting room, his remarkable story began to unfold. At first I did not realise the significance of his anecdotes and casual tales of events that happened so long ago and had been documented by historians elsewhere. The Second World War tragedies of the military campaign on the Malayan Peninsula, the fall of Singapore, the conditions of the prisoners at Changi and the Burma Railway construction will forever elicit the deepest emotional responses in all Australians. I do not think that the passage of years has in any way changed the feelings of the thousands of the cream of our young men who were betrayed, tortured and made to exist under conditions which sadly were to bring about slow and painful deaths.

This book is much more than an account of the conditions of the prisoners of war and the unspeakable cruelty of their captors. What became more and more obvious talking to Doug McLaggan was the fact that this man had kept a chronicle and diary of all his experiences. You will see how he had to improvise under the most appalling conditions, to keep his recording going, and I believe that this in itself contributed in some measure to his survival.

The real wonder of this story is the author's triumph. How did this well-disciplined, mild-mannered, and good natured family man, not particularly well-trained in military matters or survival come through to tell his tale and resume a successful life after enduring some of the worst conditions known to man anywhere? We have so often wondered what makes people survive when those next to them under the same conditions perish. Is it a biological quality or resilience or is it an acquired toughness? Perhaps it is a mental attitude that brings out a stoicism which was unknown before.

The Will To Survive is a modest man's tale of inhuman behaviour of cruel violent men inflicted on powerless prisoners in pathetic conditions. It is a story of triumph, of dignity, of decency—and for this Douglas McLaggan deserves our greatest respect.

HENRY W.FOGL, MB, BS
Local Medical Officer
Department of Veteran's Affairs
East Lindfield
November, 1994

1
Days of Innocence

I was born on the second of June 1921, nine months almost from the 19 September 1920, which was the date of my parents' first wedding anniversary. I was loved when I was conceived and I was loved when I was born: a dad happy with a new son and a mother's love as only a mother raised in an orphanage would love her newborn. From my birth certificate, Dad was 32 and born George Gould McLaggan in Edinburgh and Mum was 26, born Gwendolyn Grace Rawdon in Seaton, Devon. Neil came some three and a half years later.

Unremembered but influencial years as a small child included being carried by Dad on one of his shoulders while on the other he had a magic lantern, going off to Summer Camps of the WEA (The Workers' Education Association). My mother did not have much interest in politics but my father had a Fabian background, a respect for the Webbs (Beatrice and Sidney) and a belief in education and a social responsibility to the workers. Professor Portus of Sydney University, who, I believe I was told, baptised me, held tutorials organised by my father's circle of friends, particularly my uncle (I had a lot of honorary uncles and aunties) David Stewart, who founded the WEA. The book relating to these activities makes interesting reading.

Education and a strong work ethic were to remain with me always. There is no doubt as to the influence of my dad upon my general upbringing. He had wanted to be an educator from school but circumstances were such that he was apprenticed as a plasterer. So it was that in Sydney he excelled in the technical aspects of his trade. He did the ornamental work at the Sydney zoo: the icebergs in the seal pond, the elephant house and the decorative cement seats. He did the gargoyles and saints at St Barnabas church on Broadway and he did the pillars in the Commonwealth Bank in Martin Place, which have recently been restored. His work in cement was all over Sydney. He was a good man, good at his work and one who taught and expected others to be the same.

We were fortunate in that my father signed the pledge as a young man and remained a teetotaller all his life. His sport in those days in Scotland was Greco-wrestling, which has, for a long time, been included in the Olympic Games. In much later years going to the wrestling was a popular family outing.

The mosquitoes at North Strathfield were as big as space shuttles. Sleeping under a mosquito net on the open front verandah, with the smell of the mangrove mud flats from Homebush Bay, is among my earliest memories. We lived at 32 Consett Street, North Strathfield, an area of wide dirt roads, macadamised down the centre and I remember the beautiful feeling of squelching mud between our toes as we wore no shoes at play or going to school. I was hosed down rather than bathed at night. There is the earlier story that when going to Miss Chick's kindergarten at Concord West by myself in the bus at four years of age, I would loudly tell the bus conductor/driver that I was too young to pay. I was called a

walking gramophone by my auntie Bella and I ran, never walked, whenever we
were out. City traffic around Eddy Avenue was a lot quieter in those days or I
would never have survived running across the streets.

We kids played cricket and marbles, big ring and little ring. We played a
game too with a cricket stump and a six-sided piece of wood about five inches
long, pointed at each end. The idea was to hit the pointed end, raising it into the
air and then hit it as far as we could. Whoever it landed near took the number of
steps as marked on the piece of wood and threw it to hit the striker. If it did you
were out and the 'fielder' was next man in. Great stuff that kept us out of trouble
for hours.

When Neil was still little I remember a brown quilt on his cot. We slept in the
same room—for some years in the same bed—for the next fourteen and a half
years.

The grown-ups met with great regularity. There was a social environment
throughout my childhood. My mother met with my aunts during the day and the
fathers at billiards and cards on Thursday nights. I can still remember the giggles
one hot day when I got home from school: I walked in on my mother and her
friends with all their stays loosened and in various levels of dishabille, having
afternoon tea.

Later in the twenties, wireless sets came in and Jimmy Calder (one of the
clan) had a crystal set. He used to fiddle with a cat's whisker to get the programme
from the wireless station. I do not remember aeroplanes but Dad and uncle Jimmy
Murrell had a 1926 Chevrolet truck for their plastering business. This had replaced
the horse Flossie and sulky, although the stable and feed bins remained at the
bottom of the backyard. Last time I saw the house they were still there.

The truck took us on camping holidays in the summer and it was quite
something to have a vehicle that could get up Bulli Pass. It was more scary,
however, when the brakes caught fire going down the Pass. I was taught to swim
at Bulli and Woonoona and remember our tents—the Stewarts' (Ronnie, Lottie
and Betty) and the McLaggans'. In the wet the rains poured through our camp
and we were inches in mud. We collected blackberries in our billy cans and
played on the beach every day. Dad and his mates also went fishing at Tuross
and we got the usual fishing stories when he returned.

Another year Mum took Neil and me, with Auntie Hettie and Betty Colebrooke
to Kyogle to stay with another girl from the orphanage where she was raised in
London, Auntie Laura. It was the first time probably that I had seen a cow;
certainly the first time that I had milked one. It was good as a kid to be out in the
bush but it was a long, slow dirty train trip to Casino and an equally long return:
26 hours each way to Kyogle, only about 400 miles away.

Birthday parties were always happy events. In the morning a birthday call
came through on the wireless and the announcer would tell me to follow the
string to find a present. Later, Ronnie and other friends and schoolmates would
come and we would have dressing-up games.

Galli Curci and Caruso were big names on our wind-up gramophone, and a
boy soprano called Edwin Brough sang 'Hear my Prayer', which I insisted on
calling 'Little Boy Dying'.

Infections were rife and contagious. Impetigo was common and once my waterworks were blocked off with an infected tip to my penis, which had spread from infected hands. Styes—an infection of the eyelids—and boils on the neck were also painful. Neil and I were always told to keep clean but, being for the most part barefoot and grubby, we got everything that was going. I had worn glasses from the time I was three years old and I can still remember the pain of a particular ointment that was applied to my eyes. For what, I do not know.

Later in the thirties I had a 'Don Bradman' autographed cricket bat, his photo on the wall and, of all things, an aunt of his (Mrs.Robinson) lived in the same street, Consett Street. He was my and everybody's hero. Mum was a great cricket fan. One match I was taken to was at Coogee Oval and Jack Gregory, the demon fast bowler was playing. I remember that. Another time, too, we went to the Sydney Cricket Ground for a West Indies Test match when Learie Constantine was playing. These were legendary cricketers.

Sunday school was at North Strathfield Presbyterian Church. Acting in the Sunday school plays was a happy event and the excitement of winning a book prize had me hitting everyone over the head with it.

Talkies had started by the end of the 1920s and the earliest film I recall was *Trail of the '98* about the Yukon gold rush. More vividly do I remember *If I had a Talking Picture of You*, with Janet Gaynor and Charles Farrell. However the main excitement of going to the pictures on Saturday afternoon, apart from the serial, was when the big boys would let up a long blind, which kept the theatre dark. The irate manager made us little kids squeal and run.

Dad, Mum and particularly Ronnie's parents, Auntie Lottie and Uncle Jim, played tennis with their White Heather Club on courts at Croydon. We kids were always told to keep away from the canal but never did.

I don't know that I was a particularly naughty boy. I do remember yelling and howling 'Not on the legs' when my mother took Dad's razor strop to me for something bad. Only when I climbed up on the roof, jumped and broke some of the tiles did I really get belted—not so much for breaking the tiles as for saying that I did not do it. Eventually I owned up and had learnt a lesson.

They were good days at school, where I was not that bright but was able to pass my tests. There was more excitement in the playground, especially when it was announced that some money had been found. We would all call out that we had lost either a 1927 penny, a 1925 threepence or even a 1928 sixpence. The lucky kid who guessed the right date got the coin, and he was truly lucky, as none of us ever had any money. A penny bought a paper cone of broken biscuits. I did get a shilling from my mother one year and bought her a plate for Mother's Day. A shilling or a two shilling piece received from an uncle on a birthday was really big time—and to get a threepenny bit in the Christmas pudding was a big thrill. Dad or Mum would cut up the Christmas pudding, add lots of custard and, miracle of miracles, we kids would bite into a threepenny bit. It bought a big ice-cream cone. Others would get the wish bone, a thimble or other silver trinkets from the pudding.

Empire Day was a big day for us too. There would be special assemblies at school with flag raising and oaths to the king:

I honour my God,
I serve my King,
I salute my Flag.

Great play was made of the red areas on the world atlas, signifying the extent of the British Empire. We learnt the first verse of 'Advance Australia Fair' and would sing lustily:

Australia's sons let us rejoice,
For we are young and free...

There would be fireworks at night, cracker night, when bungers were real bungers and we blew up cans and pots and the odd letter box. There were sparklers and roman candles for the little ones, as well as Catherine wheels on the clothes post. Bonfires were more on Guy Fawkes Night in November when we had fireworks too, but Empire Night was the big cracker night.

We were growing up and Marjorie Murrell was older than Neil and me. She had us playing 'cows' in the dark of the front room at Short Street on one of the regular visiting nights to the Murrells. The game was really an excuse for her to have her fingers up the legs of our pants. When I could not find anything to pull she told me to pretend. Neil and I were still kids and it did not mean anything to us.

When the Depression came in 1929 the housing business came to a halt. Men were calling at the door for hand-outs and I remember my mother one day cutting sandwiches, putting them in a bag with some fruit and giving them to a man at the door. We saw him throw away the sandwiches and keep the fruit. I do not remember any more hand-outs after that as my mother was so upset. As far as I was concerned nothing plus nothing equals nothing. From a Calvanistic father and a provident mother I did not know luxury or extravagance—if it was taken away from me I did not know the difference. Neil and I were cared for, provided for and did not know want. In the Depression, that was known as 'well to do'. However we were certainly affected by what went on around us.

The twenties are now known as 'the jazz age', but I did not know anything of jazz or that the age was anything special. I do know that it was a period without worry among my parents' circle of friends. We were a group, of Scottish origins, bound together by the mutuality of race: the Stewarts, the Murrells, the Irvines, the Calders, the Macphersons, the Williamsons and the McLaggans. All came from Scotland around 1910 as young immigrants to Australia for a new life, a new opportunity and a new hope. As a nineteen year old girl my mother came from London, knowing nothing of what was before her. They all formed friendships and families and despite the bonds of their origins, became true Australians. We were bound together throughout the twenties, parents and children, in mutual affection and regard. It was a social era, friendships were binding and relationships were trusting. As a nine year-old I recall it as a happy time. I knew nothing of the First World War or its effects, as for some reason or other, our set had not been involved.

2
To Scotland and Back

In April 1931 a chapter closed and another one opened. House and furniture at North Strathfield were sold, two enormous chests were packed and the family sailed on the *Orford*. Neil was six years old and I was nine. We played on deck and enjoyed the six-week trip: Fremantle, Colombo where ebony elephants were bought and a trip to Mt. Lavinia, Aden and Suez through the canal, Malta, Naples, Toulon, Gibraltar finally to Southampton. Throughout the voyage Dad organised school lessons, five days a week, for Neil and me and a number of other children. Best of all and best remembered were the special kids' teas, an hour or so before the grown-ups when we had ice cream, fruit and cake.

And so to London and Ponders End, which then was on the northern rim of London toward Epping Forest. This was home to my mother's sister, we were told and to our two cousins, Diana and Bobby Rupp. Diana and I wrote notes to each other based on an advertising hoarding at the time for a brand of wine, Ruby Tawny White. I would write to her 'Ruby tawny white . . . I love you quite' and she would write back 'Ruby tawny pink . . . I love you I think'. Real romantic stuff. Bobby thought that we were just colonials.

We had trips to Epping Forest and swims at Edmonton baths but to us a ride on an open two-decker bus was really something. We went to the zoo and the Tower of London and were well looked after.

On the two day charabanc ride north we called at Stratford-on-Avon for the required visit to Anne Hathaway's cottage and then Chester and the Lake country. I was told at Gretna Green that I would see sheep with black faces in Scotland. This I thought rather silly, as they were teasing me unmercifully on the coach. Imagine my surprise to actually see black-faced sheep. And so on we went through we the border country to Edinburgh.

Dad's father had arranged for him to come home and work in his butcher's shop as long as he wanted to. So we were not actually affected by the Depression too harshly. It was different, though. For the next few years at school I was the only Australian, with a funny accent, pronouncing Kirkudbright, a Scottish town, just as it is spelt, amid much laughter in the class. The Scots pronounce it 'Kirkoobrie'.

After a few weeks we moved into a semi-detached two-storey steel house at the new suburb of Wardie, near Granton on the Firth of Forth. It had gas light and it was quite a tricky job to change the gas mantles when they became broken or burnt out. With new school uniforms we started at a new primary school. On the strength of my Don Bradman bat I went straight into the cricket team, although I missed out on being the captain.

They were good years in Scotland: adolescent years. We had school, scouts, trips to Bannockburn and Stirling Castle, to Scott country at Jedburgh, Melrose and Hawick and holidays at St. Andrews. At Easter we rolled our coloured Easter eggs down Carlton Hill, which is the custom and we developed a Scottish accent. They were growing-up years. I remember I broke a neighbour's window once playing cricket in the street. However we were taught responsibility too and I do not know that Neil and I got away with very much.

One day we were playing with our billycarts in the street and one of the boys said to a girl that she had no knickers on. It was not any lack of modesty or morality on her part—it was just that we were in the middle of the Depression and she probably did not own another clean pair. There was certainly no modesty at Broughton when the boys used to come out of school and pee up against the wall and the girls at the kerb.

My grandmother was very influential at this stage:

FEAR GOD AND HONOUR THE KING
TRUTH AND HONESTY ALWAYS

This was drilled into us, repeatedly. I earned my first pocket money doing my Grandmother's shopping on a Saturday morning, receiving twopence for my efforts. Actually I was pretty popular with my new aunts and uncles, being enterprising, voluble and snowy-haired. They were in Pilrig and nearby lived Jessie Scott, of my age, with whom I formed a friendship. Auntie Euphemia (Effie), Auntie Chrissie, Uncle Alex, Uncle Jimmie and, in Glasgow, Uncle Mitchell, with cousins Gertie and Davie, made up our immediate kin. There were cousins on the Ormiston side, being my grandmother's family.

Mum coped with a new environment and relatives, although it later transpired that she was not all that happy in Scotland. I never heard her complain at any time, though, and it was a happy childhood/adolescence. The Depression was still with us and there was never money for extravagance, but enough to maintain a family well. Dad took me to a Hearts football game, Neil and I sailed our boats on Inverleith Pond and we spent our pennies at the seaside fun fairs. We stole pumpkins from the fields for Halloween, dressing up in white sheets and with our hollowed out pumpkins and candles, going around the houses saying 'trick or treat' for halfpennies or even farthings. And I had my first bicycle. Unfortunately, the frame got broken at school.

From Wardie I went to Broughton Higher Grades Secondary School and was just above average, as I remember. I was thought to be tall for my age but never grew from the age of thirteen. It was a good school but very old. The classrooms and playground space were of a poor standard but we did get hot midday dinners, which I thought tasted beautiful. Geography, not surprisingly, was my favourite subject.

Dad was the breadwinner and Mum provided the loving care and discipline. Neil and I got plenty of both—except for one memorable occasion.

I was always the one to change the library books, my own and Mum's and Dad's. It cost a penny to replace a lost card and I had lost mine. My mother told me to rejoin, which was free. When I signed my name on a new form the librarian said that as the signature was the same as that on file I would have to pay a penny because I was already a member. I lied and said that I had not joined before and that the Douglas McLaggan was not me. The librarian knew that I was not telling the truth and after a great deal of humiliation I owned up. I was twelve years old and I have not consciously told a lie since then. It was one of the major lessons of my life.

Living in Scotland was good experience. Travel was not the norm in those days. Few in Scotland travelled far from home and even the 50-mile train trip from Edinburgh to Glasgow was a big event. I never got to see Loch Lomond, although Mum and Dad took Auntie Louie there when she came up from Ponders End to stay with us. But I wore my kilt and sporran to Scout meetings. It was at one such meeting that I practically tore my left middle finger off. Great was the consternation and amount of blood when I was taken home and off to the Infirmary for stitches. I liked the Scouts at Canon Mills, where I learnt boxing as well as all the usual scouting activities. I played outside right in the football team and now, every time that I hear 'Abide with Me' I think of the closing of Scout meetings at Inverleith when we sang the hymn before going home.

They were hard years, generally with people selling radios and vacuum cleaners door to door and my grandmother telling me I could have butter or jam on my bread but not both. Waste was a sin and the Scots were even more than traditionally frugal. However there were enjoyable outings: we were taken to see Harry Lauder, the Christmas pantomimes and, at the sea-side in summer, the pierrots and pierrettes.

I thought that I was a pretty good swimmer but came nowhere swimming for my house at the school swimming carnival. The indoor heated pool had a distinctive smell of chlorine and steam and if I remember rightly there was no mixed bathing. At Broughton School there were boys and girls in the same class although separated in the playground. Swimming at the beach in summer was not popular and the first time I ever went into the sea at North Berwick on the Firth of Forth I nearly froze. At Granton too with its stony beach, the water was always cold.

In winter for the four Christmases that we were there, the whole family came down with colds and flu and we had a nurse in to care for us. Actually, although we had icy slides on the street and lots of snow, the winters were mild. They were best remembered for the sleet and bitter winds, which were pretty miserable. We felt the cold and were chilled to the bone. The steel houses at Wardie were difficult to heat and one morning our goldfish was dead with the water in his bowl frozen over.

Scotland in the thirties was an insular country and proud of its traditions, which were still very much in evidence. History lessons at school were heavy on Robert the Bruce and Bonnie Prince Charlie and emphasised the battles against England when Scotland won. It was felt that England was still the enemy and on St. Patrick's Day there were fights in Glasgow between the Scots and Irish kids. It was always a poor country and in the Depression, even more so. Great play was made of Scottish thrift and meanness and, although joked about a great deal it was to a large extent true. But so also was Scottish generosity, I found.

The long twilights in the summer were welcome. Mum and Dad played tennis at 9 p.m. and it was still light when Neil and I went to bed. With two hours daylight saving in the summer, evenings were a time of play and recreation, although it meant that Dad had long hours of travel in the dark early in the morning when he went to the meat markets to buy for the shop in the Kirkgate. This was a very old street in Leith. There has been some redevelopment of the area but the South Leith Presbyterian Church, of which my Grandfather was an Elder, is still there.

Events in Europe were unfolding the course of future history. The Germans moved into the Saar and Nazi Brownshirts were demonstrating racial hatred in the streets. Support for the Fascist, Sir Oswald Mosely, brought this closer to home when he talked at the Usher Hall in Edinburgh. It was strange but there was something spellbinding about Hitler's voice. I did not understand a word of German but I remember hearing him on the wireless: if he had said 'jump' I would have jumped. His power and influence over the German people, particularly the youth, did not surprise me. We were certainly aware then of what was going on in the way of war, appeasement and impending confrontation.

Still my dad had a job and in the depression that was something. We kids did our homework and played in the streets. We played with old tyres, cricket against the lamp post and kicked a ball around. Outings were rare and pleasures simple. We walked the Golden Mile of High Street and visited both Edinburgh Castle to watch the 1 o'clock gun go off and Holyrood Palace to see the bloodstains still on the floor where the lover of Mary, Queen of Scots, Rizzio, was murdered. I have read that the Ormistons were involved in some way or another.

We had our birthday parties and full stockings at Christmas. At night, Neil and I, still in the same bed, used to make up stories to tell each other before going off to sleep. Henry Hall and the BBC Dance Orchestra were big in the wireless and in 1934 the hit of the day was 'The Music Goes Round and Around'. We listened to *In Town Tonight* on Saturday evenings and its theme music, the 'Knightsbridge March'.

Neil and I had to go to the Presbyterian Sunday School at Greenacre every Sunday. For a short while, when we were given a penny to put in the plate, I would spend a halfpenny on sweets and give a halfpenny to the church, however, it was not long before I was found out. Mum and Dad were not regular churchgoers but we had to go.

One summer the Australian cricket team came up to Scotland and we saw Don Bradman play. I still had my Don Bradman bat and was happy to see Australia win. At other times Dad and Mum would listen to the cricket descriptions on the wireless. In fact the wireless was the only constant form of home entertainment. I do not remember a picture theatre in Edinburgh although we must have gone sometimes as we did see *Roman Scandals* with Eddie Cantor. We all read a lot and I had my introduction to romantic novels. My favourites were *Blackcock's Feather* by Maurice Walsh and *Simon Coldheart* by Baroness Orczy. I do not remember the story but I liked all the sloppy bits. *Ivanhoe* and *Heart of Midlothian*, and all Scott's Waverley novels were compulsory and enjoyable reading, as was *Eric* or *Little by Little* by Frederic W. Farrar. This was the story of a schoolboy, who had a glass of wine after dinner and from then went, little by little, down the primrose path. Dad liked Edgar Wallace and Zane Grey and I still have the *Book of a Thousand Thrills*, which has been read often.

It was an uncomplicated life. We were fed, clothed and cared for, but Mum and Dad could not have been too happy. At North Strathfield they had talked everlastingly of 'Home'. England and Scotland were always referred to as 'Home' and among their circle of friends it came into conversation every day. Yet when in Scotland they talked about wanting to get back to Australia. In 1935 I did not want to go back to Australia at all as I was down for a school excursion to Paris—and that was something in those days.

It was a great credit to my father, who was hardworking and a man without frills, that he not only maintained a family throughout the Depression but saved enough to return to Australia, buy land and build a house and again set up a home and his business. There was last-minute packing to do and Neil and I were sorry that Dad broke Neil's boat when it would not fit in one of the cases. He was not always good. So in May 1935 we travelled on the Flying Scotsman to London.

Back we were at Auntie Louie's, this time at West Harrow. Bobbie, who was at Harrow School, had not changed and I still had a crush on Diana. As 1935 was Jubilee Year we were there to see the procession and all the pageantry, waiting for hours by the fountain in front of Buckingham Palace to see the King and Queen. It was a special treat to be taken to the theatre to see John Galsworthy's *The Skin Game*. It was the first play I had seen and left a lasting impression and a love of the theatre.

I was less popular with Uncle Bob, who was Swiss and worked in a Swiss bank in London, because I buckled the front wheel of his bicycle. I would cycle with Diana around Harrow on the Hill and on this occasion the bike got away when coming down a steep part of the road and I went into a hedge. At thirteen years of age it was an ordeal to me to own up to what I had done, but I did do so with much humiliation.

We went to the zoo, to the Tower of London and the Beefeaters, to Hampton Court and the maze and we saw the Changing of the Guard at Buckingham Palace. Jubilee Year was laid on for tourists and we enjoyed it.

And so aboard the *Hobson's Bay* at Tilbury in May 1935, bound for Australia; six weeks of deck tennis, fun, games, fancy dress and the inevitable homework and lessons. Again the Barbary apes were on the Rock of Gibraltar and the sights and smells of the Suez Canal were unchanged. The *Hobson's Bay* was a one-class vessel and, with the run of the ship, Neil and I had a good time at sea. The weeks went too quickly. We came into Sydney Heads at dawn, a sight which was as impressive then as it has always been.

In Sydney it was not long before things were back to normal. Mum and Dad chose land at Croydon, not far from Bella and Jimmie Murrell. However the partnership of Murrell and McLaggan was not resumed, some differences having occurred while we were away.

We lived first in a large subdivided house in Lucas Road, Burwood. Neil went to Croydon Primary School and I went to Summer Hill. All of us were immediately absorbed back into the circle of friends, who had then been together since about 1913. The only loss was Marjorie Murrell, who had died of pleurisy when only about fourteen years of age.

We kids picked up where we had left off: Ronnie, Lottie and Betty Stewart, Betty Colebrooke, Jimmie Calder, Neil and I. At school I was again somewhat different, this time being the only one with a Scottish accent. Ronnie was my closest friend and I remember us shooting pigeons on the roof and making feathers fly with our air guns at Lucas Road.

Dad resumed subcontracting work for Stan Grimson, who had been a builder friend for many years at North Strathfield. Land was bought at the corner of Wychbury and Alexandra Avenues in Croydon and Stan Grimson built their house, 'Ormiston'. A garage was also built but Dad had not driven since the truck got away from him at the Ryde punt on the Parramatta River back in the late twenties. Mum never had a driving licence. Although a two-bedroom house, it had an enclosed back verandah and Neil and I had separate rooms for the first time in our lives.

At Summer Hill I was able to resume in second year of high school and in fact some of the textbooks were the same as at Broughton. This was fortunate as otherwise I would have dropped a year. It was not long before the whole school, together with Petersham Boys, was moved to a new school at Homebush, we being the first class in 1936. I played tennis in one of the lower grades for Homebush but Dinny Pails at Drummoyne was schoolboy champion. He later went on to join the international professional ranks.

It was a good school and 50 years later we met at a school reunion. I was still remembered for my accent. Neil went on to Sydney Technical High School, as Ronnie had done but my schooldays finished in 1936 at fifteen years of age with the Intermediate Certificate. I passed all subjects except English, of all things.

Dad had me attend a vocational guidance session at Sydney Technical College. It was apparent that I had no technical aptitude whatsoever, so it was office work for me. Recovery from the Depression was slow but Uncle Peter Calder, who was with Lever Bros, got me an interview with Edible Oil Industries Pty Ltd. I started in my first job, in Kent Street, as an office boy in February 1937.

At EOI, a subsidiary of Lever Bros, I kept the stamp book, pushed and pulled the big ledger trolleys in and out of the strongroom and did the messages. And brought home my first pay envelope.

What I really wanted to do was to go into a chartered accountant's office. After three months at EOI and with Mum's and Dad's encouragement, I started looking around and in May 1937 I had a choice between a sole practitioner at Leichhardt and a practice in the city. I started with W.H.L.Walter and Co. in Martin Place, which was the centre of the banking and professional offices of Sydney, and so opened up a new and lasting career. Lawford Richardson was the principal. Instead of being articled and Dad having to pay a premium, Alan Hayes and I started at the same time and were paid 10 shillings per week. This provided for 4 shillings for my railway ticket, 4 shillings for board and 2 shillings for pocket money.

I was happy to be a chartered accountant in the making but it did tend to make me pretty conceited at times and something of an intellectual snob.

The degree equivalent examinations for qualification as an ACA were set by the Institute of Chartered Accountants in Australia and my studies commenced forthwith. Dad enrolled me for study with the Hemingway and Robertson Institute in a correspondence course. Every week progress papers had to be submitted for marking and I studied for my first examination, which was Bookkeeping and

Accounts. And so it was to continue through accounting and commercial law.

'A contract is an agreement enforceable at law made between two or more parties for consideration by which rights are acquired by one party for acts or forbearances on the part of the other or others.' This has been indelibly imprinted in my mind ever since.

It was a proud day when Arthur Worsley took me to The Pen Shop to buy my first Conway Stewart fountain pen and fill it with green ink. So started a wide ranging experience in industry and commerce. Audit jobs included: Workers Cash Order & Finance Company; H.H. Halls, York St wholesalers; O.T. Ltd, makers and bottlers of cordials; and Nu-Mestic Laundry at Rushcutters Bay. At H.H.Halls we would break off at 11 a.m. for coffee and dominoes at Mockbells cafe, such was the easy pace and tradition. Best of all though was to go up to Newcastle for a week on the WCO&F job. Three or four of us would leave at midnight on the steamer from Darling Harbour and go up by boat, either the *Gwyder* or the *Hunter,* arriving at 6 a.m. Prior to disembarking we would have a real sailor's breakfast of salted cod cutlets and mugs of tea. At first we stayed at the Great Northern Hotel but later at the new Esplanade Hotel, on the beach, which we thought was wonderful. Ice-cream sundaes at the Niagara Cafe in Hunter Street were a must, every visit, and once we went to see George Wallace in real old time vaudeville at its best. We boys all lied like hell when we got back as to how well we had done with the comptometer girl, who came with us to Newcastle.

On Saturday mornings we worked, it being a 44 hour 5½ day week. On Saturday afternoons in the summer four of us would go from the office to Bondi Beach for surfing and diving in the blowhole. It was a friendly office in the old E.S.A. building on the corner of Martin Place and Pitt Street, now the ANZ bank. After an expansion of the business and the admission of John Broinowski as a partner, we moved to the Prudential Building at 32 Martin Place, up the road.

Standards were high. In fact Lawford Richardson and John Broinowski were exacting bosses: it had to be right; it had to be neat and tidy; it had to be on time. The girls would set out and type the annual accounts and it would be our job to rule them up, using a mapping pen and red ink. Heaven help you if you smudged a line, not from the managers but from the girls if they had to do a balance sheet again, especially Peggy Cameron. If papers had to be submitted, the top left-hand corner had to be in exact alignment and green ticks under each other had to be straight and of the same size. We were taught the doctrine of materiality but it did not apply to us as we would spend hours, days even, to find a shilling in a bank reconciliation or trial balance. It did us no harm. I liked auditing and discovered my first defalcation at Haslam's, which was a menswear store in Regent St. Redfern.

I would study four nights a week and Sundays for four years from mid 1937 and really only came unstuck in the law subjects. These were difficult. Pass marks were high at 65% for law and 70% for accounting papers. We were sure that the examiners took sadistic delight in making the exams harder every year just to limit admission to the Institute.

Some Saturday afternoons I would spend in the NSW Public Library, which was then at the corner of Bent and Macquarie Street reading Plato and Aristotle, even Nietzche and Descartes. Maybe I had a philosophical nature; I would not know but I was a prolific reader. Saturday Evening Posts were a special favourite.

Friday nights were Ron's and my jazz nights. Ronnie was studying and doing his engineering exams but Friday nights were our night off. I would walk the mile or so from Croydon to Ashfield and we sat in Ron's room playing records and sharpening gramophone needles. We started buying jazz records in 1937 when Betty Colebrooke worked in the record department at Elvy's. The very first record I bought from her was Joe Daniel's 'Drummer Goes to Town' but it was not long before Ron and I were into Duke Ellington, Benny Goodman (Bugle Call Rag), Tommy Dorsey, Muggsy Spanier, Artie Shaw, Lionel Hampton, Louis Armstrong, the Boswell Sisters (Connie's 'I Let a Song Go out of my Heart'), Bob Crosby, Glen Miller, Jimmie Lunceford and Benny Carter; in fact an evergrowing collection of 78s, with jazz from about 1925 through to the swing era.

I had been a fan of Henry Hall and the BBC Dance Orchestra in Scotland and although the music of the British bands of Jack Hilton and Nat Gonella was not that of Fletcher Henderson and Ziggy Ellman, they did have 4/4 time and syncopation in common. By 1938 Ron and I were fans of the jazz emanating from New York, Chicago, New Orleans and Kansas City. We would play our records, especially ones recently bought, just the two of us, and listen also to a 2YA jazz program on the radio from New Zealand. We would have supper and then I would walk home. They were enjoyable and memorable nights, in abiding friendship. I cannot remember to what extent we disturbed the rest of the Stewart household, but when I played my records at home my father would say what a terrible racket it all was, it was not music and that he could not distinguish one tune from another when I changed records. He always said that this jazz stuff would not last.

It was during this period, in the late thirties, when I was earning little and certainly not my keep, that Dad had a time without work. Neil was still at school and rather than put me into a better paying job, Mum went to work as a canteen assistant at Dri Glo Towels. It was the first time that my mother had worked outside the home since 1919 but her earnings kept us going during a short recession. I know that Dad was glad for her enterprise at the time and I have remained tremendously grateful ever since for the sacrifices she made to keep me in the chartered accountant's office.

Two events made 1939 memorable. One was an exceptionally hot Saturday when, from the office, we went to Bondi Beach. It was the hottest day that I have ever known. Sydney was on fire. It was so hot that we could not walk on the sand or anywhere in bare feet. The temperature reached 114.6° Fahrenheit that day. The other was a Friday night. Ron and I were listening to our jazz program on the radio when it was interrupted by the news reader telling us that Germany had marched into Poland. Neville Chamberlain had issued on ultimatum that, unless they withdrew in three days, England would be at war. I can hear his voice still. I was eighteen and Ron was nineteen years of age. We knew that it would affect us sooner or later. We were both studying for our exams at the time and these were our top priority. But it was grim news as the armies of Nazi Germany, to that date, had a track record of being practically unstoppable—Saar, Czechoslovakia, Austria. It was on the following Sunday that Robert Menzies announced that England was at war with Germany, and Australia was too.

There were other things happening closer to home in the thirties. Big Chief Little Wolf was the villain and Sammy Stein the hero at the wrestling at Leichhardt Stadium. Don Bradman and Stan McCabe drew thousands to the cricket, especially against the Poms. Kingsford Smith and Ulm had made record flights and were living legends in aviation.

Visiting friends around Sydney was a full day's journey without a car. Florrie Cummins, who had been Mum's bridesmaid, lived at Blakehurst in an area of new houses among market gardens. We must have had to get a bus to the city and another to Blakehurst. I know that it was a long way to go and return but Neil and I enjoyed playing around the rocks in Carrs Park. There was another day when Mum took us by bus and tram to Mascot to visit Tom Barber, who was the Town Clerk of Mascot. He was also the son-in-law of a good neighbour at North Strathfield. Doug and Bobbie Barber, Neil and I walked to the aerodrome and were happy to just see aeroplanes taking off and landing. In those days I did not know anyone who had actually flown. It was exciting for everyone that new air routes were being opened up and new speed records being set. Neil and Ron modelled aeroplanes in balsa wood and Jessie Scott sent us magazines from Birmingham, where she had moved from Edinburgh. In the thirties we saw history being made in the air in commercial aviation and air races all over and around the world. On the wireless Neil and I used to listen to *The Air Adventures of Jimmy Allen.*

My mother sent me to the shops down on Parramatta Road one day to buy pads. I came home with four writing pads. Without sisters, I knew little about girls and certainly nothing at all about their internal anatomy.

Hollywood was the established centre of the movie world and weekly attendances were common at the movies. Live small theatre was also around. I went to a whole series of George Bernard Shaw plays at Bryant's Playhouse including *Man and Superman* and *St Joan*. This little theatre in Forbes Street, off William Street, only seated about 80 people on hard wooden benches. I read most of Shaw's plays and prefaces at the time.

In Rowe Street at the Blue Tea Rooms, the Sydney Swing Club held its regular meetings. Ron and I would go along there with Bill Freeman, who was to marry Betty Colebrooke, Ron Wills, a seaman later to be with EMI and his brother Merv. Sessions would be held playing records devoted to some particular aspect of jazz and then it was open forum and discussion, followed by more records. They were great nights. Bill Freeman had a wonderful collection of Duke Ellington and one of my favourite records—Red Norvo's 'I Surrender Dear'.

Borovansky had come to Sydney with the Ballet Russe. He stayed and I got to like the ballet. Later the Ballet Rambert toured and I saw them too. At the time Dorothy Stevenson was a popular ballerina and I particularly remember a performance of Scheherazade with a strong young male dancer by the name of Rubenstein. On the popular musical theatre stage Gladys Moncrief was 'Our Glad'. The Theatre Royal was upmarket and the Tivoli down.

The thirties were still a low tech period. The ice man delivered ice, the milkman delivered milk, the baker delivered bread and the greengrocer delivered fruit and vegetables—some with a horse and cart and some with a truck. The rabbitoh was still around selling rabbits and the clothes prop man, known to me as a child, roamed the street with his special call. Home appliances were mainly the Hoover vacuum cleaner and then, gradually introduced, the electric stove, the refrigerator and hot water systems. I did not know of anyone with a washing machine. The wireless continued to be the main entertainment unit in the home. Long nights were spent listening to the description of the Test matches when they were played in England and Don Bradman was batting.

Australia was still virtually a British colony. At this stage I do not think that I had ever seen an Aborigine. The population would have been 95% British and their descendants. The White Australia Policy was in force and unwanted migrants were given a dictation test—possibly in Lithuanian—which they would fail and be refused admittance. The Chinese who remained after the gold rush persecution were centred around the Haymarket area of Sydney. When the western suburbs buses to the city were diverted away from Central Railway over Pyrmont Bridge there was little, except the Capitol Theatre, to take us to that end of town. The Darling Harbour area was infested with rats and two years before I was born Australia, and the rest of the world, was devastated by an influenza epidemic. Sussex Street was still not too clean when I went there on audits to Kerridge & McMahon, produce merchants, in 1938 and 1939. In 1939 I passed my Intermediate Book keeping and Accounts examinations.

Neil and I used to go bushwalking. We would take our little two-man tent to Wattamolla and walk through the National Park to Burning Palms or we would stay at Katoomba and do the walk to Mt Solitary. A favourite place of mine was Browns Water Hole, where we would walk from Cheltenham Station through the bush and along Devlins Creek to North Epping. Neil was in a very good Scout group at St Anne's, Strathfield, and they often went hiking too. Bob Hughes and Max Viles have remained friends with us.

I still read a lot too, and after Gone With the Wind my favourites were The Sun is my Undoing, which is a marvellous saga of the Flood family, Bristol slave traders and My First Two Thousand Years, the story of the wandering Jew through history and his search for 'unendurable pleasure indefinitely prolonged'.

Ron had learnt to play clarinet and saxophone and I was learning guitar, without any real talent. We went to jam sessions in milk bars at Stone's Cafe, Coogee and a cafe at Campsie and Ron got to be quite good, even to improvising his jazz licks and solos. I had not made any real progress but we still played together quite often as I learnt the chords.

Dad was in business then with George Taylor, who had a cottage on Ourimbah Creek at Chittaway Point, Tuggerah, where we spent a holiday. I walked to Wyong and back to see Fred Astaire and Artie Shaw in a film called Second Chorus. The pace was slower in those days and the punt over the Hawkesbury River took so few cars at a time that it could take us nine hours in a truck or car to go about 36 miles from Wyong to Burwood on a holiday weekend.

A popular camping spot with the Stewarts and the McLaggans was at Narrabeen, where we would set up our tents for the summer. At night we went prawning with nets and lanterns in the lake and Dad and Uncle Jim would cook them in a big tin of boiling water over the Primus stove. In the morning we would all have to have our Enos Fruit Salts. It was a long daily journey to and from the office in town by tram to Manly and ferry to the Quay. I do not remember how Lottie got on but Ronnie came to Narrabeen when AWA closed for Christmas/ New Year holidays. They were good summer holidays though we did have problems with the fresh meat and the blowflies.

A decade which started in economic depression finished at war. It was called a phoney war then, on land anyway. We were not greatly aware of what was happening in China and Manchuria and in Europe there was little or no action. We were told of the impregnability of the Maginot Line protecting France from Germany and of the strength of the British and French armies.

The forties were wartime. The German army swept through the Netherlands and captured France in weeks. The British evacuated France through Dunkirk. Anything that floated was used to get the soldiers back across the North Sea and I learnt later that even the *William Muir*, which was the old paddle steamer we went on from Leith to Burnt Island in Fife, across the Firth of Forth, was used.

Enlistments grew for the Sixth and Seventh divisions of the AIF and some from the office joined up, including both Lawford Richardson and John Broinowski. Arthur Worsley was left to run the practice for the duration. Ron had gone into AWA [Amalgamated Wireless Australia] from school and had commenced a career engineering and electronics. It was specialist work and he was in the components laboratory. Later he was to join the navy but within 24 hours AWA had him out and back to the lab. Manpower regulations were in force.

In North Africa the British Army, including Australian divisions, and the German and Italian armies were chasing each other back and forth across the desert and coastal roads. In Greece and Crete the British and Australians took another battering and more evacuations. David Spark, who was the senior when we went to Newcastle on audits, was one who escaped from Crete.

I was nineteen years old when I was called up into the UTs [Universal Trainees] in May 1941. And so I went into uniform at Liverpool, a camp by the Georges River and over the bridge from the railway station, shops and hotel. Liverpool was then on the outskirts of Sydney with wide open paddocks and market gardens between there and Canterbury. It was an old camp from the First World War.

We did basic military training: drill, marches, guard duty and physical exercise. The scrambled eggs, army style, were an experience never forgotten, as were the quart bottles of Tooheys draught beer drawn from the tap and bottled at the Liverpool Hotel. We cleaned latrines and peeled potatoes and carried out the same routine that private soldiers in the army have always done.

At the rifle range with our .303 Lee Enfields I had a problem. I could never work out whether to shoot with my rifle to my right or left shoulder, or out of which eye I could see better. As I never hit anything I do not know that it made any difference. I do know that the Lee Enfield was a very heavy rifle, especially so on one occasion when we did a march through the Sydney city streets, with bayonets attached.

We got leave regularly. Back at the office Alan Hayes and others of the staff were in uniform too and we thought that we were the answer to a maiden's prayer;

especially Betty Gibbs, who was the prettiest girl there. There were cocktail parties to raise monies for the Comforts Fund and the war effort but the hostilities all seemed to be pretty far removed.

It was only a month or so after being called up, that it was suspected that a misappropriation of funds was occurring in the Sergeants' Mess. And there among the ranks was an eager-beaver audit clerk. It did not take me long to review the system, audit the books and discover the culprit. Not long after that I was a corporal. The day I sewed on my two stripes was the day I sat for Law relating to Contracts and Partnerships—two papers, which I passed.

At Liverpool I had a cubicle of my own at the end of the hut with a large poster of Veronica Lake on the wall. It was my task then to either lead the guard duty at the gate or call out the troops at 5 a.m. and direct a party collecting large cans or piss pots, filled overnight, between the huts.

On 1 October 1941 we were formalised as the Citizen's Military Forces for service in Australia and I was posted to HQBOD [Headquarters Base Ordnance Depot], still at Liverpool. We loaded trucks and moved supplies at Moorebank. I was then moved to the Showground, in the city, for daily duty at Victoria Barracks. This was a job on inventory control, recording stock movements from singlets to major items of equipment, in handwritten ledgers.

We slept on straw palliasses in the pig pens and cattle stalls at the Showground, which have not changed to this day. Each day we would march across the road to Victoria Barracks, then the army headquarters in Sydney. This routine was kept up for all of October as N250229 of the HQBOD, with a promotion to lance sergeant. The war was on the other side of the world and my future in it, as planned by the army, was to be in stock control and accounting at Victoria Barracks in the Ordnance Corps. It was certainly what I was best at, audit and systems analyses. No doubt this was an important aspect of war service but not exactly exciting stuff to a 20 year old.

I made up my mind to volunteer for the AIF for overseas service and on 3 November 1941 I enlisted at the Showground and became Private NX50016.

When on leave, Ron and I, with Betty Colebrooke, still went along to a Sydney Swing Club meeting but we were getting more into classical music. I had bought Greig's Peer Gynt Suite and Ron had Mozart's Concerto for Clarinet in A Major with Reginald Kell. The larger works came on 12 inch 78rpm shellac discs. Great was Ron's disappointment when he glued the covers together with an acetone-based adhesive, which combined with the shellac and ruined the records. While on leave, we still had our Friday night sessions, but at times strictly classical.

The Kirsova Ballet, who were an advance on the Borovansky, were at the Minerva and I took Betty Gibbs. Jessie Scott still wrote often from England and sent us Melody Makers and other magazines. Unfortunately she lost a brother, who was bounced off the tailboard of an army truck and killed. Ronnie's cousin from Melbourne, Alan Stewart, was also accidentally killed with the RAAF in Aden when doing loops and hit the deck.

In mid-November 1941 I was moved back to Liverpool, still with the Ordnance Corps and acted as orderly corporal. I was sent to a school for evaluation and special training and was told that I was being considered for Officers Training School. I expected that this would eventuate. The school, homework and exams were on ordnance and accounting systems for war within the army. I progressively came fourth out of 200 with 85% in the first exams and third in the second lot. A great deal of study was involved over about three weeks and I finished up coming second out of the whole group at the conclusion of the course on the 5 December 1941, expecting my commission eventually.

And then on the 8 December 1941 the news came through of the Japanese entry into the war. Fantastic furphies were flying about: We're going to Bathurst; we're going to Townsville; we're staying here and doing nothing; it's all baloney.

I was back on guard duty with the news that I must sit and wait a while. And then the news came through that all previous plans for the future were cancelled. Such is the army. After weeks and months of specialised training, study and examinations I was loading 44-gallon drums at the Shell depot onto railway trucks. On the 19 December 1941 I was transferred to go on draft after we had been training with rifle, light machine-guns, bren guns and even bayonet training.

It was December and it was hot. I thought the field training out in the paddock was good stuff and that draft training was much better than the depot work of loading drums and counting singlets. On Christmas day Hong Kong was captured and that day, in camp, I thought to be probably the best day in my life. I was fixed up to go to NCO school on Monday 29 December, but on Friday the 26th I was suddenly notified to go on four days pre-embarkation leave.

Leave was spent with Neil in town shopping, playing pontoon, doing Dad's books, playing records with Ron, saying goodbyes at the office and having lunch and dinner with Betty Gibbs, having taken her to the pictures in town. Ron gave me a very good pencil and Dad gave me a leather writing set. Our pay was not much but it bought 1s.6d. for a haircut, 1s.10d. for cigarettes (50 State Express cost 3s.3d.), 1d. for matches, 6s.6d. for two of us at the theatre and 8s.9d. for each of three records of the Tchaikovski Romeo and Juliet Overture; 2s.1d. for a quart of beer, 3d. for the phone and 1s.1d. for razor blades. I was either broke or in debt. It was a good leave and on 1 January 1942 I arrived at Dubbo, having been switched from the Ordnance Corps to the infantry and drafted with reinforcements to the 2/30th AIF battalion. I volunteered for the infantry. I knew a crowd of us were about to be shanghaied on the day I came back from pre-embarkation leave so I got in first and put my name down. I felt that it turned out for the best and, although I did not bargain on getting away quite so soon, I was pleased.

2
The Japanese Drive South

For the period from 1942 to 1945 these recollections, for the most part, are taken word for word from the diaries I wrote and kept with me throughout those years. I have altered the present tense to the past tense to maintain the narrative. Some events, not recorded at the time, have been included from memory but I have not coloured or exaggerated any of the text, as now transcribed from the diaries. Occasional explanations and later perspectives are between square brackets.

I arrived at Dubbo on 1 January 1942 and was put with the 5th reinforcements to the 2/30th Infantry Battalion AIF and next day promoted to acting corporal. There was not that much doing actually and it was very hot. Quite a few, whom I knew with the Ordnance unit at Liverpool, were at Dubbo too. In fact it was like old home week—George Smith, Doug Morriss and China Hall. In the evening we went swimming, there being no further training at first. Then it was for one day only at the rifle range and an eight-mile march. That was it. In all the first eight days at Dubbo the actual effective training done would have fitted into about nine hours. It was an incredible preparation for actual combat as we received virtually no real training at all. It was quite a muddle, too, equipping us and passing us through the staging camp although it was obvious that the time for departure was drawing near.

On 9 January we were on our way, leaving Dubbo by train with full kit, straight to Darling Harbour. Next day we were ferried on to the *Aquitania* at 3.30 a.m. and I kicked off on duties immediately. We did not know where we were going and with Sydney fast disappearing that afternoon I was not in the slightest bit affected or apprehensive.

The weather was perfect and the sky a vast expanse of blue as we sailed south and west, sighting the Victorian and South Australian coastlines with HMAS *Canberra* for company.

I was made Mess Corporal for the trip. There was the inevitable dice, two-up and penny poker going and I won and lost but hardly a fortune changed hands.

At Fremantle on 15 January quite a few of the boys went AWL and were brought back next day in naval boats. The attractions in Rowe Street [the brothel area] had the men queuing up, with the cops maintaining order. We did not know it, but that day, the 2/30th had gone into action in Malaya as the first Australian unit to come up against the Japanese.

When we left in the afternoon of the 16 January a Wirraway saw us off with quite a bit of stunting and that was our last sight of Australia for a very long time; for quite a few, forever.

For sheer unadulterated blackness I had never seen anything like a black-out at sea. I had had a cold and been chesty since Dubbo and it was not long before I was sick of the job in the mess. We did not know what was ahead of us but I was told that three stripes were in the air for me when we landed.

We anchored in the morning of 20 January in what we thought to be the prettiest spot in the world. Islands were all around us, which rose straight up out of the water and kept going up. Wild jungle was on the land with little beaches and native huts along the shore—all very tropical. We were in the Sunda Straits, between Sumatra and Java. Later we trans-shipped on to small Dutch boats, which were clean but crowded. The meals were awful.

We stayed a couple of days in the Sunda Straits while a convoy of six ships assembled with our escort of HMAS *Canberra*, two Dutch cruisers and three destroyer/gunboats. Air attack was expected but everything was very quiet. With the sun overhead it was hard to tell our direction when we put out to sea again. The *Canberra* soon left us but it was an uneventful two days on the small boats.

On 24 January we arrived and docked in Singapore at 9 a.m. By 11 a.m. we were ashore, marched to the railway station and were off. I saw little of Singapore and what I did see was dirty. We passed through Johore Bahru, detrained and then marched five miles, stumbling through rough terrain with full pack to our base camp. I was a bit weak, we had an air raid that night and I had no idea where we were. It was obviously somewhere in Malaya.

Next day we learnt that the Japanese were about 40 miles away. It was a quiet day, with no further training scheduled but we had a bit of a lecture as to what was happening. Rumours were abounding but it was best to ignore them all. Despite the air raids, which got on our nerves somewhat, we had a good night's sleep.

Monday 26 January was Australia Day and I was transferred from the 2/30th to the 2/29th Battalion with most of our boys. This was a Victorian unit, also in the 27th Brigade. Only about 150 men of the unit (except D Company) came out of Muar, on the west coast, where they had been surrounded by the Japs, with a loss of about 700 casualties. They had been rescued, five days earlier, by the 2/19th Battalion, who themselves had fared even worse. Both units had been badly knocked around.

I was appointed a section leader of 1 Section, C Company and still had my two stripes on. We moved forward about 20 miles and set up a temporary camp nearer to the action, which was fast coming down the road. AIF and British forces were retiring about 15 miles away, while we were getting instruction in fieldcraft and I was learning to use a tommy gun. On our patrols, seeking forward Japanese scouts, I was always the breakaway, about 40 yards behind the section. It was not the best place to be.

We did get more training over a couple of days, sentry duty at night and I got to be quite proficient with the tommy gun. We were close to the Japs, on the lookout, expecting attack but in fact the closest I got to danger was a live round from one of our own boys, which he let off and missed me by only six feet.

The Japanese air formations of 27 and 35 or more planes, doing regular air raids on our sector, were a grand sight but somewhat ineffective. One day we saw three of our Hurricanes, but RAF aircraft were few if non-existent in the skies above us. Brewster Buffalos and other small fighters were no match for the Japanese

Zeros and had got shot out of the sky. In one air-raid, shrapnel came very close, only a few feet away from where I was standing, but none of us was killed.

We were in Malaya, up against the Japs, for only four days because the troops were evacuating the mainland for Singapore Island. We moved over the causeway on the 28 January and were quickly disillusioned as to the impregnability of the 'island fortress'. At the causeway they had to dig slit trenches and wire the beach.

I was in love with my tommy gun but had to take off my two stripes. The 2/29th, due to the heavy losses was regrouped and the new sections were made up of two originals and nine reinforcements, the stripes going to the acclimatised boys, who knew more of what it was all about. Alan Ralph was made the new section leader.

The AIF was given the north-west coast of the island. At times I was up to my waist in mud as we did patrols and waded through mangrove swamps and creeks. We were there to defend that part of the island, should the Japanese cross the dividing channel between Malaya and Singapore Island. This they did with their main force. They were down to Johore Bahru by Saturday 31 January and the causeway was blown up. Half blown up actually as the job was never done properly.

From the landing at Kota Bahru the Japanese had rolled over the British and Indian forces all the way down the Malayan peninsula. There was no defending air force to speak of and two major battleships, the *Prince of Wales* and the *Repulse*, with two destroyers had been sunk off Kuantan on the east coast. The Japs were checked at Gemas by the 2/30th Bn, 2/15th and 4th Anti-tank Regts, and at Muar, but by the next day they had gone around them and the withdrawals continued. This was the pattern through the state of Johore, which had been given to the Australians to defend. The 2/30th and the 2/26th would meet the Japanese force advancing with tanks and on bicycles and then fight their way out of a defensive position from the rear. They would regroup and meet them further down the road again and again. The Japanese were simply better prepared soldiers, prepared to wade through swamp and crash through jungle to keep their advance on the move. The 2/26th met them on the east coast, the 2/29th and the 2/19th on the west coast and the 2/30th on the main road down the middle. There was no stopping them and they reached Johore Bahru, with fewer numbers than the defending British forces, from 8 December to 31 January, in seven weeks. It had been an incredible advance. The Japanese soldier was more experienced, better trained and better disciplined to cope with the tropical terrain.

On the island we had set up defensive positions and were doing constant patrols of 4 and 8 miles each night, through jungle and swamp, expecting infiltration. It really was a two-day crash training course on what to expect. We were even fired upon by one of our own sentries one night on our way back to camp.

I had been in Malaya and Singapore nine days when I came down with dysentery, discharging blood, after drinking stagnant or polluted water some days before and reported to the MDS [Medical Dressing Station]. I had been having diarrhoea for some days but had still gone on the patrols at night. That night, from the air, everything was thrown at us—bombs, machine-gun fire and shrapnel. A lone Tojo, as we called their planes, came in with engines off and flying just above the rubber trees. Two miles away it bombed an oil dump at Bukit Timah. The tanks were burning and my inside too when I was moved to a CCS [Casualty Clearing Station] and then to the AGH [Base Hospital] just out of Singapore. This had previously been a cathedral. I was getting better though, being dosed with brandy and castor oil. I felt terrible. The bomb-happy cases however were pathetic.

I could not get over the 'fortress'. There was nothing there. The big guns pointed out to sea, all wire and pill boxes, were on the southern shore and food dumps were even in the open.

Frequent artillery duels were going on between Johore and Singapore Island, which were only a half mile apart. Holding the island was going to be a hell of a fight, whichever way it went. I wrote and sent letters home but it was doubtful if they ever left. The medicine I was taking was making me feel much better and the sisters and nursing staff at the hospital were excellent and efficient. They were in fact quite wonderful.

On the night of the 9 February, the Japanese attacked the island after intense shell fire and bombing all the previous day. The moon did not rise until 3 a.m. and in pitch blackness the patrols had no hope of stopping them. They came across in boats at 2 a.m. on the western shore of mangrove swamps and mudbanks, in front of the Indian sector and near the 2/29th and 2/30th positions. They just kept coming across and through the mud, in force, securing a beachhead on the island before dawn. And I was still then in hospital.

The boys were being shelled and dive-bombed all day on the 9th, with the Japs holding a strip of the western shore. The AIF and British troops settled in around them. I did think that we would lose the island but that it would take some days yet and be a great fight. The landings just could not be stopped without an air force. Japanese parachutists were expected although it would have been a difficult operation over the rubber trees. The defence was disorganised and next day the Japs were down about five miles from the causeway. They had an observation balloon up from Johore for their artillery and we could not even shoot it down; presumably because our guns did not have the range or elevation. They also had Malays and Japanese planted on the island carrying out fifth-column work, indicating our positions and cutting wire. Our old camp site was quickly overrun and some of the 2/29th were mixed in with the Argyle Highlanders.

When the Japanese were pushed back at one stage below the causeway by the 2/30th it seemed that there were brighter developments but next day reports of the fighting were contradictory. The Japs were landing tanks and their advance continued.

The big oil dumps and tanks off Keppell Harbour were set on fire by our own gun fire and the Japanese bombings were getting closer to the city. Great columns of smoke hung overhead. A ship just off the shore was bombed too, with huge fountains of water going up as it zig-zagged and got away. There was no sign of our air force although the ack-ack was busy firing upon theirs.

On the night of the 12th the women and nurses were evacuated and I had been moved again.

An order from CICs Percival and Wavell, which I read not knowing if it was official or a pamphlet, stated that the British armies, including the AIF, were just not good enough: though greatly outnumbered they were always on the defensive:

there was no spirit of attack or zeal. This was true [except the being outnumbered] and in only isolated instances was any offensive action taken. The general outlook was to look after your own skin first and maybe your mate's after that. The dive bombers were the cause of that and the fact that this was the first action of the great majority of the troops involved. It also seemed to many that there was nothing of Singapore worth fighting for. We were, by then, 13 January, herded closer to the city.

Of the 350 men in the convalescent depot where I then was, only 40 of us volunteered and tried to get out to a composite unit of AIF men defending the city. I went into action. I soon realised what we were fighting for—it was for our bloody lives.

I was given a rifle and 100 rounds of ammunition and sent forward, coming up against the Japs and sniper fire at night. There was a general air of despondency everywhere, aggravated by the statement by a Major Hunt that for us the war was over. But we were not beaten yet and though we were surrounded we thought it quite false that we would all be prisoners of war.

Very early in the morning of 15 February my position was heavily shelled and mortared with crossfire from Bren guns on our flank. The shelling increased during the morning and it was almost unbelievable. I lost seven of my remaining lives (only one left). In the afternoon English Sherwood Foresters raced through us during a barrage, leaving us, 30 in number, in front to defend our part of the line. We stuck and were pretty game, waiting for the Japs and odds we thought would be 30 to 1 against us.

By that night the position was impossible and the cease fire order was given.

At that time Singapore was a picture of grey. Everything was grey. The Cathay building stood out grey against a grey background of grey smoke from other burning buildings and the burning oil tanks off the shore. What isolated air defence we had was grey ack-ack fire against a grey sky. It rained frequently—rain, rain, rain. The sight from our position in and around the Botanical Gardens of a defeated city was quite dramatic and it left an indelible impression.

3
On Becoming Prisoners
1942

At midnight we were withdrawn and disarmed.

So it was all over and I only had done some 30 hours in actual action, plus a lot of patrols looking for advance scouts. But even then I did not see a Jap or fire a shot. I soon met up with one of our boys, Jim Carr, and learnt that the 2/29th was again knocked out but saved by the Argyles.

The Japanese soldiers did not immediately come to claim us, although there were signs of peace everywhere. The arms and equipment we had given up were enormous, even from our sector alone. There was no official news but certainly the war was over for us. On the previous day the convalescent depot and the hospital at Katong, which I had left, had been bombed and shelled and there was talk of atrocities through the wards of a nearby hospital by Japanese soldiers, who were cleaning up the whole area.

The news was that we would be returned to our units. The Japs we met up with were very civil and gave us cigarettes. There were certainly plenty of them in town but neither us, nor the civilians that I saw, were molested in any way. The area where we were to be congregated was a 17-mile march from where we were, in the Botanical Gardens and it took us from 3.20 p.m. to 12.30 a.m. on the night *Feb.* of the 17th. We had been raiding the nearby houses and establishments for food and what supplies we could lift while we had the chance. It was just as well that we did so, for a lot of the stuff we carried with us on the march was to come in very handy in setting up a prison camp and hospitals. We got some waves from the Chinese civilians as we walked through the streets, especially from one group of girls on an upstairs balcony. I could guess what they were. All the AIF were put into English barracks at Changi. Ours were the Selarang Barracks and although food and water were scarce we were otherwise quite comfortable, even if on the floor.

We were told that the surrender was because of cholera in town, that the water was cut off by the Japs from the reservoirs and that the hospitals were in a bad way. With no air force, an evacuation to Java would have meant mass drownings and sheer suicide. There was no comparison to Dunkirk and Crete. It was my opinion that it was never the intention to hold Malaya or Singapore but to fight a losing battle for as long as possible and at the cost of as few casualties as possible.

Back with the 2/29th I was told that Cook, Kelly and Rainbow, mates on board the *Aquitania* had been killed. I was somewhat unperturbed as by then we were callous bastards. The shot up and burnt bodies still lay beside the road as we marched from Singapore to Changi.

Our clocks were then placed on Japan time with sunrise at 8 and my first job, in that first week, was in a party wiring around the perimeter of a coconut plantation.

We marched in proper formation to the job with our own officers and worked under them. There were no Japs standing over us and everything was run with normal army discipline. This was to be the pattern within all the camps, as we were always responsible directly to our own officers and NCOs, who took their orders from the Japs.

On the last day in Singapore, prior to the march, when everything scroungable was scrounged, we had obtained a gramophone and some records. It was good to hear 'Twelfth Street Rag' and 'Shoeshiners Drag' by Lionel Hampton and 'Louise' and 'Whispering' by the Benny Goodman Orchestra. Within a week of being at Changi an education scheme was started to fill in our time and this was very good. There was a persistent rumour that we would be back in Australia by Easter but I did not really believe it. It was hot though and at times I was pretty weak.

On our first Sunday we had an excellent church service in the morning and it was noticeable that there was no mention of King or National Anthem.

Summing up our first week in captivity I honestly believed that the AIF (approximately 14 000 of us) were being the best treated of the prisoners. We had three fair-sized meals a day, were quartered in the healthiest part of the island and had no interference or standover by the Japs. When we did come in contact with them they were civil and friendly. Many spoke English. Actually we were better off than the English and Indians and, to that point, had no reason to complain. We wondered how long this would last.

On 23 February I was in the first working party to move back to Singapore, 350 of us in batches of 50. The Japanese soldiers accompanying us got us food at every stop and even gave us a lift for eight miles of the way to our new quarters in town.

We started work by being taken by lorry about a mile to the job, loading trucks with foodstuffs being sent to Japan. Japanese soldiers worked with us too. We worked hard, getting fed at lunchtime with tinned pineapple, biscuits and condensed milk and with buckets of coffee all day. Coming back a Japanese officer said: 'Japan—Australia' (handshake) 'Japan—English' (throat cut) We agreed.

There is an international understanding between one soldier and another, irrespective of uniform or which side he is on, especially between the privates or ordinary fighting men. One Japanese soldier made us laugh when he put his forefinger tightly into a circle of his other hand and said 'Nippon'. Then he again put his forefinger into a loose and floppy circle of his other hand and said 'Ozzie'. These soldiers were fighting against us only about two weeks before.

We worked in different bulk stores and godowns (or warehouses) each day, loading cases and pinching stuff as we got the chance. I filled my tobacco pouch again when working in a tobacco store (Virginia House) and the boys had the Japs playing two-up for cigarettes and they were winning too.

I thought that the camaraderie with the Japs was becoming too much of a good thing when some were forgetting themselves and taking their charity like bloody natives. In fact one day we were with a pretty unintelligent lot and they thought that we were a huge joke. It was apparent that these Japanese soldiers were unused to any of the goods around us before the war and had not got over the novelty of it all. They would take hair oil and put it over themselves because it smelt nice.

Having got over the surprise of being prisoners, and the relief from being in action and shot up, humiliation generally set in. The YBB (yellow-bellied bastards), sons of Nippon, were still fair to us in their own way but in their propaganda they made fun of whites being naked to the waist and doing the work of Chinese women.

Though our cooks were able to make bread it was actually a pretty soggy, doughy mess and we were soon on rice three times a day. We got to hate the stuff.

We saw most of Singapore in the working parties, except around Raffles Hotel and the commercial district and it was quite apparent that the city had had a far worse bombing than, I was sure, any city in England, including London. Singapore of course was smaller and so the bombing was more dense. Had it not been for the ceasefire on the 15th I was sure that the Japs would have carried out their threat and flattened the city completely in the course of another few days.

It was significant that the first Japanese word I picked up was 'arigato' (God knows the spelling far less the character in Japanese), their word for 'thank you'. They were giving us things all the time, mainly foodstuffs and tobacco. Most of their officers were learning English words and we had a bastard tongue in common for what they wanted done and getting it done.

It was always manual work, loading trucks with cases and bags. I thought it inevitable that when the food stores were packed up and sent away, things were not going to be nearly as good. The work was making me fit though, fitter than I had ever been but my lack of weight and height made things pretty hard.

We would be up at sunrise (8 in their time), breakfast at 8.15 and be on the job from 9.30 till anything from 5 to 7 p.m. It was dark at 7.30. We were threatened with searches at night after being caught stealing on the job but as yet that had not been carried out. No doubt they were going to get a bit tighter on us.

I had quite a few sores on my face where the chinstrap of my slouch hat had rubbed into the mosquito bites, but it was more the itching that was driving me mad. There were still some ointments and medicines then to treat the sick and the cuts and bruises.

The news around the camp in early March 1942 was very interesting—or rather the complete lack of real news. Among the more important rumours were:
• England and America are fighting in Belgium and France.
• The Russian army was in Warsaw.
• Turkey was for the Allies.
• Churchill's solemn reassurance that we would be relieved very shortly.

More important to me, though, was being hungry in the afternoons. The rice was filling but certainly not sustaining. Another 200 men came down from Changi and our work party was now 600 strong. Another 600 was expected soon. We were still handling foodstuffs with a lot of work to do, loading the ships. On 11 March pay commenced and I was able to fill myself with condensed milk but could not get onto a toothbrush. With the pay, a rollcall was introduced.

The Japanese method of attacking a job was different from ours. We would take time working out the best method, organising time and labour for their best use and planning to set up the job to be done as efficiently as possible. Long before we were ready to start, however, the Japanese NCO in charge would give us some stick and we would wade into the piles of cases individually and in no time they were on the truck. I knew which method was the quickest.

There must have been something pretty big going on in the world around us, what with increased tank and shipping movements. We were speeded up as well and I got my first belting on the behind for taking a smoko. An ammunition dump went up too that afternoon while we worked from 9 a.m. to 1 a.m., 16 hours, getting the next day off.

Food was on our minds and in our dreams every minute of every hour of every day and did so for a long time to come, completely eliminating girls as the subject of our thoughts. Not that we were then starving but there was never anything solid to sink our teeth into. I dreamt regularly of meat pies and plum pudding. If there were any thoughts left they were always of going home.

At times I was dead beat by the time I got back to camp, especially after working on 200 lb rice bags from 7 p.m. to 9 a.m. next morning. Four of us would lift a bag into the air and one of the bigger blokes would take it on his shoulder to the truck. Quite a few were wheat lumpers before the war and it amazed me what they could carry. Eventually their strength was abused and they could not sustain the weight loss. [The whole of the 2/30th football team died].

I later recovered from the previous days' exertion by taking leave through sheer hide. I saluted the sentry at the gate as if I did not have a care in the world and took an hour off in the town buying pancakes (chipatties?), biscuits, cake and milk. Though still tired I was myself again. There were days, however, when everyone was beginning to crack up, getting snappy and sarcastic, not about food but afraid anyone would get something that they did not get. The sores on my face had spread and I was covered in ointment every day. But still it was 'off to work we go' every morning. For a week we had been lifting and loading the bags of rice on to trucks. Then we moved about a mile to the 'Great World' amusement park on St Patrick's day, 17 March. There we slept on beds (charpoys) and although uncomfortable they were still beds and we were off the floor.

4
The Great World

We were quartered in the various stalls of the old amusement park and from there we would go out to work each day.

We did have our good days, such as the day at the racecourse. No horses but we had tinned M & V [meat and vegetables], bacon, cheese and biscuits. Not so good was the news of Alan Ralph, who took over my section as Corporal in C Company of the 2/29th. We were told that he had made a break for it from Changi and I did not think that he was ever heard of again. It was easy to get out but impossible to get anywhere. [This was not so: he died in Thailand.]

By this time, in March 1942, I was a mess. The sores on my face had turned to impetigo and I had not shaved for eight days and looked a wreck. Sores under my arms were Dhobie's Itch. A sore on my leg was an infected pimple. Sores between my legs were a form of tinea. And I had a sore of some sort at the back of my neck.

There was quite a collection. We were easily subject to infection, what with the workload, sweat, the humidity and, try as we might, it was impossible to keep clean every day. I was very brown though, never wearing a shirt, day or night, sun or rain. I weighed 8 stone 9 lbs, which was the same as when I was passed for the UTs about twelve months before. *14 × 8 = 112 + 9 = 121 lbs.*

Japanese methods continued to be unorthodox. They would tear into anything with little apparent thought but to get the job done. Working at the railway station, a train would come in and we would have it unloaded and stacked with our bare hands and backs and the train would pull out again in two hours.

I had variety. One day I was working in a Cold Storage Depot, shifting frozen beef, and it was so cold at -15°F. By then our crowd had grown in numbers to 1700 AIF men and we were a permanent 'Delivery Party' on all the food.

Pay was a Japanese dollar or 10 cents a day. Though probably not worth anything it was accepted in the shops and by the local people on the road. Actually the Japs had paper money printed for Malaya and Singapore while they were still fighting down the mainland and spreading it everywhere. For all that, the Japanese prohibited us from buying anything from anybody, but of course the AIF is the AIF. Bread was the main thing we bought and the rest we 'obtained'. Some of the Chinese gave us doughnuts for nothing when they were not seen doing so. We had the highest regard for the Chinese people. In all, we thought then, we were quite well off except for meat.

Our routine had settled down for what seemed to be a very long stay. Most of the boys expected to be home by Christmas but I thought it was more likely to be 18 months or 2 years. The lack of confirmed news made it hard to conjecture. We pretty much knew what was going on in the world around us but of course it was all second-hand.

Over the seven weeks to 28th March:
- I had been on the working parties for 6 weeks.
- I lost my glasses the first day we started work in Singapore. One of the boys trod on them.
- I lost Dad's tobacco pouch. I just laid it down and some bastard swiped it. And it full of 'Three Castles' ready rubbed tobacco.

At the Great World we were told that conditions at Changi were terrible.

- Food was scarce because there were so many prisoners—just rice and tea.
- Prices for food outside were prohibitive: one loaf of bread (about two slices) was one (Japanese) Singapore dollar.
- There was nothing for the men to do. The Australian officers, under Black Jack Galleghan, held parades and enforced a discipline, worse than we had in Australia.
- Some men had tried to break out but Indians (Sikhs) were guarding them and when they were caught they were either shot or imprisoned.
- They got no pay. The Japanese principle was 'no work no pay'.
- There were no recreational facilities or amusements except probably cricket matches and 'Changi University'.

All this in seven weeks. What would it be like in twelve months?

Easter 1942. By pure coincidence I tasted an egg, which I had managed to buy. It was no holiday but I wondered how Neil was and if the Easter Show was on that year. Actually to celebrate the occasion we had our rations cut. A canteen was started in the Great World camp mainly selling bread and tobacco. It was expected that I would be the auditor. Where we had measured our wealth in shillings before, we were reduced to a unit of 10 cents (3½ d.), our daily rate of pay. Balancing the budget was a problem but made easier by getting used to having so many threepence halfpennies to spend.

I started working in the camp for a few days, in the new store, as a break until I was fit again. Rumour was persistent that the Chinese were fighting up north; that fighting was still on in Sumatra; that Britain had opened up a second front. We could not get any confirmation but it was so universal that it did seem a fact.

I was soon out on the work parties again. Nothing changes. Just after Easter we had some music to break the monotony: an Indian family with a tom-tom, a combination of piano accordion and organ plus two child dancers. There was a snake charmer too, which was really interesting, especially the guaranteed genuine cobra. The boys who had come to Malaya earlier had seen it all but it was new to those of us who had arrived in January.

Tich Martin scrounged a pair of sunglasses for me, which I really needed. Not having my glasses my eyes had ached a good deal from the brilliant sunlight and glare. Scrounging on the job for myself too, I pinched quite a haul of cigarettes, papers and tobacco. We were not happy however learning that the Pommies were getting 20 cents a day to our 10. It was bad enough before the surrender and the English making such a mess of things but now they still thought that they were superior. There was bad feeling around, me included. On 11 April my whole worldly possessions were:

My clothes: slouch hat, 3 army issue 'bermuda' shorts, 5 pairs of socks, 2 shirts, puttees and boots.

Dad's leather writing case, money belt, diaries, wallet, pay book, water bottle and gas bag, my mess kit and Ron's pencil.

Cash	23 cents	Cigarette papers	8 pkts
Tobacco	6 ozs	Hair oil	1 jar
Cigarettes	8 pkts	Soap	2 cakes
Matches	½box	Sugar	1 lb
1 book	(Arsene Lupine)		

I was rich but still no toothbrush.

On that day too I had my first haircut in three months...since 6 January.

It was still pretty hard work carrying hundredweight cases all day. At 112 lbs that was almost as heavy as I was at 121 lbs. I buckled at the knees. There were no hand trucks or trolleys and we used to argue with the Japs '2 men 1 case': we tried but it did not do us much good, '1 man 1 case' was all we got back...'Speedo speedo'. We did get the occasional day off, which I spent reading, glasses or no glasses. However, my eyes were getting sore. But when we had stolen some beer on the job and shared it around it tasted good. I celebrated my birthday in April while I had the opportunity.

Feeling at times was not too good between the 2/29th (Victorian) and the 2/30th (NSW) men. Our work party was made up of both. The 2/30th were more disciplined and we of the 2/29th were (without their training) a wild bloody mob. It was thought that there would be a blue when they tried to stop us scrounging on the job and to maintain better discipline and order. At the railway station though it was work together as hundreds of thousands of tons of rubber came down.

In a lecture from the Japanese CO of the camp it was explained to us how we were getting a fair deal. And we *were* getting a fair deal by their standards. He looked upon us as Japanese soldiers and treated us as such as far as possible and not as captives or prisoners of war. That was very good but our lack of discipline in not saluting got us into trouble. This we tried to improve. The Japanese CO could call our treatment 'fair'. It may not have been fair by our standards but it was the same as the way they treated themselves. They had corporal punishment in the IJA [Imperial Japanese Army] from formal beheading to physical beatings with heavy sticks, chunkel handles, baseball bats or whatever came to hand. A Japanese NCO would beat up all Japanese privates, a first class private would beat up second and third-class privates, a second-class private would beat up a third-class private. Our only problem was that the third-class private had nobody to beat up except us POWs and Chinese civilians.

At times we overstepped the mark and the big stick would come down to speed us up and it seemed that they especially picked on the tall chaps like Stan Arneil, who was well over six feet, as an example. We never did seem to improve much, however. In mid-April I had stolen some pork and beans and a bottle of French champagne to share around. I had met a British soldier from Birmingham called Ron Noakes and asked him across. He had been telling me about Quinton, where Jessie Scott lived. Five of the Pommies came to share the wine.

I was working harder than ever and with the help of some Scotts Emulsion (cod-liver oil; also scrounged), was actually filling out. One day at that time we made an early start at 6 a.m., two hours before sunrise and it turned out to be a pretty eventful day:

- We witnessed a Japanese morning parade with them facing the rising sun.
- A hell of a lot Japanese wounded were brought in by boat from heaven knows where.
- Tich Martin and a couple of mates were beaten up pretty badly when caught stealing some tinned fruit salad.
- A guard went berserk at night, taking a stick and bare bayonet to us for smoking in bed.

We worked because we had to but we were somewhat intractable. We watched Singapore come out of its holes and slowly get back to normal, almost; yet with many bare shells for buildings as reminders of the recent past. I often thought of London and the time yet to come when it would have that greatest of pleasures, filling in its air-raid shelters. It was the experience of a life time to watch the fires go out and a city come back to life.

During this time, despite having been working right in and through the disorganised food position, I was satisfied with my lot. I did not expect it to last and it didn't. We were lucky then to be in a work camp with the respect one soldier has for another, even an enemy—not treated as captives but actually as soldiers who had fought and lost. We felt that we were respected too, even sympathised with. The Japanese soldiers in command of our working party in those early months were fighting soldiers and the Australians were the only ones who had stopped them, no matter for how short a time.

I missed Neil and Ron, although I certainly would not have wanted them with me. I worried about Mum and Dad wondering if I was still alive. I worried over how long it took to assure them of my safety and prayed that the Japanese, the Australians, the Red Cross or whoever was responsible, hurried for once to get news through. Memories of so many things in the past crowded my mind and meant that on some nights, because of them, I did not get to sleep until 2 a.m. Long waking hours thinking of home.

On Anzac Day, 25 April, we held a minute's silence at 9 a.m. but 29 April was a more eventful day as it was a holiday to celebrate the Emperor's birthday. Everyone had to give three cheers for which we received a cholera needle plus half a tin of pineapple. Both were welcome and the needle was not painful at all. The town was decorated and it was a big day for the Japs.

I had two particular mates of the 2/29th in the Great World, Curly Avard and Tich Martin but both were to die later. They were great scroungers too and they had a quite a holiday on the Emperor's birthday.

My legs were still pretty bad where an acid treatment was painted on the tinea. Medication was whatever was available or stolen and I do not know that there was ever a Japanese army issue. My skin was burnt and had started to break out in a rash. Ringworm then broke out all over me. One really had to be sick or have a camp job not to have to go out on the loading parties though, and out I went. Torrential rain, solid blocks of water for half an hour at a time did not help. In

Singapore it rains often and hard.

We had started taking vitamin B tablets, when we could get them. We were lacking in meat and I thought the tablets might do me some good. Our meals were then:

Breakfast : Rice (nothing else) and a cup of tea (no milk or sugar).

Lunch : A jam tin full of rice.

Dinner : A plate of rice and a ladle of 'stew', with every night a tablespoon of meat in it. Tea.

This we supplemented with bread, bought with our 10 cents a day at the canteen and at night a tin of condensed milk between four. Because of the lack of variety in our diet beri-beri and meningitis had broken out in the camp. This brought about a further issue of vitamin tablets from the stock of medicines, which was brought from the hospitals at the time of the surrender. Mumps had also made itself known but the fear of cholera seemed beaten as the result of another inoculation. We ate what we could get. I had eaten some jam, which was blown and it made me pretty ill; crook enough to go to the RAP [Regimental Aid Post].

On the working party that day, shifting heavy loads, which was our daily chore, I had worked till I dropped and had actually laid down on the job. This was a risky thing to do. Depending upon the urgency of the job and the character of the Jap overseeing the group, no matter what condition you were in, you were soon on your feet if they shouted 'Kura' and the stick came down.

At the RAP I sat down next to a man named Bobby Logan who had been in an accident (one boy was killed). Getting into conversation with him I learnt that he came from Hamilton, in Glasgow, and worked in the Council there. Who should he know but my cousin Gertie and her fiance. It seemed a small world.

Still weak, I was put in the working party orderly room by the Camp CO, Major Schneider, so I could stay inside for a while. It was a change for I had been working solidly for going on three months, not always in good condition and hardly physically fitted for the heavy manual work.

We got news of a big naval battle off the Australian coast and of probably being sent away from Singapore. We wondered if it would be Manchuria or Formosa. It was thought that some of our boys had already sailed, maybe to Saigon. However in our camp we got a raise from 1 May to 15 cents a day. Only those at work collect a day's pay except for a small number on camp duties, me included. There was also an increase in our meat ration, which played up on me for a while. Already we had weak stomachs.

The news vendors were running riot again:

• The naval base had been bombed.
• Churchill had again assured us that we would be off soon.
• The Japanese had landed at Darwin, Wyndham and Broome.
• The Allies had won the naval battle of course.
• The British forces were in Sumatra and Java again.

We wondered how the rumours started but they did, however, build up morale. Most of the boys were betting everything from their shirts to their deferred pay that we would be home for Christmas dinner. I could not see how America would retake Singapore and that the Japs would let us get away. 3000 had already been taken away to South Burma. The thought was that they were splitting us up and despatching us in all directions.

Lights out, in fact a black-out was then put into force at 9 p.m. instead of 10 p.m and there were a few other signs of Japanese apprehension. Even the *Syonan Times* was toning down a bit.

Shaving once a week and reading very little to save my eyes, I had almost cut out smoking as well to try and look after myself. I had not cleaned my teeth, though, since before the surrender. I had quite a job convincing Bobby Logan that I would soon be 21. I had changed in a lot of ways by May 1942. I had dropped all that swelled-headed and sarcastic stuff, in fact the same thing in some of the smart-alecs annoyed me like hell. I was still pretty quiet but not silly like some of the kids and although I kept to myself a bit, I was still one of the boys. Most took me for being a bit older but I had had a lot of sense belted into me over the last six months. I had seen a little of what I joined up for...a little of what life was all about and a helluva lot of what it wasn't. It was Tich Martin's nineteenth birthday and he had been in the AIF for two years! He too had seen a lot over the last six months, from prostitutes to week-old corpses.

We learnt too that the last draft of men had gone to Burma but there was still the belief that Java was being retaken and that the Yanks would be in Singapore and rescuing us very soon. It was even rumoured that leaflets had been dropped with 'thumbs up', 'cheer up, you'll be home soon'. We were prepared to believe anything.

Typical of the boys:

Tich: L.R.A.Martin from Mentone

A little beauty. Now nineteen and has got all the hide and cheek of it, especially after two years being one of the boys. Everybody's mate but as good as the best of them at yarning, drinking, scrounging etc. In fact those yarns Tich? At seventeen years of age. But the confidence and the cocksureness of it!!

Huggie: Jack Huggins from Townsville

A very good soldier and a better mate; tall, dark, well-built, honest and unafraid. In fact every bit another 'stout fella'. A banana-lander and L/Cpl too.

Maurrie: M.F.J.Ferry from Kensington

A journalist on the Sun, an intellectual cuss, used to knocking around a lot and now amused and disgusted by the petty discipline and airs of some of the officers. Knocked back the Mr Ferry title himself. Now wild and haunted by this horrible waste of valuable time.

Codger: Forwell from Brisbane

A real digger. The biggest bloody rogue and the worst bloody drunk in the 2/29th Battalion but still one of the best liked. He'd take the shirt off your back and then innocently ask you to sew the buttons on. Past all redemption, Codger was just Codger.

JACK: J.Cressdee from Chatswood

Another good soldier. In the Light Horse in the last war and did great work in this one. Steady and dependable: a solid man in a Section.

Whit Monday, 25 May was a most eventful day. We were woken up and paraded at 1.30 a.m. Three men had been caught in town after a little 'nocturnal amusement'. A fourth escaped but gave himself up in the morning. From the cries during the night the punishment was made to fit the crime. The boys, four Australians, were taken away somewhere. As a result, the canteen was cut out. We expected that our rations would be cut down as well and that we would be placed under an armed guard at night.

The four men got four days without food, followed by five days field punishment, whatever that was. Their lives were promised them, however. It seemed that we would miss out on our pay and no extra bread because of the incident, which we thought a pity as we had been having a great spin. There were only five guards to the 1700 men at the Great World Camp, no barbed wire, our own discipline and no parades. We were more like civilians in some respects.

After a few days the canteen was back and things almost back to normal. The boys ragged me about having a cushy job, without any nastiness and reckoned I was one of the luckiest in the camp. I was too, for the work was only taking me an average of an hour a day. The name 'Argus' was stuck on me. They were always asking me questions and had not tricked me yet.

I met up with Curly Hardman at the Great World, who was to be my closest mate for the duration. It turned out that he had lived in Blaxland Road, Ryde for some time and he knew Jimmie Calder and Auntie Queenie, as well as the McPhee girls. A group of four or five of us would yarn away for hours in the evening, reliving the past. Bobbie Logan would reckon the Australians to be the most arrogant, conceited, vainest, self-opinionated soldiers of any army. We stood up for ourselves but he was probably right the way we had ourselves on that we were the world's greatest.

The officers' conduct we thought deplorable. They forgot which army they were in and Churchill's order of 'defiance in defeat' was completely ignored. The last lot of reinforcement officers were the worst.

On my birthday, 2 June, I received 'best wishes' from the boys and 'many happy returns', God forbid. I thought of the twenty-first birthday I was going to have. That day we didn't have a meat issue. Maurrie Ferry and Bob Gibbs (from Liverpool days) celebrated the day with me and we had two duck eggs, three slices of fried brawn, a tin of bully beef and a loaf of bread, which I had accumulated. It was beautiful and we finished it off drinking coffee. However, to cap the lot, my pay was cut down to 10 cents a day.

I was not always in the camp. At work one day 2250 cases of sake weighing 100 lbs each were shifted. It tasted terrible and I could not have picked a harder day.

A four-day air-raid precaution scheme had been in operation for some days, which we thought may have had some significance. Some of our men were always hoping and expecting that the Allied forces would come in and retake the island as part of a general push north from New Guinea.

I would have been surprised, myself, if ever hostilities again broke out while the Japs were still in occupation. Singapore had settled down to as near normal as possible. All essential services were in operation again: law courts, banks, water and sewerage, trolley buses, the brewery etc. For us it was pretty monotonous. Our theme song was:

> *I've got the POW blues,*
> *Everlasting rice and stews.*
> *I'm just wasting my time*
> *In this tropical clime,*
> *Singing POW blues.*

We would repeat this over and over. A concert party was started and every night we would have mouth organs, a couple of soloists, dirty jokes, etc. We even had a cricket match in the street outside our hut, just like in Wardie.

We questioned the news that Sydney had been shelled by Japanese submarines and one ferry boat sunk. This came with the news that 400 000 Yanks had landed in India, Burma was lost and that huge British bombings of Bremen and Cologne were carried out with 1000 and 1500 bombers.

Certainly it was better that we be under the discipline of our own officers, when back at the camp and not on the job, than directly under the Japanese, but the unthinking and unimaginative way it was carried out was beyond my comprehension. Curly Hardman had been on sick parade for three days and did not get a chit to get off work for the day. For that, he was put on a charge sheet:

AAF A4

No.NX50687 Pte. Hardman of 2/30th Bn AIF

CHARGED: with that on 4th June 1942 at Singapore whilst a Prisoner of War did fail to attend a place of parade appointed by his Commanding Officer in Dispatch Party parade ground at 0845 hours.

WITNESS: NX67414 Sgt Rowe K.W.

AWARDED: Forfeiture of four days' pay (Japanese)

But a worse occurrence was when one of the boys died from a crushed pelvis in an accident. Another sustained a crushed liver. We had no accident prevention methods.

A new screed had come out in regard to saluting (our most prevalent misdemeanour) and forbidding communication with the native population. An order forbidding the excessive ill-treatment of us must have come from a high source for it was far from Japanese practice to treat prisoners well. Bashings were usually only meted out for stealing or for not working. Earlier Maurrie had come down with 'malaria' on the job and a Japanese NCO paid to have him sent back to camp in a rickshaw.

Our concert party was getting more professional with a stage, backcloth and costumes. We lacked a piano but had some excellent talent in jokes, sketches and singing. For an hour we would forget that we were in Malaya.

After four months the weeks and months seemed gradually to get longer and longer. At last I cleaned my teeth, Bobby having given me a toothbrush and a full container of Gibbs Dentrifice. A quarter of an hour of scrubbing did not get my teeth clean. Soap was not too plentiful either. Bedbugs were throughout the camp and spreading sores. We painted the beds with oil and creosote but we were to take them everywhere from then on. They were into everything, try as we might to squash and kill them. The smell was all-pervading.

We seemed to have been classed as being in the Nippon Army. Machine-gun posts were built around the camp, mounted with Vickers guns and there was ack-ack practice going on. We did not know the significance of these moves but we were required to mount our guard, Jap style, complete but for rifle and bayonet, being on alert 24 hours a day.

At our work base, (the 'Bottle Yard'), to which we marched from the Great World before being sent to various jobs each day, we were made to dig and make a machine-gun post. When we had completed it the Japs set up a brand new Browning LMG — made in USA 1937. If we had had that turned on us we would not have been too happy.

We were Tomi No. 2308 detachment. Our officers were responsible for our behaviour in the Great World camp, which had an unprison-like atmosphere. We might as well have been back at Liverpool for the concerts and canteen, which, as far as we knew, was the only one on the island. We even got our hands on a piano and drums for the concert party. The Padre had an excellent library too of about a thousand books. I read *Lost Horizon*, two Shakespeare plays and Omah's *Rubaiyat*.

The good news also was that we were told that arrangements were being made to write home. Along the road the Chinese were still very good to us, often giving us food and money. I was back on the work parties as well as working in the camp. I even learnt to type the pay sheets. It meant that I did not have to go out on the back breaking work every day, for which I was just not strong enough.

On most evenings we would yarn away before lights out. We all came from a great diversity of backgrounds, each with our stories to tell. Curly Hardman was one of the great yarn spinners of the camp. I would imagine him as David Gordon (Blackcock's Feather) in a lounge suit and a motor car: having to work for a living but hating it and avoiding it at every opportunity. We planned what we were going to do and how we were going to spend our deferred pay. I drew up plans for a boat and to have a VS [Vaucluse Senior] built: *Virginia*. Wanting something out of the army life was one thing but I thought that I would be lucky if kept my life. Meanwhile we developed a circle of mates, shared life's experiences, our meagre possessions and made the most of it.

We had a brown-out for a week but at the end of June we had no lights in the camp at all. Machine-gun and weapon posts were set up at corners all over town. Events, of which we were unaware, were no doubt causing the alert. Work was slack as there were few boats at the wharf although an aircraft carrier was in, which we thought was interesting.

About 1500 men, mostly Pommies, were taken up north somewhere by train and we were on stand-by. The 53 000 of us taken at the surrender were all over the place by then. An Indian Regiment had turned traitors and their officers and sergeants were acting as pro-Japanese police. The Sikhs were hated by everyone.

We were not happy when our officers meted out punishment for transgressions of the Japanese rules and regulations or for our conduct, when considered unmilitary. Tich Martin was on a charge sheet for buying a loaf of bread along the road and Curly Hardman was fined 60 cents (40% of a week's pay), which was a lot of money.

Major Cousins (Charles of 2GB radio in Sydney) returned through town on his way to Tokyo, probably for propaganda broadcasting. I believed that he had made some recordings at Changi, after the surrender, for some purpose or other.

The bedbugs were getting worse and I threw out a mattress I had managed to get my hands on. I had a table and a chair for clerical duties in the camp and they had to be debugged and moved too. On 1 July 1942 the long-awaited postcards were received to be made out and sent home. We had no idea how or when they would be delivered, though. My card ran as follows:

Mum and Dad
Was not wounded but am now a prisoner of war and am quite well and happy.
All the love in the world.
Douglas

Flour was unobtainable by the native population from the Japanese, except at an exorbitant price. I wondered how they were living. All the food was seized at the surrender and most of it shipped away. Milk was to be cut next and then frozen meat, which would reduce us to just rice and vegetables. The civilians would have only pineapples and coconuts.

The Japs were getting very cocky. I thought that things were not going too good. Excerpts from the *Synonan Times* (*'Comic Cuts'*, printed in English):

• British destroy Suez Canal to cover army retreats
• Axis forces 50 miles from Alexandria...Tokyo predicts fall within a day or two
• Nothing can save Britain...neither changes in fighting personnel nor reinforcements. The British Empire is now definitely on the wane...the British position was hopeless in the face of the inevitable trend of events. For the first time in history the British Empire is tottering and falling. In the end if India stays with the British Empire she will find herself among the wreckage when the Empire crashes as it inevitably must.

We wondered how our forces were actually faring in the various theatres of the war: the British in the desert; the Russians after Sebastapool; the Yanks in Australia and the Pacific; the Chinese up north.

A mock invasion stunt was carried out on Singapore. Coast guns, ack-ack fire and about 100 bombers and fighters were let loose. It brought back the exhilarating feeling of the three weeks of concentrated noise and death, which was indelibly in my memory from January/February.

I was shocked though to learn that our officers had instituted a 'hostage list', in which was entered the names of 'criminals' in the camp. If ever the Japanese were to ask for men as hostages, etc, these men would be given up. It seemed incredible.

We were taken to see the site of Japanese executions—block, blood and heads on the railing -so we would know what to expect. One of our boys was caught selling bike chains to the native traders. He was not taken to Jap HQ but it was left to our own crowd to deal with him. One of the officers wanted him thrashed but he could think himself lucky that the boys did not do him over. For the duration many of our bastard officers were reviled only a little less than the Japanese bastards.

With the general alert in the first half of July, beatings up and general bashings had become considerably harsher after the executions. It had been a daily occurrence since March, that one or more of the boys had been beaten up by the guards on the job. The insane temper into which they flung themselves meant that they did not know the extent to which they went.

On Saturday 11 July one of the boys was unconscious for two hours after a blow from a steel-shafted golf club. Some weeks previously 'George', the Jap guard, came at Collins with a tomahawk, hitting him on the head with the flat of it and then twice broke a broom handle over his back. He was taken to Jap HQ, thrashed, half drowned and tied up in the sun all day. We received a letter saying that he was treated lightly. The worst I knew of was when a guard attempted to open Roy Poy's skull with a piece of two-inch pipe and then a with a piece of three inch timber.

We were POWs and if we were caught we expected to pay for it but not to the lengths they went. We expected, as sure as rain on eight-hour day, that one of us in the Great World was going to be shot or executed as an example. It was no longer worth the risk to even look at a packet of cigarettes. At Bukit Timah the Sikhs had bashed one of the boys to death.

And yet, only a week before, Snowy Stevens got 'sun stroke' on the job at the Bottle Yard, causing the Japs so much concern that they organised a truck especially to bring him back to camp.

The Japanese on the job tried to speed things up and we tried to slow things down. It was a classic confrontation. Our officers were in the middle, but at that point I had never heard of one of them being hit. With scrounging pretty well discouraged, a tin of tobacco would last me eight days. Most of the boys would run out quickly though, including Curly Hardman, so I only smoked half of my tobacco myself. Our rations were cut and we were getting half of the meat and vegetables that we were getting two months previously. In fact we were back to the gruel with the rice and maybe three or four small bits of meat and onions for tea. It was a lucky dip, the broth would be vigorously stirred up, the ladle would go in and on to your plate or mess tin. The luck of the draw got you a couple of bits of meat or nothing. That was our main meal of the day. Lunch was then plain rice and a tin of Rosella baked beans between ten men. Breakfast remained plain rice and tea. Things were grim and every night I slept in an Indian burial sheet.

A typical day's work at Virginia House [W.D. & H.O. Wills' former warehouse] was: Fifty or so of us carrying cases on our shoulders from the trucks outside, down some stairs, up one flight and stacking them. The line of bodies would be going up the stair, others coming down, the endless cycle going on and on all day. The 'Two-bob Lair' would be doing his block with a broom handle. His foreign language and features were strange to us and in the heat and humidity we were stripped to the waist. It reminded me at the time of a story in the *Boys Own Paper* of slaves to the Spaniards in South America.

The Japanese saw some trading of razor blades going on from the back of a truck. They came to the camp and demanded the man. Our CO (Schneider) called for him (a Pommy) and threatened to hand over the first man on the hostage list if he didn't come forward. And at the Jap HQ they made an example of one of the boys, caught with a tin of milk, in front of our morning parade. They had him tied up with wire and at one stage it seemed that he was to be shot in front of us. At the same time we were shown how to bow and salute, Japanese style and we had to bow and scrape for half an hour in front of the Japanese lieutenant.

We would often work out how much our deferred pay was going to be. The optimists still thought that we would be home by Christmas, but still thinking that it would be two years, I would calculate my accumulated pay on that basis. Meanwhile I still kept my cash book record of receipts and payments, religiously accounting for every cent received and spent. I had done so since before leaving Australia. I hoped that Australia would not be broke when I got back and it was time to square up.

The concert parties were then on twice a week. It was surprising how good they were; better than at Liverpool. Of course girls are girls and there we had only imitations.

There must have been some dirty work at the crossroads somewhere in July as about 150 tanks, up to 35-tonners, were unloaded. These we thought came from Java and they were taken to the railway line for railing up north. The work parties worked 24 hours a day non-stop, unloading and storing Japanese foodstuff. It had been obvious for some time that the original Japanese soldiers in charge of us had been replaced with garrison men but we thought that they were going to again be replaced with fighting soldiers. Rumour had it also that 3000 of our men, probably tradesmen and technicians, were soon to be taken to Japan.

We at the Great World did not know much about what the rest of the boys were doing or getting. Changi, we thought, was pretty well deserted except for the hospital, to which we sent 18 cents of our pay each month. There was a big mob at Bukit Timah on the roads and on a big memorial to the killed, both Japanese and British. Quite a few, we thought, had been taken to Kuala Lumpur and Malacca as well as the crowd to Burma. It had been in the newspaper that a Yank submarine had sunk a prison ship, drowning most of the 1000 POWs and civilians. Certainly we were working for the Japanese war effort and releasing their men. With the private soldier's disinclination for work and our anti-Japanese sentiment we did resist.

We were a varied and human crowd. I took a school textbook on algebra out of the library and started studying my $a^2 + 2ab + b^2$. It was quite interesting and kept my mind occupied in my spare time. I also read *Insanity Fair* by Douglas Reed. Maurrie Ferry was funny and exasperating. He had missed some tobacco out of his tin after I had got a smoke from him and he accused me. When someone had taken four tins from his tobacco plant (he had more than anyone else) he got the sulks and wouldn't talk to Curly Hardman or me. That a man of 26 would carry on like a schoolgirl, 'I won't talk to you', surprised me. There were some mad and funny bastards in the collection we called an army. We would yarn away and reminisce. I was always thinking about the good times with Neil and Ron; from when we went to see *Brown on Resolution* at the Embassy to the three of us at the Prince Edward at Christmas 1941. Curly sketched the boat (*Virginia*) for me, which we both hoped to build when we got back. It was to be a 20-footer, to be built for £70, and would take us to Broken Bay and Port Hacking. I hoped that it would appeal to Neil too. It was such incentives and promises to ourselves at the end of the war that kept us going. We needed something like that to work and hope for in order to stop ourselves from becoming morbid and more dead than alive. The rot had already set in with some of the boys, who could not stand the routine and the mental state of mere existence.

Things were pretty grim by the end of July. I smoked my last shred of tobacco and we ran out of fat and flour, so no more fried rice or flapjacks. Plain rice was well nigh inedible. It was what we had been expecting for some months past but it would take more than slow starvation to kill us.

Breakfast	Rice and 1/2 ladle vegetable gravy and tea.
Lunch	Rice (fried) and tea.
Dinner	2 rice cakes and tea.
Supper	A cup of re-heated tea. It was not much.

I felt that I would like to go to sleep for twelve months. The work was exceptionally heavy, with the wharf and harbour full, and some days we worked all day and night till 10 or 11 o'clock. I was lucky that I still had my pay job as well and so some days stayed in camp. Air-raids were the last thing the Japs were frightened of as the city at night was lit up like Luna Park (pre-war) and the wharves were the answer to a bomber's prayer.

When we could get our hands on some flour, etc., Curly would knock up a flapjack or rissole for supper. One night, however, a Jap sergeant stirred things up over our fires at night. He kicked pans, billies, contents and all, over the fence and took cooks and culprits to HQ. It knocked our (illegal) cooking on the head for a bit, which was serious as the small extras to our thinned-down rice and stew had kept us going.

Four days later the twelve men taken to HQ over the fires in the camp at night came back. They did the four days in the civilian gaol on four biscuits and a bucket of water. And we had never been told that we were not allowed to light fires in the camp after dark until the twelve were taken away. Again, for the umpteenth time, we were warned that we would be shot next time for disobedience.

When wondering how Dad's and Mum's birthdays went (31 July and 4 August) I thought of what things would be like at home. I couldn't see Australians worried or concerned, even if the Japs were right at the front door. I supposed that I saw quite the wrong picture of conditions prevailing at home but I felt that I knew the Japanese better. Most of the boys were glad that General Bennett got home, much as he deserted us. It was never an issue.

On 11 August we had our first contact with civilisation. Two hospital ships had come from Mozambique with food; super concentrated soups, jam, meal, caramel, etc. We thought that we might even get some of it too, though individually it would be very little each. But it would be something and it made me hopeful that our letters would reach home.

Things looked bad in the Pacific according to the *Syonan Times*. Much as we would have liked to be home, most of us would like to have another crack first, only under more even circumstances: and against the Germans.

Some Japanese civvies came and inspected the camp, particularly the canteen, and asked what prices we paid. It turned out that the bloody natives had been lying to the Japanese and profiteering on us. They were forced to lower their prices. We were midway between two pays and were nearly all broke so we could not take advantage of it anyway. But Curly made up for it by being given a tin of sausages along the road; the first for some time.

Wouldn't it bloody well root ya,
Wouldn't it make ya scream,
Ya think ya back in Orstaylya
And wake up and find it's a dream.

That's the way we were—just plain homesick.

The canteen came back to normal. We were too hungry to boycott the bastards. If they had been reported they would have been kicked out and we would have been worse off. However, stoves and fireplaces were built for us for cooking at night when we came back off the job late. Not that many of us had anything to cook. We did have showers and beds and I had my Gibbs dentrifice. These were among our last pieces of civilisation and we were living pretty close to nature. My eyes were getting worse, having fallen off noticeably over the last six months.

Two naval men had been picked up in the Indian Ocean and taken to Changi. They had left Australia on 23 July and were giving talks on the latest news.

• The Japanese submarines story in Sydney Harbour was true.
• It seems we have got a pay rise.
• There is a fair sized army in Australia as well as the chocos (chocolate soldiers. Citizens Military Force, CMF, looked down upon by the AIF).
• Those who ran to the wharves and cleared out of Singapore before the surrender are being hailed as heroes in the newspapers and may get off scott-free. We called it sheer desertion in the face of the enemy and they were lucky they were not shot by our side when they were leaving.

There was always something going on around us. Officers above the rank of colonel had been taken to Japan and Black Jack Galleghan of the 2/30th Bn was OC of the AIF in Changi. We were glad to be on the 'delivery party' in Singapore as troops in Changi were being drafted to work forces and taken away. We seldom wore more than football shorts and a hat and so sores and burns were suffered from carrying lime bags on our bare backs. In August it was surprisingly cold and wet and there were cases of TB in the camp. We assumed that the 'comforts fund' parcels from the Hospital ship were being processed at Changi as we had not sighted any. The Japanese on the job were getting stricter and more interfering. All the things we thought we must have and could not do without, we had learnt to do just that in less than six months.

On 22 August, in the newspaper, we got both sides, German and British, of the Dieppe stunt. One, sarcastic and laconic, was of Churchill's disregard of his soldiers lives for purely show purposes: the other, very boastful, that they had just carried out a raid and all went well. For something that was heroic but a disaster 'well' seemed hardly the right word. 26th August was my 'good fortune' day:

• Bananas for breakfast.
• At 10.0am a Japanese was shot by a local civilian right outside our gate.
• At 11.30 Curly came back from work with some condensed milk

and Irish stew.
- Later Jack bobbed up with some of the cook's cake and Norm Allen with some tropical fruit.
- For tea we got two good ladles of stew.
- I entered a quiz competition at the concert party and won 20 cents for knowing who formed the Salvation Army.

It was one of those days when things could not go wrong.

Maurrie Ferry had come round from his sulks but he was in a pretty bad way. Some tropical skin disease had covered him over every square inch of his skin, especially between his legs and on his left ankle, where the skin has just rotted away and decayed. He went back to Changi Hospital with Jack Greenwood. Meanwhile the dice made their reappearance after a six-month break. We played with local cigarettes, which were well nigh unsmokeable, at 10 cents a packet of ten. Curly Hardman borrowed 50 cents and we finished up even, so we smoked our chips. I would have preferred a Capstan.

I was able to fix up the pencil Ron had given me last Christmas. It had been out of commission since the surrender. I never let the pencil, my wallet or my diaries out of my pocket on patrols, through training, in hospital, in action and then in the work camps.

The Japanese guards in camp had never really troubled us except with one or two notable exceptions. At our first camp in Singapore we did not have any at all, not even a sentry. In the Great World there were only six Japs under a superior private. Each hour one would tour around with a rifle and bayonet. We did not worry him and he did not worry us. When a couple of Japanese guards came through on one occasion, they started to shake things up about our smoking and one of them clouted down on one of the boy's cigarette lighter. We reported him and he was thrashed.

On 1 September 1942 the first census was taken and we were paraded outside the camp and counted, simultaneously with every other POW. The reason was that two Australians and two British were caught 200 miles away and nobody knew they were missing. On being brought back they were court-martialled strictly according to international law, found guilty and sentenced to death. The executions were correctly carried out and witnessed by Lieutenant Colonel Galleghan for the Australians and a British Colonel Holmes. The Japanese drew up a paper for every POW to sign, promising, in the event of future hostilities, no attempt to escape would be made nor any sabotage carried out. It had not yet been presented to our detachment but those refusing to sign were compounded at Changi under severe guard and discipline. 18 000 men were confined in quarters originally built for one battalion and reserves of Gordons—2½ square yards per man. Deaths from dysentery occurred at the rate of four a day. Of one party of 14 000 only three signed. It was believed that Black Jack Galleghan stated that those voluntarily signing would automatically forfeit their pay and deferred pay by being traitors (as they would be). Those at Changi were on quarter rations (the Japanese were not supplying rations) and Black Jack said that they would last out a week, when the paper would have to be signed under duress. We were told that the Japanese threatened to shoot ten men a day until the parole form was signed by every man, leaving Black Jack no alternative but to order the signing of the form. [It turned out that this information as regards the ten men was not correct.] I did not have the slightest doubt of their carrying out the threat if it was so, for it was for just such a purpose that they demanded that the hostage lists be prepared, given to them and kept up to date.

We had not signed the form by 8 September, when things were back to normal at Changi but it was supposed that we would be ordered to sign without a fight because of the threat over us when they did arrive. Actually quite a few of us were sorry that we weren't at Changi as it would have eased our consciences and made us prouder.

Meanwhile the Comforts Fund issue arrived. I got half a tin of grapefruit marmalade, five caramels (with milk content) and seven lollies (vitamins A & B); soup and oatmeal we got through the kitchen. It was all very welcome but we wondered, why jam?

There had been many thousands of Japanese troops brought on to the island. These were raw rookies and we watched them train. They got to know the island, to defend it, much better than we did. It was not a pretty sight to see them learn to handle a Bren gun, although I was glad that they were preparing for defence.

Our CO Major Schneider was a good man. It was the best bit of luck we had had, that a man like him had been put in charge. Without being pugnacious he stood up for himself and us and if unable to get the Japs to meet us halfway he did his best anyway. It was his understrappers who caused us trouble at various times. When Black Jack Galleghan (ex-2/30th CO), a dogmatic, aggressive old bastard was made GOC of Australian forces I could see sparks flying in his dealings with the Japanese. He started with a bonfire. Stories were that he would inspect the Japanese guard outside the wire at Changi and admonish them if they were not properly dressed.

It seemed a miracle at the time but one of our men, Hyde-Cates, was on a working party job when a Jap came up to him. It turned out that they knew each other at Mockbells [coffee shop] in Bridge Street. The Jap returned to Nippon just before the war, was attached to the army and sent to Singapore and Athol was put in the 2/30th, in our detachment, our work party and on our job when they met.

Curly was yarning with a Pommy, who was in the Changi affair. For four days they (20 000 AIF and British troops) were compounded on the Selarang Barracks square, in the face of machine-guns and gun posts, unable to put a foot over the drain acting as the border. The men were all defiant as they were making history.

Exercise or movement was impossible as men even had to sleep over the latrines dug through the asphalt. Ill and dying were not allowed to go to the hospital and one operation for appendicitis was carried out on a table. They were threatened with the shooting of nine men and one officer a day and that the hospital would be brought to the barracks if the papers were not signed. That would have been murder so every man signed and the party disbanded. Nearby the four men (the escapees) were marched off, untied not blindfolded and faced the firing squad, it taking four volleys to shoot them. After the third volley one of the AIF, rising to his feet yet again, shouted 'for Christ's sake shoot straight'. It was thought that Black Jack would get him a VC for it.

On Sunday 13 September I signed (in duplicate):

> No. ....
> I the undersigned, hereby solemnly swear on my honour that I will not, under any circumstances, attempt escape.
> Signed
> Dated
> Nationality
> Rank or Position
> Ordered by Lt.Winchester 2/30th Bn., by Mjr. Schneider 4th A/Tank, by Lt Col Galleghan 2/30th Bn. O.C.Troops Malaya.

And thoughts of home persisted. I hoped that my things were kept for me.

War memories were already forming. The most gruesome and disgraceful affair in the whole campaign was at Alexandra Hospital. The Japs were chasing some Indians who took refuge in the hospital. The Japanese soldiers entered the hospital, smashed all the X-ray and operating equipment and went through the wards with grenades and bayonet, bayoneting those in bed who did not seem wounded. Later a higher Jap officer came up and shot his men but this did not atone for the slaughter, mainly among Indians but also of a few Pommies. The most peculiar thing I saw was a dead native, with no apparent wounds, lying on the road with his feet still in the pedals of his bike and his hands still on the handlebars, lying on his side, instead of being upright. It must have been concussion. The most maddening sight was that of the Brewster Buffaloes at the civil aerodrome, just bombed and riddled with machine-gun fire in their camouflaged hangers, even before they could leave the ground. It was pathetic to see them in action. The Japs just flew rings round them but the New Zealanders were the gamest ones there. I'll never forget the Cathay Theatre, a symphony in grey; a modern seven storey building with a large slab on top. On a hill, it was painted all over grey and as they came from Katong, it made a majestic sight, defying the bombers. As I saw it, looking up, it was silhouetted in grey against the smoke from the oil dumps, all on the grey background of the sky at dusk. The gun boat being attacked by two dive-bombers just off-shore was the sort of stuff you see in the world's newsreels. Bombers came in over Singapore in formation, just scorning the ack-ack. They dropped their bombs in clumps, when over the town, carefully avoiding the wharves and the railway station and making the ground around us simply toss and heave. I could not talk about planes being shot down as I never saw one. I kept a piece of shrapnel, five and a half inches long with me for some time. It was almost red hot when I first made its acquaintance about two feet from my side (this was one of the lives I lost on 15/ 2nd), when it smacked against the wall I was leaning on. I thought it would make a good paper weight. Snipers were something we all had memories of. Mine were of fifth-column work in Singapore, letting fly at every truck that passed, including us in an ambulance. One thing I did not wish to be repeated, was the march to Changi after the surrender. Thirteen miles it was and there were men three abreast along every inch of it, in fact it would have covered sixteen miles or more. Many were dead tired and quite a few drunk. Very few of the God knew how many thousands of us had ever put in a worse 24 hours. Those who couldn't make it lined the roads over the last five miles with the overturned trucks, fire-gutted tanks and unburied corpses, no longer recognisable as Indian, white or Japanese. Our thoughts were, may Buddha or Allah bless his subjects who put out water for us. And when we came back into Singapore a week later, buildings and ashes were still smoking, the wreckage still littering the streets and the civilian population still stunned. In fact it took fully six weeks or more to clean the city up and the smoke pall hung overhead for a month after the last shell.

Memories...memories.

On 2 October 1942, of all the grand sights I had seen throughout the world, the Sydney Harbour Bridge, the Suez Canal, Mount Vesuvius, the Rock of Gibraltar, Tower Bridge open, Edinburgh Castle floodlit, St.Andrew's, York Cathedral, London at Jubilee time, the Mediterranean fleet in Valetta Harbour, tropic atolls, and Singapore aflame, I saw the grandest sight of them all—four truckloads of South African and Australian foodstuffs, stacked near the kitchens. Fruit salad, pears, milk, cocoa, meat and vegetables, sugar, caramels and cigarettes, etc. etc., all for us.

And because the Comforts Fund goods arrived the Japs halved our issue of tea and sugar, quartered our salt and cut out cigarettes altogether. As we had no idea when another batch would arrive our MOs and officers decided to spread the stuff, after giving the milk, cornflour and a few other things to the hospital, over the next 90 days. It is a private's golden rule that a bird in the hand is worth a flock of flamingoes in the scrub and we objected to it lying around in the QM store over a long period as we would not then get our full entitlement. We thought that, if the Japs saw foodstuff around they would not put our rations back; on the other hand if we got through it too quickly they may leave us to starve. Major Schneider and the MOs compromised so we got some of the stuff straight away.

Beri-beri, a vitamin deficiency disease, again appeared with swollen ankles and numbness of limbs generally. And there was a spate of accidents; in one case four pairs of broken legs.

Comic Cuts was not reporting much from New Guinea or the Solomons but rumour had it that Rangoon and Penang had been raided. We wondered when we would see the red, white and blue. I also wondered how Germany would stand the coming Russian winter as it would be the greatest test of the war. The boys admitted that we only played at being soldiers compared with the Russian Campaign. We heard little of Libya or the threat to Alexandria.

On 18 September another Comforts ship came in and we looked forward to some bully beef and fruit, even clothing. We had been getting little or no breakfast since before the last ship came. I was down to grinding rice to flour between two stones, revolving them in the same way as the most ancient of Egyptians.

There was no doubt about some of the 'Jap happy' bastards amongst us. One of the crawlers even carried a photo of a Jap around with him. In quite a few cases they crawled in so far we only saw their boots. It maddened us to see some of the boys playing with the Japs and making themselves ridiculous. Some of the country boys reckoned that they worked harder and longer back in the bush. Types were beginning to show up. To the young fellows it was still a lot of fun, making the best of it, even if pleasures were simple; some of the men around 30 were doing it harder, more inclined to mope and take a material view of things; the few even older plodded along patiently. It was interesting, no two were doing it the same, we had the dreamer, the yarner, those who wrote letters home all the time, the news fiends, the concert fiends and the blank—the man who just sat.

At work I witnessed another Sikh affair. This one arrested an old (they always pick on the old ones) Chinaman for picking up a butt he threw away. He tied his hands cruelly tight and would have taken him to the station and undoubtedly framed him to make a big hero of himself had we not got a Jap to have him released. It was the Sikh guards at Changi who had shot the four escapees there earlier in the month.

Malnutrition was attacked scientifically. The two MOs drew up lists of the thousands of calories we were and were not getting and what we should and should not buy at the canteen. At Changi there were four cases of blindness due to a lack of vitamin A (some film formed over the eyes) and beri-beri too was rapidly increasing. We got no cooperation from the Japanese medical authorities, in fact we could not get near them. So we started contributing one cent a day from our pay to buy palm oil, which the MO thought would do us the world of good. We were a study on the effect of a lack of essential vitamins on health because of the monotony of the rice diet. We were getting plenty of some but absolutely none of others. One budding expert discovered that we were sterile due to a lack of vitamin F.

Communication was getting formalised with the Japanese in charge of us, as we further developed a more or less bastardised tongue to understand each other:

Dicika	Go home
No. Oneika	The best
No. Tenika	No goodika
Speedo	Hurry up
Chui	Officer

Boxu and *trucku* were self explanatory

They had learnt our swear words too so we had to go easy when we were talking about them. 'Kura !' was the word we dreaded most for it apparently meant 'cop this you ******** Aussie bastard', as with it came a bunch of fives, a pick handle or a bayonet on our heads, backs, sides anywhere it landed.

The level of illness in the camp was increasing. Work hours were long, till three and four in the morning and as a result, in our particular party of 205, only 120 (down to 100 on 15 October) went out to work each day. A pretty high sick rate. I had piles, which became slightly painful. The MO offered to send me back to Changi Hospital for an operation. I put it off to see what ointment and an oily five cents worth of peanuts would do. Talk was of arrangements being made to send some of the boys home. Of 600 men totally incapacitated at Changi, the Japs passed only 146. I later learnt that a consultation was held over Maurrie's leg as to whether or not to amputate it. It was deferred but showed the rottenness of the conditions we were under as anyone could have picked up the same infection or disease.

I did not know what the weather was like in Japan but the Japanese soldiers in Singapore wore singlet, long underpants, 'cholera' girdle wound around their waist, shirt (sometimes two), cap, shirt-tunic, knee-pants, puttees (long) and boots. Their officers wore a heavier tunic, breaches and leggings, with their swords down to their ankles. I did not know how they did it as I was hot wearing only boots, socks, shorts and a hat. We felt the cold when it rained though. We thought we would freeze in Sydney; more so in Melbourne.

Out on the Bukit Timah road job, the transport fellows were caught selling their petrol to the Chinese. I believed they had been making a great deal of money and had handled the job well. But the Japs were tipped off. They took one of them, a Pommy, and squeezed his head in a vice and later, when he was in Changi, he died. The rest who were caught were put in the gaol. (This was the old Outram Road gaol for criminals before the war and used then by the Japs for the worst offenders.) A later death was that of a Sikh. They were on guard duty and between the Great World and another camp there was a Sikh making the civilians bow to him. He tried to make a Scotty of the other camp bow to him too, although he was inside the wire and going for a drink. He refused to bow and the Sikh beat him up three times. The Scottie was taken to the Jap HQ to show them what had been done. The Japs sent for the Sikh, who lost his temper apparently for a Japanese officer split his skull open with a rifle. We felt that the traitorous bloody Indians had had it coming to them for a long time. Quite a few had gone over to the Japanese, the Sikhs early in the piece, of their own accord. The Punjabis and others went over later. Mainly their jobs were ack-ack and guard duties.

Notwithstanding our situation I noticed that, with Tich Martin and Curly Hardman, in those few months after the surrender, I had never laughed so much in all my life before. We were young and we had a helluva lot of fun just fighting, yarning and acting the goat amongst ourselves; pinching stuff from the Japanese for the hell of it as much as for anything else. It would have taken more than the conditions of the last eight months to get us down. The Japs caught one of the officers sketching. He was placed in solitary confinement and when they came to collect him, found him fast asleep. They just could not comprehend it.

In the newspaper, along with the world news, spread across the front page was Nippon's profound gratitude for the return of their Sydney Harbour dead. At the same time a reign of terror was on at the different jobs and the Japs were getting stuck into whole platoons of the work parties. At Virginia House the 'Lair' took his belt, or rather the buckle end and belted everyone, including Rex Mason, a 2/29th lieutenant and 'George' went berserk at the Bottle Yard. It was rumoured that we were to be shifted soon and so the Jap overseers were doing our party over to reach their targets before we went. On the Bukit Timah job, we learnt, they simply went insane, causing broken arms and legs and one more death over the trading there.

At the Great World camp one day the problem started with us intending to go to work with only 83 men out of 198 on morning parade. The interpreter came to investigate where everybody was and while we were on parade, 'Fuji', the

Japanese sergeant-major, inspected the camp. He found primus stoves, immersion heaters, toasters and loads of goods we were not supposed to have, up in the eaves of the various structures/amusement stalls in which we lived. He also found Curly Scott planting his boots and Carroll, an NCO, not reporting him. They were both tied to trees in the sun. Later a search at the gate of the work parties coming home caught two of them with good hauls and they told the Japanese officer that they had intended bartering the stuff at the canteen. They were tied up all night. We expected to lose our canteen privileges for good after all that. If the Japs could not understand us, we could not understand them either for the canteen came back into operation next night, for which we were grateful.

It seemed that the cause of the stir was that a new set of Japanese were to take over. We were told that we would be moving camp and the Great World was to open up again as an amusement park. We were also told that we had to leave the place exactly as we had found it. This was a bit of a joke considering the firewood shortage we had had over the last eight months. We received our pay after a lengthy delay and then were told that all the books in the library were to be censored for any anti-Japanese sentiment! At this time too some of the boys were making really beautiful ornaments from the mica taken from Japanese bombers. The ingenuity and talent amongst us was quite outstanding.

On Neil's eighteenth birthday, 23 October, I wondered if he would have had to register for military service: it may have been that his job would claim him. I expected that, otherwise he would be in the Signal Corp by the time his nineteenth birthday came around. I had had no regrets and hoped that Neil would be in the war too.

The 23rd was a big day for us too as we moved to a new camp, not that far away in River Valley Road (still in Singapore), a move that was uneventful except for a couple of search scares. And so we left the Great World, where we had really been somewhat fortunate and could consider ourselves lucky.

5
Behind Barbed Wire

If we weren't really POWs before we certainly were after the move. We had barbed-wire, Sikh guards and we lived in dilapidated double-decker attap huts, about four feet per man along the entire four rows, top and bottom. I would climb up the ladder to the six feet top platform, Curly Hardman on one side and Ron Cruickshank on the other. According to Curly the bedbugs were under, over and between us in thousands. In the rain the mud was inches deep. So, except for leg irons, we were the typical prisoners of war as people would imagine us.

Work was quiet, only about 100 of our party going outside each day. Meals were the same, rice and weak vegetable stew three times a day. The canteen arrangements in the new camp were poor as well. I took orders each night, handed them in to be given to the civilian trader and when we were lucky the goods arrived. That was the best we could get.

There was quite a lot of movement of our troops going on. Indians on the road may have been going off the island and a large batch of Pommies were inoculated and medically examined before going on a boat for Tokyo. They had already been on the boat once. It seemed that there were to be 5000 Poms and 2500 Australians left in this camp to work in Singapore. All the other troops were to be taken away. There had been quite a few new prisoners brought into Singapore too, possibly from New Guinea, Timor and Java.

Things came to a head in the cookhouse soon after we moved camp. Breakfast was to have been at 8 a.m. one day instead of at 7 a.m. Our own cooks made it at seven and let it go cold. After a word or two about their ancestry, they were kicked out and a fresh lot of the boys took over the job, including some ex-pastry cooks. We started getting pies and biscuits made with rice flour, the first I had seen for a long time. But up to then the cooks had not tried to help us at all but had been living like lords themselves, which they claimed was their prerogative. We were sure there would be some improvement and there was. We even got on to some shark, mutton and pumpkin and we thought it beautiful. The cooks had a very important job in the camp in trying to vary our meals with whatever was provided. They were also required to exercise a high degree of honesty because of the unique advantages they had over the rest of us.

I got news that Maurrie Ferry was pretty well better again. Getting the right treatment had left only a patch on his leg. He was lucky. He had had a wart removed and was three months on his back through picking up some infection. It showed what could happen. We could not be too careful once the skin was broken as the slightest cut became infected. We thought that nine-tenths of all the flies in creation were in Singapore to torment and infect every sore like hell. Our teeth were in bad shape too. Eating a biscuit, I took one bite and broke a lump off a back tooth. It was the first hard thing that I had bitten into for fully three months. Having to go on sick parade before the dentist I saw the MO and, in passing, he questioned the tinea on my feet. He slapped me in hospital for treatment. The dentist had a portable foot-operated pedal drill, pretty blunt, and cocaine for anaesthetic. However he did do a fair job. I was glad that I had seen my local dentist while on pre-embarkation leave.

I had my first mix-up with a guard that night. In the pitch dark I did not see him. A 'Kura' pulled me up for not saluting. I was lucky that he was not over-zealous for he did not get stuck into me. The lot we had then were Korean and pretty nasty.

Syd Grounds was older than most of us. I would never forget him sitting on the floor over a mug of tea one morning at the Great World, lecturing Tich Martin (19 years) and me (20 years) on the absolute impossibility of platonic friendship. And he an old bachelor! He would calm Curly Hardman down too, when he was ranting and raving i.e. going crook in his usual style. Syd was a really good mate and a calming influence to us all.

November 1, 1942. The last twelve months had sped the fastest in my life. It was a year since I had signed up and enlisted in the AIF. The time factor in the work camps was peculiar to say the least, the day being divided up between rice and stew in the morning, rice and stew at midday, and rice and stew at night. And work...work...work. We had nothing to fix the time of day by (often we had to think whether we had had lunch or not) and every day was exactly the same. You could not split the time up into weeks and months. No one ever knew what day it was or could say that a certain thing happened last week because there was no such thing as a week. There was no difference in the months even, as the climate of Singapore was the same all year round. So for sheer timelessness that was it, for there were only the two headings—night and day. As it was 'lights out' two hours after dark we knew little of the night except to sleep or work.

The tobacco we were smoking was terrible. Cigarette papers were scarce but the leaves of the Bible made excellent papers. On Melbourne Cup day, 3 November, I was smoking the First Book of the Corinthians. When tobacco was really scarce the boys smoked anything—dried tea-leaves, pawpaw leaves...anything.

At the Havelock Road camp, across the road, the officers intended, one day, to hand over one of the boys to the Japs for general bludging. The boys threatened to hand the officers into the river. True to algebraic theory, the equation cancelled itself out.

The prison camp at River Valley Road was reorganised along unit lines. The AIF were the 3rd Battalion and we of the 2/20th, 2/29th and 2/30th were C Company, which was split up into three platoons and HQ, in which I was included. We were *never* a rabble. My job was kept for me while I had been in hospital and I then had more work to do. I was virtually the Orderly Room clerk, carrying out pay, personnel records, canteen duties and general office work. I was glad of the inside job as it saved me a lot of worry and was better for my health in more ways than one. We thought that there must have been a union working for us. Basic pay was 10 cents a day, an extra 15 cents when on heavy work and another 10 cents if working over eight hours, making a possible total pay of 35 cents a day. The officer who carried the flag at the surrender was in the camp with us (Major Wild) and worth his weight in gold. He spoke fluent Japanese and was able to get the boys out of some awkward blues at times. He was one of the few English officers I respected.

Another crowd of 600 men moved off north and they were really loaded up. That was the pattern; everything that could be carried or loaded was taken, especially by the officers. The most rumoured destination of the work forces was Bangkok.

Our meals continued to improve with the new cooks and at times we got a bigger meat issue from the cold stores. We were getting beef or mutton every two or three days and fish, which was quite a change. Lunch was cut out, though, both on the job and in the camp.

After working from 9 a.m. to 11 p.m., Curly Hardman and the party, 30 of them, were called out again at 9.30 a.m. next day to work at Virginia House. Curly lost count of the number of thousands of boxes that came into the place, to be packed on the first floor. They worked through to three the following morning and at one stage, when it was raining heavily, they had to run, bringing the stuff in out of the wet. It was the worst two days ever and a promised 35 cents a day was little compensation.

The officers had been receiving $25 a month regularly and were going out on work parties as little as possible. I thought it laziness and sheer cowardice as they were sending out sergeants (in many instances mere boys) in charge of small detachments to face the Japs on the job. Of the eleven officers in our company on the 9 November, two officers went out with 28 NCOs and 173 men: on the 10 November, three went out with 28 NCOs and 211 men. I observed some instances of an officer in the 2/30th in a state of sheer funk whereas others, like Rex Mason and Arch Thorburn, did their best.

A thousand or more Dutch troops, both white and native, from Java were brought into the camp. The Javanese with their dark green uniforms, together with the English, Scots, Aussies, Yanks, Chinese, Japs, Malays and Indians made us a pretty mixed and colourful lot. Many of the latest Dutch prisoners spoke English and they were surprised that, in the AIF, we drew no colour line whatsoever.

One of the Dutch officers told us that the Japanese troops have actually set foot in Australia, north of Perth somewhere, after three unsuccessful attempts. In Java, as in Malaya, he said that the fighting, the cruelty of the fifth column and the steamroller tactics of the Japanese soldiers was just the same. After the capitulation the troops disbanded and returned to their homes and it was not until 25 August that they were again rounded up, designated prisoners of war and brought to Singapore.

The newspaper was full of news of a landing and a new front by the Americans in Algiers, Morocco and Tunisia; of the mystery of what happened to the French fleet and of the German occupation of the rest of France and Corsica. We hoped though that the British had cleaned up Egypt and Libya.

We were on two meals a day still. The Comforts Fund issue of cocoa and sugar helped a little but lasted only two or three days of each ten-day period. As far as our ten cents a day went, it bought five bananas. Curly and I would pool our pay. Apart from buying tobacco (35c), cakes (10c), pies (16c), peanuts (15c), bananas (6c) and bread (10c), Curly would win or lose on the two-up and pontoon games. I still kept my cash book going; once an accountant always an accountant.

We had cleaned up most of the bugs in our hut by encouraging ants and lizards. Unfortunately the rats ate the food we left out for the ants but the scores of dogs and cats kept the rats in check. Anyway we beat most of the bedbugs.

Unfortunately at this time, November 1942, somebody stole my slouch hat, and with it the only decent puggaree in the camp.

Lieutenant Colonel Pond of the 2/29th Battalion was widely disliked. I was told that, as CO of the Thompson Road job, his behaviour was despicable. The boys from Thompson Road came into our camp, having almost completed the shrines and parks at Bukit Timah. The whole thing was done with chunkels (large hoes) and small shallow baskets and involved the slicing off of the top of the hill. They used perangs to make the approaching roads and drives. There was one memorial to the Japanese dead and another to our own. After Kranji the stiffest fighting was at Bukit Timah and many of the boys, and the Japs, buried there, had been taken to the respective shrines at the top of the hill. These were opened ceremoniously. The Japs were strong on ceremonials.

The greatest thing in the world for us was meeting mates whom we had not seen for some time. A group of us, who were at Liverpool, Dubbo and on the *Aquitania*, met when some came in from Thompson Road: Jack Cressdee, China Hall, Jimmie Carr, Don West, Norm Waugh, Bob Watson and Wal Davis. We lived it up all over again. We yarned all about those still with us and of Cooky, Kelly, Rainbow and Pete Lennon who never would be. Some of Curly Hardman's transport crowd came in as well and I met the legendary Bill and Mick Bailey, the oil barons.

Work had not changed at all from the first day that we shifted pineapple cases back in February. If it wasn't pineapple cases it was rice, sake, lime, caustic soda, anything up to 200 lbs. We ran the transport within our own jobs, releasing more Japs. With civilian internees, some of the boys had jobs in town as electricians, lift mechanics etc. From other camps they made and repaired roads which were damaged during the fighting in January and February. The LCM [lowest common multiple] of it all was that we were just coolie labour, seven days every week, except for the break on 29 April for the Emperor's birthday. There was nothing voluntary about it at all as it seemed it should have been, according to international law. The fact was that our officers fined us four days pay at least if we did not go outside to work when we had to. Lieutenant Colonel Pond reached the lowest point when he fined men for leaning on their shovels for a minute at Thompson Road, one morning. In our company of 350 men, 29 of us had jobs inside; cooks, hygiene, company sergeant major, clerk and (3) batmen. We got on to some records and I thought of Ron as I listened to Duke Ellington's 'Blue Serge' and 'Jumpin' Punkins', in the 'Gal from Joes' style. It was good to hear all the Ellington soloists again. The lack of glasses affected my midrange and distance vision but not close-up sight. I still read a lot when not actually at work. I had read all the Shakespeare plays in the library, including *Twelfth Night*, which Neil had done at school and a book on Homer, his life and times.

By 25 November confusion reigned supreme in our camp. The personnel at River Valley and Havelock Road camps were split up and reorganised into our original units. The 2/29th were gathered together under Pond and in the mix-up I found myself without my inside job. I had been unobtrusively taking care of myself, getting the occasional promotion, for seventeen months in the army up to then and I did not think that the new circumstances would get me down. But that day the boys were not happy and jacked up over the Comforts Fund foodstuff, which had been kept too long and had to be buried. It caused quite a bit of discontent.

One of the officers was concerned for me going out on the docks and offered me a job in the camp as a batman, the greatest bludge of all. I was too proud to take that job so refused. There was no way I would be a batman to anybody. And so out I went; a six-mile march, no lunch and on to the wharves loading scrap iron—still no glasses, covered in sores and really not big enough for the work involved. There was the usual 'woof ******* Kura' to speed us along, armed guards kept their eyes on us to and from the job and yet we whistled and sang on the march, the same as ever.

We were interested in a huge floating crane down on the docks. I understood that it had got away before the surrender as far as Sourabaya where the Japs caught up with it and brought it back. We also saw that they were raising the ships which had been sunk off the wharves and we watched the divers with interest. I wondered if they had raised the dry dock at the Naval Base. This was a massive affair, the second largest in the world, and had been sunk by the Navy in February 1942.

Meanwhile we had a beautiful description of Singapore: that when you die you have to take your overcoat to HELL to ward off the cold. I was only out again working for three days when I brought up some very big blisters and sores on my feet. The boots I had were a broad 7 on one foot and a narrow 8 on the other. My size was a 6. They were all I had and had gouged bits out of my feet.

Other working parties were much worse off than we had been at the Great World. The Argyles, Leicesters, Indians and a few AIF had a terrible time at Kuala Lumpur, in the gaol there for the first three months after the surrender. They were lucky that they were not shot or beheaded as so many of the 2/29th and 2/19th men were when the Japs caught them after the Muar engagement and while the fighting was still on. There were 109 prisoners at Kuala Lumpur and 10% of them died with cholera and dysentery due to a complete absence of any medical supplies. For food, at one stage, they were eating boiled pineapple stalks, which was a similar situation to the hibiscus leaves and lemon-grass stews they were eating at Changi in March. Things did improve at KL in May, as they did with us, and they were brought down to Singapore.

I met up with Bernie Smith of the Ordnance Corp, with whom I was in action in the last days of the campaign. We lived it all over again; being mortared in the dark, no slit trenches dug and the Pommies streaking through our line. I was still of the opinion that I probably would not have been alive next morning but for the surrender. There was a gap a mile long in front of us, we were in the middle of a Vee and facing directly on the Japanese advance. Not that they could advance much further for they already had us in a position where we could not retreat any more.

I was in the camp for about eight days as my feet got better and I could walk again. During the time I played chess and Bing and Bob Crosby's 'Delores' over and over again on the record player. We were also moved once more and I was back with Curly Hardman and many of the 2/30th. We did feel that the conditions would never really get us down with boys like Bill Bailey to put new life into us. [But he later died too.]

After lights-out one night, four of the boys got stuck into a corporal who was throwing his weight around too much for his own health. This happened just outside my hut and they were choking him pretty proficiently. [I will never recall what the outcome was as edges of the pages of my diary were affected by sweat and damp and this obliterated some of the writing.] Life in the camp was never dull, even to soccer matches at times. I was still dreaming of having a boat, *Virginia*, built, living at Double Bay when the war was over and the conditions under which we were then living would be just a memory.

There was no let-up on the work parties. The 'Lair', who was one of the worst Japanese gang bosses, went to town on the team at Virginia House and it was the same at the Customs House, with one of the boys having to go into hospital. That was bad enough but what upset us more was the situation in the camp. The boys pulled down the recently built barbed-wire cage, about the third built for various offenders. The man then in it was doing 28 days for not shaving and then abusing an officer. I had no doubt that it might have been necessary in extreme cases to enforce discipline but using it for that, I thought, was pretty bloody wicked. What with the stunts such as at Havelock Road where they were going to put some officers in the river, doing over the corporal and dismantling the cage, we were asked to tone it down a bit; with the threat of the 'Riot Act' in the air. The constant stream of petty exasperations we had to put up with from officers who practically never soiled their hands on the job and stayed in camp every possible day, were certain to lead to something explosive before long. After a three-mile march home from the wharves, probably scarred and bruised, arriving back sometimes almost out on our feet, we were not happy to be ordered to 'mark time in front, left turn, block up, dismiss'. Major Schneider was respected at the Great World for recognising us as working parties to the Japs and doing as much as he could for us, letting us have as much rest as possible. Lieutenant Colonel Pond, on the other hand, treated us as if we were still at Bathurst and as though working for the Japanese was just a sideline. We could not be both, what with lime burns, sore shoulders and feet and having ill-fitting boots or none at all. We found the childish parade ground treatment hard to suffer under the circumstances. It appeared to us that the real cause was that the officers had found themselves to be inferior to Japanese privates and they did not like it.

Though I was still supposed to be off, I volunteered to go out to work for someone else and out I went in Cyril Battie's boots. I had thought that there were no seasons in Singapore but I was wrong. There is Wet and Dry. In December it was wet.

When in camp I had been manually grinding rice and I thought it wonderful when the cookhouse got on to an electric grinder, saving a lot of wear and tear on backs, shoulders and arm muscles. The hut we were in was a disgrace as most of it was without walls. As I was on the wet side and the rain just drove in, I had to patch it up as best I could with bits of tin, gas cape and attap [woven palm fronds]. We all did the same. But the cockroaches were not as bad as in the last hut and the bedbugs, while still around, did not worry me as much. It was all very primitive. For months I had eaten out of a large pineapple tin with a spoon. They were all I had in the way of mess gear.

We did receive a sort of 'corn sack' jacket affair from the Red Cross issue, which we thought was a sheer waste until we felt the cold, working and living in so much rain and under the damp conditions. Often we would go for some days and not really get dry. But I did find my slouch hat, minus the 'rising sun' for which I was glad.

At work I got the usual 'Kuras', shoves and searches but luckily was at Nestles House, which was one of the better or say lesser sadistic spots. Nothing further was heard of the repatriation scheme at Changi. The problem with the wounded, amputees and gangrene cases was that there was insufficient tissue-building foods and equipment to effect a proper recovery. I was very happy to receive a Comforts Fund issue of a pair of boots. This made a big difference when out working on the wharves and in the godowns. I came across a 1941 *Sydney Morning Herald* and a Sun too, on the job and was interested to read about parcels being sent to POWs abroad. It mentioned that after food and tobacco, music was the biggest thing to the men. It was so true. The gramophones were going every day, the concert parties were packed every night and we sang in the hut at times until nearly midnight. We sang on the march to and from work also; 'Reilly's Daughter', 'The Ball of Claramore' and 'Ivan, Navinsky, Navar'—pretty earthy stuff. In camp it was 'I'll Pray for You', the 'Maori's Farewell' and 'When They Sound the Last All Clear'. The newspaper was right about the music.

A German tanker was in at the wharf where I was working. The Huns were certainly big and we still had strong feelings about white supremacy. The boys could not resist lairising a bit, strolling around and smoking cigars in front of them. They were amazed until the Japs decided to do a bit of showing off themselves and did a few of the boys over.

There was strong talk that our work party would be ceasing soon but as we never knew if we would be alive or in one piece tomorrow we let the future look after itself. The weather had been terrible, a lot of the island was flooded and the camp was under inches of mud. We would come home up to our knees in water. It was like Melbourne or Edinburgh, cold, windy and wet. At work we were going through a minor reign of terror but as Christmas was approaching we appointed a committee to try and make it a festive season. The super-optimists who thought we would be home by Christmas had despaired, although the 'before Easters' were still noisy. I thought it would be August '43/February '44.

Extract from Routine Orders 15th December 1942:
NOTICE The following punishments have been awarded:
VX28431 Pte Grimison H.J.

disobeying a lawful command	14 days detention
disobeying Bn. S.Os.	14 days detention
conduct to prejudice	Fined £2.10.0

WX16347 Pte Watson W.

disobeying Bn S.Os.	14 days detention

VX34845 Pte Devery
failing to appear on place of parade   10 days Jap Pay
WX 13161 Pte Wright
disobeying lawful command   7 days extra duty

These were things to wipe out dissent within the camp. God knew where the dissent was but we thought it a vicious circle as it was likely to cause 'dissention' trying to wipe it out. I thought that I would be arrested and charged with disobeying SOs [standing orders] and given fourteen days detention for not having the correct dent in my hat. It was incredible what Pond and Major F. Hove, or maybe it was Black Jack, were like.

At work on the godowns by the wharf I was on a party shifting rice. The bags weighed 224 lbs (10 to the ton) and as I could not carry one I was in the team lifting them from the trucks on to the boys' backs, four of us, one at each corner. My voice, being the 'Hup' man suffered most. It was hard work and consistent all day. We did get some lunch and sweet tea, smokos and no interference so, getting a truck home, we thought it a pretty fair day; but still very heavy.

After a similar dress rehearsal the day before, we had an inspection through the camp by a Japanese general. We were on parade for four hours until he arrived and were lucky that it was cloudy as we were all dressed up in shorts, shirt, hat, socks and boots. Curly had the right idea and volunteered for work. Only half of us were going out each day as it had become considerably easier. One thing we had not been loading and unloading was bombs, as had others.

Work continued with its variety. I spent a day pulling out the iron piping from around tennis courts at Tanglin for scrap iron. An all-in war for the Japanese meant all in. They were moving out of the homes they had occupied and we were told that we would cease work soon. There appeared to be a general stir all over the island.

Shaving and haircuts had been a problem for some time but two of the boys had set up a barbering business. For ten cents a pay we got a shave every second day and a haircut when we wanted it. It was important that we stay as clean as possible. Personal hygiene helped allay sores and infection. A less important enterprise was the tattooing business in the camp. I was tempted but when I thought I may get around to it the two proprietors were under detention.

We had our own rogues in the camp and two 2/29th boys broke into the 2/19th cookhouse. They were caught at it and thrown in the river. Without having any sympathy for them and their fourteen days in the clink, I thought it a pity that the legalised robbery in the camp by men taking advantage of their position was not equally dealt with.

The Dutch troops moved out. Probably they were taken by boat somewhere but we never knew exactly where anyone went once they left us. It was so on all the work forces; you found where you were going when you got there and there was little or no communication back. The Dutch were inspected for dysentery and, not too thoroughly, medically examined. We had given them a good go while they were with us and being mostly Javanese, they had been a novelty to most of the boys. We had not previously associated with native troops.

On 22 December the white labour forces in Singapore were discontinued. It was ten months to the day since we were detailed to go into town as a working party (we thought for only a few days). Many were the things I had seen and done since then. I had been lucky but was not really sorry to be going back to Changi. Certainly we did not expect it to be as comfortable or as informal as it had been at the Great World and River Valley Road. We thought that the move was probably a preparation to move elsewhere. In feeling that we would be disappointed if such a move *did* take place, most of the men by then were resigned to just patiently wait it out; as I had been all along. There were few of us not prepared to take whatever the future may have held.

And so on 23 December 1942 I was on the road to Changi again, a road which always brought back bitter memories. As when we came into Singapore, we were transported for half of the way by trucks, for the Japanese did not want us to march through the city. The one and only time I did march the whole way along the Changi Road remains a symbol of the allied capitulation.

Gwendolyn McLaggan and infant Douglas.

George McLaggan

Dad with Flossie at the house in Consett Street, North Strathfield.

1920's scallywags.
Lottie Stewart, Me and Neil, Marjorie Murrell, Betty and Ron Stewart.

Another budding Bradman. . . Neil and I with Bobby and Doug Barber

In Edinburgh.

My grandparents, Edinburgh.

Aged 13 in my local Scouting uniform.

HQBOD (Ordinance) AIF

On final leave. Back in the office at Martin Place

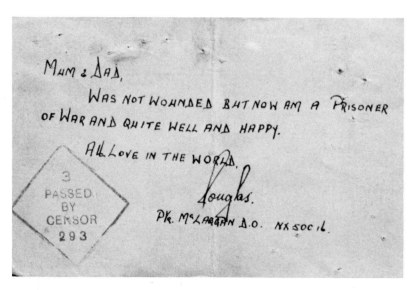

Mum & Dad,

WAS NOT WOUNDED BUT NOW AM A PRISONER OF WAR AND QUITE WELL AND HAPPY.

ALL LOVE IN THE WORLD.

Douglas.

PTE. McLARREN D.O. NX 50016.

3
PASSED
BY
CENSOR
293

My first letter home as a prisoner — July 1942.

27th Brigade parade at Changi — Australia Day 1943.

Meanwhile on the home front. . . A Christmas party for the children of POW's.

My wartime diaries.

When the diaries were filled I began to use whatever paper was available. In this case on the back of a letter from Grandma.

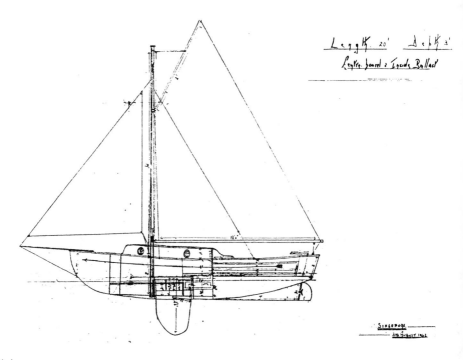

Virginia
A plan for the yacht I hoped to build with Curly Hardman. Just one of the many ways that we kept our minds focussed on the future.

The Selarang Barracks Square incident, September 1942. Over 15 000 men were kept for four days in a space usually accommodating 1200. They had refused to sign a document promising never to attempt an escape. This photo and others on following pages were taken in secret by Australian POW George Aspinall.

The Thai/Burma Railway

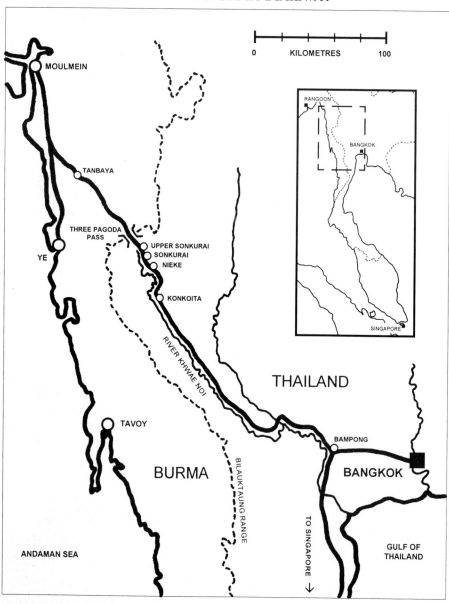

THAI/BURMA BORDER (ALONG MOUNTAIN RANGE)

- - - - - - - - -

RAILWAY

En route to Thailand

On the march — F Force in Thailand.

A welcome wash after a day's work on the railway.

The cholera clinic and open-air operating theatre. Shimo Sonkurai No.1 Camp.

Carrying logs for bridge construction. Pile-driving on such bridges
was the hardest work I've ever done.
By POW artist Jack Chalker.

Laying the track. The latter stages of the Burma Railway.

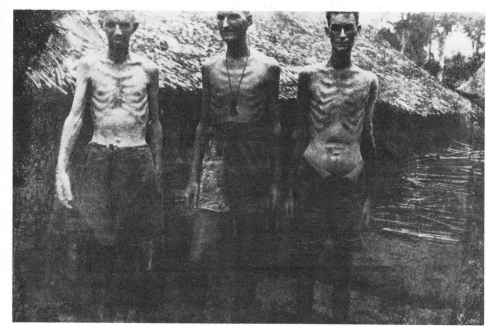

Typical 'fit' men.

Burial service. . . Every man got the 'Last Post'.

Back at Changi.
A Christmas card from Pieter 't Hart and Lex Noyon.

MESSAGE TO PRISONERS OF WAR

from

GENERAL. SIR THOMAS BLAMEY GBE KCB CMG DSO ED

Commander - in - Chief, Australian Military Forces

I extend to you on behalf of all ranks of the Australian Military Forces our congratulations on your final release from captivity.

Everything possible has been and will be done to ensure you rejoin your families with a minimum of delay and that in the interim your comfort and your needs are thoroughly cared for.

Many of you have suffered severely at the hands of the enemy while others, due to variations in conditions, localities and the quality of your captors have been more fortunate. But now you are free to resume the peaceful lives of which you must have thought so often in your captivity and we rejoice with you in your freedom.

You will find Australia is mindful of and grateful for the sacrifices you have made on her behalf and I trust that you will find great happiness and full compensation for the difficult times you have endured.

Good luck and God speed to all of you.

TcBlamey,

General
Commander in Chief
Australian Military Forces

Drs. Fagan and Bye, Heroes of Changi Hospital.
Of all the POW's taken by the Japanese, if an individual had to be picked as having done the most good for all, it would have to be Billy Bye.
Below. A letter from Dr Bye's British colleagues.

CHANGI P.O.W. CAMP,
SINGAPORE,
10/8/45

Dear Bill,

With the termination of three and a half years association in the practise of medicine under unique circumstances your undersigned British colleagues feel compelled to express their admiration for you, especially during the period when you were responsible for the sick of all nationalities in the jail area.

Your constant devotion to duty, your absolute professional honesty, your determination to give fair play to all with the limited means at your disposal, have been transparently clear to all.

Your example has borne its inevitable fruit in the work of your subordinates, and in later years when time has dimmed the memory of the cruelty, the hardship, and on occasions the apparent futility of the struggle, you can recall with pride a task nobly done and they can recall the high privilege and opportunity offered to them by their association with a gifted and humane man.

We all wish you a long, full, and abundant life in the profession which you so adorn and which you so whole-heartedly practise.

Yours sincerely,

First time home for the day. 1945.

Below: Stan and Vi Grimson, Mother, Neil, Mrs Hickson (neighbour), myself and Dad.

Curly Hardman at Lilli Pilli.

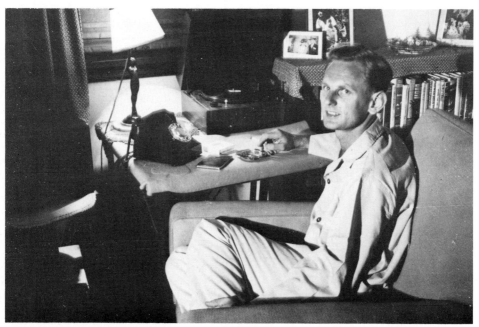

Back Home. My records, books, photos and lamp 'Diana'.

7
Changi

Selarang Barracks had changed little except that there remained evidence of the latrines and cookhouses dug into the asphalt in the previous September when there were so many men congregated together over the parole form. I did find it hard to realise that it was ten months since I was there last, the time having flown so quickly. On Christmas Eve 1942, there I was, sitting in the tropic sun, bug-hunting in a prison camp. I felt that if anyone had foretold my future last Christmas, correctly, I would have had him run in for fraud. Certainly the circumstances of the last twelve months were something that I could never have visualised.

I put in to transfer back to the 2/30th Battalion. This was a tough unit but I knew more of the boys. The 2/29th was not really a unit, as such, being a mixture of Victorians, New South Welshmen and Queenslanders, originals and reinforcements. All were a bit jealous of each other. The 2/30th were a homogeneous lot and as solid as a brick.

I did learn at Changi that :
- We had got the Japanese to forbid the Indians laying a hand on us.
- Black Jack Galleghan had been delegated all the powers of a G.O.C.

Christmas Day 1942 and I was stony broke. I went to church as I thought that Mum and my grandmother, in particular, may be thinking of me. Confidence in our release during the new year improved things considerably, which was half the battle. The excellent menu anticipated at River Valley Road fell through due to the lack of comparable facilities in the cookhouse at Changi. At breakfast we had rice and porridge with possibly milk although I did not know what it was. At dinner we had a tin of M & V between two men, a few chips plus some Red Cross fruit, which was not too bad. We had a good tea also, including beetroot, a rissole and cocoa. To make my day Jimmie Foster told me that my name was on the notice board of the 'Lost Property Office'. This was stuff recovered from our kitbags, which were discarded somewhere along the way. I picked up my leather portfolio, which Dad had given to me a year before. It included all my ordnance papers and a photo of myself taken in the office. Of all the AIF only 100 or so of us got anything back so I was lucky.

But I went on sick parade next day as I had strained myself the previous week lifting the rice bags and brought up a varicocele on the left side of my testicles. Hot foments and rest were the answer to the problem. There was slight and persistent pain but not enough to give me much trouble.

It was a totally different world at Changi from that on the work forces. Just after Christmas I was at a baseball game, the AIF versus the US. I wondered if there were many Yanks in Sydney but in Singapore they got on my nerves. We could not shut them up as they thought that we loved them as much as they loved themselves. We were thankful that there were only about 600 of them. They were an artillery unit from Java and the survivors from the *USS Houston*, which was

sunk in the Malacca or Sunda Straits. I had not met many seamen from the
HMAS *Perth* as they kept pretty much to themselves. There were a few air force
men in Singapore too, some Dutch but very few of the 7th Division men from
Timor. They were in hospital and I did not know where the rest of them had
been taken to. Many of the white prisoners were being brought to Singapore
from everywhere and I hoped to see the Burma lot again. The Japan party, of
course, were gone for good. We never let up on the Yanks for the cat and sparrow
stew they once made and ate. Even at our worst we had not come at that and
never did. Rump steak of dog had been discussed more than once but never
seriously. Not that I thought that we may never have to. Curly Hardman and
some of his fishing mates were working out how to net fish in a fairly large tidal
drain by the wire as a few of the boys had been successfully doing so for some
time.

At the concert party the orchestra was very good, playing popular classics and
light pieces. It comprised of an alto sax, two clarinets, violin, two trumpets,
euphonium, piano, guitar and drums. I was amused that I had been trying for
three or more months to think of Bing Crosby's big number from *Mississippi* and
just couldn't. And then it dawned on me—'It's easy to remember...and so hard to
forget'. Quite ironic.

I was still without glasses and called at the hospital in the hope that the pair I
had left in my portfolio might be around. They were not there but fortunately I
was able to get another pair which were reasonably close to my own prescription.
On the way back I witnessed the march past of two burial parties. Between the
AIF, the Pommies and the Dutch, especially the latter, there were deaths every
day. There were going on for 80 in the AIF cemetery which, considering the
circumstances, was very light. This was due to the standards of hygiene enforced
on us by our medical authorities, which were the highest there. The hospital was
completely isolated from the main camp and there were about 4000 there all
together at the end of 1942. Dick Trew was there with a bad case of dengue
fever.

It was Curly's thirtieth birthday, on the 30th, in the 30th. The days had not yet
really started to drag:

Up at 8 a.m., wash and breakfast.
Read till lunchtime, lunch with a bit of stew.
Read till tea time, tea.
Yarn away all night after being paraded and counted. The Japanese
were then coming to check the count more often than not.

We had a lot going on at Changi. There was sport, lectures, plays, concerts,
recitals, both recorded and orchestral, and the library. In all, our time was well
organised and every effort was made to remain alert and positive in our thinking.
Changi University ran training classes in a great variety of subjects with our
future in mind. On New Years Eve it was twelve months since Mum, Dad, Neil
and I had bid our most casual of farewells. Most of the boys had told me of a
deluge of tears and a myriad of kisses when they left but in fact that Wednesday
morning twelve months before had never ceased to amaze me. We were all so very
calm. To celebrate New Year's Eve there was an issue of brandy (?). It was only

a fairly large nip but Des Gee, Mark Wilson, Syd Grounds, Curly Hardman and I drank quite a few toasts before downing it all. It was lights-out at 10 but we still made a lot of noise in traditional New Year's Eve style with sing-songs and bagpipes. And next day we made our resolutions:

No gambling;

No swearing;

No talking about women;

No more lies or fish stories;

No growling, on parade or off.

In fact we were going to be good boys from then on; or until they were all broken of course. On New Year's Day I spent the afternoon chipping cement off old bricks. It was a job I had not done since 1929.

The gardens had come on well at Changi. These were commenced shortly after the surrender and by then 80 acres were under seed: spinach, chillies, yams, tapioca root etc. They were terraced, irrigated and sheltered and the experts had done a really good job in providing crops for the various kitchens. In looking over some of the photos, which the boys still had with them, a lot of us had lost some weight. Curly was about a stone lighter at ten stone. I was glad that I had little to lose and yet some had actually put on weight.

Shortly into the new year, four MPs, followed by two staff officers and a Red Cross officer from Division were whizzed off to the gaol, about half a mile away. Black Jack Galleghan and Major Wild followed. In a search, the Japanese came across cameras, maps, compasses, plans and God knew what. All our gear was then searched by our Company Commanders in the presence of Japanese with fixed bayonets. We were told that the position at Division was terrible. Things could not have been too good as we were on parade for two hours instead of the usual one. There was an air of jitters in the camp. But nevertheless we would spend hours at night playing animal, mineral or vegetable, arguing and abusing each other.

Is the groove in a screw made of steel?

Is a footprint in the dirt made of dirt?

I had them guessing for a while with the neon gas in the COR sign at McMahons Point.

I worked out that in 1942 I had had six haircuts and no more than 70 shaves since the surrender. Water was not a problem at Selarang Barracks though. I would do my washing, shower, shave, have a haircut, clean my teeth (while rationing my toothpaste) and feel like the proverbial new pin. I still had a cold from sleeping on the outside verandah of the building and getting soaked through every time it rained. But there were always camp duties to do: one day on rice grinding and another on boreholes, 22 feet deep, in three shifts of eight hours. One day one of the boys fell down an old one and what a mess.

Into 1943 I still had a pen and ink to write up my diary every day. These I had managed to avoid being discovered in the many searches in the camps so far. While writing one day, I thought of Ron as I listened to a Telefunken recording of the *Peer Gynt Suite* ('Anitra's Dance' and 'Solvieg's Song') by the Berlin Philharmonic Orchestra. I did not think it as good a record as ours.

There was a robbery at the canteen in the early hours of one morning. We did not know if it was an inside or an outside job. Cigarettes and a large sum of money were taken, the loss of which would have to be made up with increased prices. Actually the profit at the canteen was like a 'purchase tax' and was distributed among the kitchens. Canteen arrangements, however, were pretty poor; even peanuts were then unavailable and coconuts were rationed. There were a few hundred coconut palms in the camp but they always seemed to be green.

There was always something wrong with one of us in our close knit group of mates. Curly was down with a helluva temperature, cold shivers and a sore throat and Mark Wilson was pretty bad with a swelling under the eye. The eye tooth had to come out. Nothing much seemed to happen to Jack Cressdee though. Being in the PMG he told me that Neil was on to a good thing in the Department with their cadet scheme.

Boys of the 2/40th (23rd Brigade, 8th Division), some Pioneers and CMF arrived in the camp at Changi on 7 January 1943 from Timor and Java. The crowd also included those who had skipped from the *Aquitania* in Fremantle when we were there in January and did not get back to the ship in time. I had not yet got on to them to get their stories as to what happened after we left. Meanwhile my transfer to the 2/30th was knocked back. I was not that sorry but being mates with Curly Hardman and Syd Grounds and others in the 2/30th and also with Jack Cressdee, Tich Martin and Curly Avard in the 2/29th was a double-barrelled affair, I thought, and was not right. Whatever I had I shared with the boys but somehow when I was broke and others like Jack shared their stuff with me I was uncomfortable. Jack claimed that I had been good to him and Les Cook on the *Aquitania* and what was his was mine. It was the way we worked. He had collected more than one watch and lent me one to wear. I timed myself one day:

0805	Awoke
0810	Up and dressed
0815	Wash and roll call
0845	Cleaning up, taking canteen orders, breakfast
0915	Writing up diary, listening to Bix Beiderbecke and Red Nicholls records. The record was cracked and it was an ancient portable with a faulty soundbox and half a spring—it was cruel.
1000	Trailer party for wood for the kitchens. This was a flat-top truck chassis, pulled along by a dozen or so of us.
1300	Lunch
1330	Writing up diary and more records
1440	Making a 'cake' mixture with stuff we could buy from the canteen.
1520	Still writing up my diary for the last four days and getting my 'cake' back from the kitchen (baked).
1800	Tea
1830	Dressing for parade.
1840	On parade and retreat at 1900.
1920	Dismissed (this was a record). Hunting around for change as I was still holding the money for the QM and taking canteen orders.

2000   Yarning with Curly Hardman and the boys of the 2/30th.
2215   Made up the bunk and yarning with Jack Cressdee.
2245   Lights out
2315   Asleep

We were not actually overworked. When I was not writing up the diary I was reading or just yarning with the boys in the sun. We got a job about every second day. I felt that it was the sort of life millionaires paid millions for. It may have been better still if the meals were more satisfying and thoughts of home not so worrying. The beer, women, pictures, telephones, trains, motor cars, in fact all those things that make a civilised world and which seemed so important to us once, were not missed in the slightest. We found that all the important things in life were very simple: sunshine and friendship being the first two, then music, books and a smoke. These we had, even in a prison camp. What more could we ask for, we thought but pay, food and a letter from home. We were going 'troppo'.

January was the season for the north-west monsoon and for days a northerly wind blew continuously over the camp. It was freezing. A year previously we would have called it a cool breeze but our blood had thinned, we were carrying less fat and we felt the cold.

It was mid-January: not being occupied by work parties and with insufficient other activities to occupy us, squad drill was started. It was soon cut down from two hours a day to half an hour a day, however. We were told that the 27th Brigade would put on a show at a Review Parade on Australia Day, 26 January. Trust Black Jack. We were not enthusiastic and thought it pretty scandalous that we would have to repeat the first two weeks in the army all over again and in a concentration camp of all places. I felt that if I was to go on parade I would like to do it properly and have it look good. I was not, however, for drilling men who did not want to learn and could not be taught in a million years. The review would not involve all the Australian units, for at least those remaining at Changi under Black Jack Galleghan included :

Infantry	18th, 19th, 20th, 26th, 29th, 30th Battalions
Artillery	10th, 15th Field Regiments and the 4th AA
Motor Transport	2, 3 and 4 Companies

All the Corps Units including the AASC, AAOC, the medical, engineers, provosts, the 4th Machine guns and others.

They were all real men that I was with and I was proud of the friendships made and being one of them—Curly Hardman, Doug Morriss, George Smith, Jack Cressdee, Tich Martin and Curly Avard to name just a few.

We were given to understand that the Indians who went over to the Japanese shortly after the capitulation were behind wire again. The Sikhs had been taken off the job of guarding our camp at Selarang and it was rumoured that some of the Indians sent north had escaped to India. We had Korean guards at Changi then. One day when I was outside spreading gravel on a road, we had an interesting conversation with one of them who could not speak a word of English. His acting was good and his ideas as a soldier were the same the world over. At least we got paid. We were told that Christmas Day and New Year's Day were declared as holidays and that the Japanese sent no money for those two days. Typical.

Sunday 17 January was upheld as the anniversary of the battles at Muar and at Gemas. Some of the boys, who had been florists before made really beautiful wreaths for the memorial services. It was arranged that we would go to the cemetery as a Unit.

Another job I was on was pulling down the wire around the camp and bringing it closer in. Our own engineering officers conducted the job, without a guard in sight. You would have thought that we were wiring Bondi Beach from the way we were taking our time and having our own standover merchants.

Our views on the Provosts [MPs] were typical and unwavering. I thought, may Curly's favourite oath strike all those 8th Division provosts. They were purely and simply the same stooges and pimps as in any gaol. The bloody bludgers patrolled in and around the perimeter of the camp and gardens just looking for and making trouble. We could not insult them, they had hides thicker than Jessie [the famous elephant at Taronga Park Zoo] and it was maddening to see the big bastards lounging around with simply nothing more to do. Of course we were better off with them than to have an increase in the number of Koreans but we resented it when the provosts were around. It was bad enough having physical training sessions, squad drill and starvation rations on Tuesdays and Thursdays without standover tactics by provosts. The disgrace of there being a gaol within a gaol for offenders was worse than ever and we blamed Black Jack Galleghan for condoning it, not the Japanese. Private soldiers and the lower ranks of NCOs are not the most tolerant of people and the AIFs resentment of authority was no less by being in confinement.

On the lighter side the boys held an old time dance in the 'hut' one night and it was a helluva lot of fun too. Bert Sporn raked up a trumpet, an accordion, drums, the old two spoons and a couple of crooners. It went over well and I was sure that it would not be the last. Light was the only trouble, as after dark we had only some oil in a tin and a wick. The previous night Jack Haig had given a talk about his job as a screw at Coburg Goal and more of the boys planned to have a go along similar lines. All this was within our own C Company in the 2/29th. We were on our own, without officers, who were segregated from the troops (and for the most part were not too bad) and with our own cooks, who were doing a good job with the pitiful rations and the money we put in. We were certainly better off than the rest of the battalion and the 2/30th, especially in that 'the Bull', our Company Commander, held no unnecessary parades. The distinctive character of the 2/29th arose from the fact that such a high percentage of the unit was killed in action at Muar and that there was a more egalitarian attitude among those remaining.

We were told on parade that the Japanese offered Black Jack the chance of broadcasting messages home. This time he accepted and it was planned to pick a balanced group from the men in the camp to send the messages. We were concerned that they would be used for propaganda purposes, but nevertheless thought that they would be wonderful in the homes they reached.

Malaria had become common by this time and Syd Grounds had gone off to hospital with a temperature and all the symptoms. It was under control before the war broke out but apparently the mosquitoes again were starting to spread. It was a debilitating sickness and Syd had a terrific dose, although we expected him back soon as large as life.

I learnt that the vegetable gardens, which were then the largest on the island, were mainly for the benefit of the Japanese, our officers, the hospital and the permanent gardeners. A part also was set aside for the civilian internees. The officers certainly knew how to look after themselves. They even had chicken runs, as did the hospital. Day-old chicks were available at the canteen at times; as were 1943 diaries. Though broke I set about seeing what I could do about ordering one. I did not know if the Japs knew they were to be available. If they were recognised in a search they were confiscated so they were not left lying around. It was later that they were actively prohibited, when searches would be made for cameras, diaries, weapons and knives, with severe punishment if caught.

The bedbugs were still bad throughout the barracks. We lived on a wooden floor and they were in, under and through everything we possessed: boxes, clothes, gear and beds, if you were lucky enough to have a bed. I was on the floor. I could feel them biting me at night when they were at their worst. We applied an oil and other deterrents when we could get something to put down, but for the most part we just had to live with them. [And did so for the duration.]

When I went over to see Snow Pannowitz he told me about the Timor show. They only lasted about two hours. Some of the Timor boys told me that before they surrendered themselves they were critical of the 8th Division, as probably were the rest of the AIF, but when they also capitulated after the fighting they could understand the hopeless job we had. It might have been thought that we threw in the sponge too easily, but it amazed me really how the boys held out so long. We *never* had a thing, not *one* tank and the RAF then told us that for only one day did the infantry have air support (at Gemas). The only effective work the air force had been able to do was to bomb the troopships up north, early, and to protect our landing, in January—the only day that Singapore did not have an air-raid.

On 23 January 1943 our camp was inspected in the morning by what must have been a very high Japanese officer, probably of royal blood. We had to conform with Japanese custom in that no one was allowed outside the huts or to show his face. It was the first time that they had gone through that procedure, though I believed it was common in Japan. It was an extraordinary performance and just another incident which we, of the white races had to go through and which we thought to be unique in world history. The day also was my 365th in Singapore. So much had happened but I had to admit that the war and the period since had done me the world of good.

And next day I came off the rehearsal for the Review Parade thinking that there was no doubt that Galleghan certainly liked a show. I thought that all the baloney on Australia Day was only to please his vanity as on previous occasions he had been merely a battalion commander and was then an acting divisional commander. Quite a jump. But of course it was more than that. It was to show the Japs the pride and independence of the AIF. And at the end of the day we had another beautiful tropical sunset. A cluster of palms on the orange red horizon would forever be one of the prettiest sights I have known. And even more beautiful was the same thing set against a big full moon.

The Brigade Review on Australia Day 1943, on Selarang Square, was complete with all the trappings except rifle and bayonet. We had to give it to the old bastard that he certainly had a lot of nerve. As usual we felt that the 2/29th put it over the 2/30th although I did not really know which was the better. But I still could not get over it, a ceremonial parade to celebrate Australia Day, in a prison camp!

After the parade I had my first swim since being at Dubbo, twelve months before. The first dive in the water was beautiful. We went down to Changi Beach, a couple of miles from the barracks for the usual buckets of salt water to boil our vegetables in and to crystallise for the salt. The water was not as salty as in NSW but where previously I had missed out on a swim I did enjoy it that time.

In every camp we kept the lines clean every day. It had been a big factor in keeping down sickness and death. Wherever we were, cookhouses, latrines, drains and showers were cleaned and washed down and the huts scrubbed regularly. It certainly paid off and I was sure that one result was fewer numbers in the cemeteries. We visited them one Sunday and they were well cared for. In the AIF section there were then 78 graves compared with 100 British and 150 Javanese. These were as the result of wounds, disease, accidents and executions. The graves were covered with lawns and each had a cement cross. The whole was set out among palm trees, paths and gardens. It was quite remarkable in that it was all started from scratch, with first having to clear the scrub and root out the trees. Diseases were always on our minds and when we did get a dysentery needle or other inoculation, on an irregular basis, it was welcome. So much could happen to us. Jack Cressdee went to hospital as his eyes had been getting very bad. It may have been infection or as the result of a deficiency of vitamin A, which caused a loss of sight until treated with a vitamin supplement.

At the end of January we wrote out our messages for broadcast home. We doubted that our individual messages would go as, at the same time, Company messages were written, containing as many names as possible. We thought that these more probably would be sent. I wrote: 'Mother, Dad and Neil and all concerned, I am still fit and happy. Do not worry, all is well. Love, Douglas'. It was a terrific exaggeration if not an outright lie but it served no purpose to worry people at home more than we, no doubt, already had.

It rained all that day too and we were glad it did not become a swamp, as did our previous camp. The boys, who had been at the Caldecot camp on the Bukit Timah Shrine job, told us of the frog races they held in the wet. With good nags, good form, good pedigrees and good prices, the meetings must have been a lot of fun. 'Fiver' out of 'Pay Book' by 'Col. Pond' was a typical example. The meetings were properly run with stewards, starters and bookies and plenty of punters. Quite a few owners however were suspended for running crook, a hooked pin tied under the frog being one of the favourite ways of making him jump.

At this time too a camp boxing tournament was run. I thought it absolute pure stupidity. There was not a man in the camp in a fit condition to fight on the food we were getting, no matter how good he thought he was. But mostly the bouts were pretty poor. We had reached a sad state of affairs. Due to the cigarette paper position (and the complete lack thereof) we had to resort to Curly Hardman's letters from his wife. It was sacrilege but all for a good cause. We were sure that Beatrice would forgive him.

But we were forever thinking about food. I preferred salt to sugar and would suck on a lump of salt like a lolly, enjoying it infinitely more. We would go for days without salt in our meals. Sugar was scarce too, though we did get about a spoonful per man each day. This went into the biscuits the cooks made, even the crumbs of which I did not waste, picking them up to get their full taste. We did however think that the lack of salt was bloody wicked. Meat I had forgotten about.

The series of lectures and tuition, on a campwide basis, continued. An excellent series on Economics was started, being given by a BEc. from Sydney University. The first lecture was 'Capitalism in Great Britain and Australia' (private property, enterprise and laissez-faire). This was explained simply and was easily understood. With the best part of 300 men there it was obviously going to be a successful series. I was pleased but for the fact that they were to be held over twelve weeks, which considering the ever uncertainty of our position, was ridiculous.

When visiting Jack Cressdee in hospital I was told that they were doping his eyes with drops. I also learnt that his name had been drawn out of the hat for sending his message home. It had a good chance of going. I hoped so as he had included my name, although of Kogarah. I was sure that anyone hearing my name, who knew me, would pick the error and realise it was me.

Duties on the garden party were coming around regularly and were to be our principal occupation. All the Dutch had moved out. I was inclined to think that our days on the island were numbered although I had little to go on. I had been back at Changi for six weeks and did not expect the situation to last.

My 1942 diary ran out on the 4 February 1943 and I received a new diary as a gift from Curly Hardman and the team. At $1.55 it was wasteful, considering all the calls on what little money we had and Syd Grounds, jokingly, would not let me forget it. It was good of the boys, though. The year in the diary being 2603 will certainly make it a good souvenir of Singapore's occupation as Syonan: an English diary in Japanese years.

Black Jack had by then, in no uncertain terms, set himself up as an absolute dictator. No more nor less than a monarch of all he surveyed. On him entering the concert hall everyone had to stand fast. One 2/29th lad was fined £5, 20 days' Jap pay and 28 days detention for chiaking in his presence. And against Major General Callaghan's orders on his leaving for Japan, promotions and reversions went on. We thought that he would have a lot of explaining to do on our release. He was in a position to take a better and more far-sighted view of things but I thought that most of his disciplinary actions were entirely without reason and unnecessary. He and his subordinates always had the threat of putting us on three meals a day of dry rice in the internal gaol, in a situation where we were already underfed and did not know what was before us. I had not the slightest doubt that he would carry it out if his authority or word was questioned. He was cunning though; his heel was not continuously on our necks—only resting there to be clamped down at the slightest wriggle. As a soldier before, and more especially after the surrender, there was no man commanding more respect in all Malaya than Black

Jack; as a disciplinarian this respect tended to be cancelled out.

On more general matters at the time, I wanted to make a bat pie but Syd said that I would have to catch, kill, skin, gut, cook it and then dish it up without telling him what it was. I was prepared to be in it but not on my own. And smoking newspaper was pretty wicked, burning my throat and, I thought, could not be doing it any good.

We certainly developed a lot of 'types' in Changi. We had a stir over a man brought into the camp claiming that he came from Australia but was shot down over Timor on 27 December last. He was given the world until Black Jack and a flight-lieutenant started questioning him and it proved all hot air. Later when they tried to question him again he could not be found, causing not a little concern. But he turned up in the news again and was put in the 'boob'. His news nevertheless spread like wildfire: that still in Australia no real news of the 8th Division had been received. That this *could* have been true really worried us.

Meanwhile we had a visit to the camp by a pretty high Japanese officer, one with a red pennant on the shining new Buick. We thought that probably he was the new CO for the area. He was, incidentally, very small. Next morning we had a 'humiliation' parade before him. We were up an hour before daybreak and breakfasted in the dark (and really in the dark for we had only two oil lamps in the whole of the gym, in which we were quartered, an old bully beef tin of coconut oil and a bit of rope for a wick). On parade just on daybreak, we were on our way to the AGH padang about one and a half miles away when apparently pity was taken on us and we got the order 'Battalion will retire—about turn'. It had been raining like hell for some days and not all the boys had a groundsheet or cape. Everyone was required to be on the parade, sick paraders, cooks et al. The language that morning would have warmed the air and could have brought a corpse back to life. And so the whole thing was called off. Two days later another attempt was made at a 'humiliation' parade. About 20 000 AIF, Pommies and Malay Volunteers were on the padang when it was again called off until next day, when we could expect to be up once more at five o'clock in the morning. Next day I was on a garden party and missed the parade after all. It became apparent that the reason for the assembly was for the taking of propaganda films, 15 000 of our fellows having to line up and have their pictures taken. On the side, scenes were taken of Japs dressed up as wounded, rallying around their mud-stained flag, stalking in the bushes, etc. The faking was obvious and all together from our point of view it was a pretty disgraceful show. We were glad it rained and the light was dull. Even so it took all day and no lunch.

Meanwhile we, on the garden party, had nothing to be proud of. We were cutting lalang [high grass], the job previously carried on by the lowest caste of Tamils. I was feeling miserable. On an earlier visit to the beach for salt water, two of us carried a ten-gallon drum nine-tenths full, up to our ankles in mud. Then we stood for a TAB needle, which was put off and then on the evening parade we stood again for an hour being counted. The weather cleared but it had been a miserable 24 hours and I was just down in the dumps. The lecture that night was 'Big business and the State in Industry', which cheered me up a bit and was certainly informative.

I still wanted to transfer back to the 2/30th. It was expected that we would soon be split up and I really preferred that I be with the 30th crowd. Curly and I saw Captain Macauley, who undertook to follow the matter up and see it through.

The session of the miseries was not helped by having to watch all the food, rissoles [which we called doovers] and puddings go by us to the 2/30th officers' formal dinner. I had not the slightest doubt that, when it was all over, we would hear how much the officers did for us while we were prisoners: how they preferred to be with us than be detached on their own. Bloody liars. Undoubtedly they did do some things for us and I was not one of those who imagined that we would be better off under direct Japanese control. However, as far as I was concerned any exaggerated and extravagant claims of sacrifice or effort on our behalf would fall on ungrateful and unappreciative ears. I was steadier and considerably less prejudiced than most but the lack—especially under the circumstances that we were in—of that comradeship between officers and men of the AIF, or even brotherhood of fellow Australians in times of 'distress' was, if existent, certainly not apparent. There were individual exceptions, of course but as a whole, no. I made and recorded a vow at the time: 'There are some good officers here, a few very good officers but in Australia I will never drink with any man who held a commission here, apart from official reunions'.

And so our first twelve months were up on 15 February 1943. All the novelty, all the holiday feeling, all that expecting to lay back until the war was over, living like lords, all that 'we'll be home soon', 'it won't be long now', 'we'll do it on our heads', had entirely disappeared. Some had come a helluva thud. I was glad I was never one of the optimists, though I was then inclined to think that my two years was a slight underestimation. But all the same, morale was extraordinarily high. Time did not travel as fast as it had on the working parties in Singapore as we were away from the hurly-burly of the city. Even so, most of the boys agreed with me in believing that we still had our worst times before us. Although morale was high a steadier and less juvenile outlook was adopted toward our future.

It was winter in Scotland and I thought of my grandparents as their diamond wedding was due. I was fairly sure that it was about February 1943. But it was not winter in Singapore as an all out war against flies was started. It was the breeding and dysentery season. We did not want a recurrence of the spread of the disease as had occurred in the previous year and from which many of the boys did not recover. The blowfly was our worst enemy. One man died of dysentery weighing 3 stone [19 kilograms].

We were still a mob of gamblers, though. Our group would pool our pay and Syd Grounds and Curly Hardman would give it a go. When we won we paid our debts and it provided for a couple of suppers and some tobacco. On pay night of 18 February we had fish soup and plain doovers for our supper, made of fish heads, maize flour, rice and oil. Except during our 'out' periods we had been having supper ever since we had come back to Changi. Curly had the job of chief chef, with only minor competition.

Milk had given out and our diet was just rice and vegetables (of some grass variety). Occasionally we had fish (sometimes a whole shark) but as it was bad (without refrigeration) when it came in we only had the parts that could be saved.

We could buy some things at the canteen like coconuts, bananas, dates, peanut toffee, gula malacca, maize and sago flour, even pineapples, if we had any money. Pay was something less than $3 per month. We were, however, without the three staple items of our normal diet—meat, milk and bread. The produce from the gardens supplemented the plain rice but it was typical that when pumpkins came into the 2/30th kitchen the men had pumpkin peelings stew and the officers had baked pumpkin.

When the Economics lecturer was in hospital I would go to other lectures at night or listen to records (Beethoven's Fourth) at the Education Centre. It was beautiful lying on the lawn under a palm tree, a big full moon and just listening to the music above the breeze. I was mainly working during the day in the camp gardens, trench digging with the best of them. Working without a shirt, I had a colour which I would have been proud of on Bondi Esplanade. And after having used blunt razor blades for some time, using a cut-throat razor, when given the chance, was less painful when shaving. We still tried to look as good as we could.

Postcards to home again made their appearance. Possibly they were only to keep us quiet: I did not know. I made mine out to read:

Dear Mother, Dad, Neil and all concerned. I was unwounded and am
still fit and happy. Do not worry all is well. Love Douglas O.

Rumour had it that a Repatriation ship would arrive soon and possibly the postcards were connected with it. It *was* about time another Red Cross ship arrived. We thought that maybe the only thing preferable to a Red Cross ship would be an air-raid, well almost. The last Red Cross shipment had made a big difference to us, particularly in saving the lives of a considerable number of men with dysentery. When we did have tests taken for dysentery we all lined up, trousers down, having our 'maidens' taken. There were the inevitable comments:

• I've got a feeling he's fooling.
• Don't go with your hat on, he'll knock it off.
• Are you going to have a back-up?

There was no doubt about the army but how a glass rod up the backside was a test for dysentery, we never knew.

At the hospital Jack Cressdee was coming on well with his eyes and while I was visiting there Syd Grounds was admitted. It seemed that a man had more mates in hospital than in camp. I met up with Roy Williss again, who I had not seen since the dressing station in Johore. He recognised me straight away. We were told that the deficiency diseases were getting more serious and we often got lectures about vitamins, proteins and carbohydrates. We were short of these in our diet and it was the cause of beri-beri, pellagra and loss of sight. It seemed that rice polishings were the best we could get for vitamin B. When it was available to us we got a little each day. It tasted like pollard.

I had written a pretty critical few lines about Pond, the previous November, from hearsay. Since we had been at Changi and the 2/29th all together again he had done nothing to justify or substantiate the poor opinion. In fact, apart from his stern appearance, I was sure that he was as lenient and as fair with us as would normally be expected. So, though others had known him longer than I, from what little direct connection I had with him he appeared definitely to be a good CO. It was an opinion I kept to myself.

On 28 February I went on morning sick parade. My big toe was infected right in the corner of the nail. Next day I was put in the MIR [medical inspection room] and Captain Brand, the MO, thought that the nail may have to come off in order to get at the root of the trouble. Syd was in hospital, Curly's mouth was sore and his eyes not the best and Mark Wilson was back on sick parade also with a bunged-up eye. I did not know what had come over all of us. Young Johnnie Clune, who was a good kid, was over to see us a fair bit. Des Gee, whom I had little time for, was the fittest of any of us. The boys on a wood party were bucked up though when they saw the women internees from the gaol lying down on the beach having their regular swim. In good spirits, the boys reckoned it was a wonderful sight for we had not seen white women for more than twelve months.

In a talk given by an American lieutenant, who was dropped off in Singapore by a German raider, we were assured that 8th Division casualty lists or nominal rolls had been broadcast over Australian radio. It was a great relief to us to know that something about us was getting through. Altogether it was very interesting to hear someone who recently had been in civilisation. The existence we were leading was not civilised: sleeping and living on the floor, every meal eaten on the ground with a tin or dixie between our legs, a spoon (in my case a fork) the only implement with which to eat, shaving with very common washing soap, the communal tongs or showers, the extraordinary motley of clothes and patches we wore, the garden and trailer parties and the *diet*.

Generally, however, we were pretty pragmatic in accepting our condition. We were told that there had been 5000 cases of dysentery and, since April, 1000 with deficiency diseases, 500 of which had previously had dysentery. As well as the cemetery we had our own morgue and an asylum for mental cases, chronic masturbation etc. Surprisingly enough, apart from general rumours over at the Pommy's camp, I knew of no cases or practice of homosexuality in the camp. I thought it may come. [For the whole of the duration I never heard of a single instance of it among the Australians.]

A very few of the boys at Changi, mostly Pommies, had received letters from home, dated since the surrender. How we did not know.

For the most part, among the men, we were all treated the same in the camp. We paid in a levy from our pay to the canteen fund and in turn, from the canteen profits, 25 cents each pay day was paid to those not in receipt of pay, that is, men in hospital and no-duty men. In hospital or not, it was important that we keep our minds and bodies occupied. I read a lot, read up on yachting, did crossword puzzles, wrote up my diary, kept my cash book going, attended lectures, worked on the various parties and yarned with the boys. Not everyone was as industrious. We often thought that we would be bored to death if we did not die of starvation first.

One afternoon, in the MIR, I had nothing to read, went to sleep for half an hour and woke up starving. I did not know how some of the boys could sleep all day. Their wives will ask them 'what was it like in a prison camp?' and they will have to reply 'I don't know, I never woke up'. When I did get a book from the library it was the *Compleat Lover* by William Godfrey. It was a compilation of extracts from the writings of Plato, Shakespeare, Aldous Huxley, Dorothy Parker and others. A couple of the verses amused me:

'No, no not my virginity, when I lose that', said Rose 'I'll die.'

'Behind the elms last night', said Dick, 'Rose were you not extremely sick?'

Nancy Trollope climbed so fast she caught and wed an Earl at last.

A bigamist she came a wallop back to plain and simple trollop.

Besides occupying our minds and keeping active it was important to have something to look forward to. *Virginia* was settling down to a 25 foot fore and aft boat, gaff and headsail (and extras of smaller jibs, ballooner, stormsail and maybe a spinnaker), an 18 inch deadwood keel and auxiliary engine: half decked, side decking and cabin forward 15 inches above the deck: copper bottomed, carvel built and canvas covered decking and cabin roof: all white but for below the waterline, which would be either green or black. Estimating the ballast at 12½ cwt [hundredweight], the total weight would be between 2 and 2½ tons and carrying a normal sail area of around 250 square feet. She would be no baby. This was mark 2, an increase proportionately on the plans previously drawn up and with which I grew so much in love. She would take some building but not the frightening job I first imagined. Twenty-four hour cruising would be done in comparative safety, which I actually looked forward to. This I had made my reward for the miserable existence as a prisoner of war. However the estimated cost kept going up. I hoped to stir the kind of enthusiasm that Curly Hardman and I had and enlist help in getting her built. I still thought it could be done for under £150. It was what kept me going. It seemed from the news that we had got a rise in pay to 9s.6d. and 4s.10d. deferred: 14s.4d. a day was all right to us and I calculated that I had £261 17s 1d in the pay book. Like a miser I often counted my accumulated pay and thought about how I would spend it. I felt that I would be rich for the first time in my life and I looked forward to enjoying it.

In early March everything seemed to be happening at once.

• A draft of 2500 men (excluding dysentery and malaria cases) was being prepared to go away. We did not know where to. It seemed that they got the number wanted as volunteers.

• 70 men (technicians) were to go as replacements to Blackamati Island. This was an island south of Singapore Harbour. It was an oil and ammunitions dump and some 500 men had been there over 12 months. It was a terrible place to work, not only for the isolation but the nature of the work was heavy and dirty.

• Letters had been received for us all and distribution was expected without too much delay.

Bernie Smith told me that he was going on the first draft and in the 100 AAOC men there was not one officer going. It was a bloody disgrace but consistent with their form. Thirty men left for a job at the Woodside camp and not an officer nor a sergeant went, leaving corporals again to handle the boys, the job and the Japanese. It may have been Japanese orders but it was still bloody disgraceful.

We received orders 'If allied aircraft appear overhead, no man is to signal or behave conspicuously. If arms, food or pamphlets are dropped no man is to pick them up. The IJA [Imperial Japanese Army] have been given orders to open fire on any one disobeying these orders'. We believed that enemy aircraft were expected and that preparations were being carried out, especially searchlight practice at night.

Jack Cressdee came back from hospital and although there was some improvement in his eyes they were still far from good. Syd Grounds was picking up too but would never be right until all this was over. I had one side of my toe nail taken off by a chiropodist and expected it to clean up in time. Curly's mouth was still sore. Deficiency diseases mostly affected the eyes, mouth, scrotum or feet. With all our problems I thought a lot about how so many that I knew from the office, home and friends were getting on. I hoped that all were well and that we would be full ranks when it was all over.

The first mob of 500 (of 2240) left on Sunday 14 March for up-country. We understood that most likely it was a four day train trip to Bangkok or to Jitra. It seemed pretty definite that it was a railway job, cutting and repairing lines up north somewhere. We thought that the draft may be relieving or reinforcing the crowd that left Changi the previous May. If that job was in the jungle we felt that they must be nearly wiped out with malaria. The team that left had four needles and a vaccination.

Our meals at that time were no good, which meant we were throwing half of them away. It was a camp crime to kill cats and dogs, which was only right, although I knew that we were a bloody sight hungrier than Black Jack. Turtles were the latest that the boys were getting onto and they were still getting fish from the drain. But it started then that the boys dying of dysentery were cremated, or rather crudely roasted, in a small oven, which had been built in the scrub behind the camp lots. This was probably a Japanese order to prevent a breeding ground in the cemetery. In March/April 1942, when the boys were at their absolute worst after being concentrated at Changi, Major Gunther had about twenty pits dug, approx 20'x3'x10', down by the wire. We were positive that they were for mass burials in case of plague or dysentery going through the camp. It so easily could have happened in their weak state of hunger and despondency. We thanked the Lord that they were never used and since had fallen into disrepair. But the pits represented the saddest and most miserable time of many men's lives. Digging them was undoubtedly near torture, the way the men were and realising what they were for.

I came out of the MIR with my toe better although it took a long time for anything to heal. I was marked 'A', so was still off duties. I was not impressed with some of the doctors, who had taken over the medical unit where I had been treated and who previously had been at the Great World camp. It was however the nature of the private soldier not be impressed too easily by those in authority. The MIR had been free from bugs however and that had been a relief.

Life had become very monotonous and dreary; everyone was affected. On a trailer party for wood it was a long haul back with 25 men pulling the trailer. These old truck chassis were getting stiffer and harder to pull. Sometimes two tons of wood was loaded on with 40 men in the hauling team. As always there were people worse off. I saw a man at the Convalescent Depot playing cricket with a leg off. The amputees played tennis, cricket, quoits and billiards and did not let things get them down. It was Sunday 21 March: Curly was screaming again. The 2/30th held a compulsory church parade when he wanted to visit the hospital as it was his afternoon off. Compulsion was not his idea of religion so he just walked off the parade.

I visited the hospital myself next day to see Syd Grounds and the boys. Syd was improving and Mark Wilson was due to return to the camp at Selarang. Syd and I yarned the time away, arguing whether the growth in secondary industry in Australia over the last few years would collapse after the war or not. I was pro and he was con. He was a good 'stick', old Syd, fourteen years older than me.

Coming back to the 2/29th hut I was 'nabbed' to do picket duty at the gardens from 11 p.m. to 1 a.m. Going down there I tripped over a wire in the dark and landed, elbows first, to save my watch and glasses. It gave me a shock and, while falling, I sure abused the wire. I hoped that I would never trip up in George Street.

It appeared superficially that you could just walk out of our camp as there was only one guard visible on the opposite hill. Actually around the whole area there were three perimeters of wire, which were densely dotted with guards. Their headquarters were at the nearby gaol. It was plain stupid to go through the wire and get into trouble over a few vegetables from the gardens. Some bastards just had no sense.

The mail arrived in the camp and I was pleased to get a letter from my mother dated 16 May. I knew that she always had a good reputation for writing wonderful letters. Reading mine I hoped that she did not cry and worry over me at the time of the capitulation. I was worried enough that at the time she would have. There was news of Dad, working down the south coast, of Neil, of Jimmie Calder getting married, of Judy Gray, her young 'niece' and good wishes for my twenty-first birthday. I was sure we would make it up with an accumulated party; it was just up to me to keep my health and to stay alive. I did not know how true it was but one man got a letter from his wife saying that she had adopted a two week old baby (Oh Yeah). Another's fiancé, had married his father. And one of the boys received three letters, the first from his girl saying that she is going out with Bob as she is lonely, the second that she has married Bob, the third from Bob asking him to keep his allotment going until they get on their feet. Army humour.

I tried to get in touch with Harold Wright, Ron Nokes and 'Twink' Wintle. These were English soldiers I had met at the Great World but I found out that they had gone up north. I would have liked to have seen them again but we were not allowed 'leave' over to Southern Area where they were camped. The British and Australian areas were divided at Changi and some distance apart. I thought that I would like to get in touch with Bobby Logan of Glasgow too. I still thought it a miracle that I would meet someone in a God-forsaken labour camp, who actually knew my cousin Gertie. I was looking to her to make me an uncle. There was no doubt about the army. Altogether I knew over a 100 men by name and twice that easily by sight. And every time you passed you nodded and made some remark like 'How are they hanging?' or 'How are you putting it in?' etc, etc. Undoubtedly there was camaraderie in the AIF. Unfortunately it was abused so much and so often by a minority of selfish, unintelligent bastards. It was so, especially at Changi, where humanity was at its absolute worst and the instincts, normally under the surface, were brought to the fore by hunger and greed.

I was back on duties and one Sunday I finished up working in the kitchen after seven days of cleaning grease traps, peeling vegetables, grinding rice and swatting flies. During that time, to maintain my self respect I had not taken anything out of the place, no odd peanuts, rissoles or vegetables, which were always going off, not even a cup of tea. Nothing sickened me more than the snivelling, crawling rats who hung around for scraps and what they could get. The bastards were no hungrier than anyone else.

When I got back home I thought of cooking a POW meal for the family:

4 ozs of rice (before cooking), boiled or steamed.

A condensed milk tin of stew, made of sweet potato tops and the stalks of some vines, precious little beans, potato and pumpkin, thickened with rice flour. No salt.

A rissole of rice flour, cooked rice and a few peanuts.

A cup of tea, no milk no sugar.

Of course it must be eaten off the ground and out of a tin. That was what 90% of our meals were like although at times, much worse. It kept us living and working but we had no reserves. If something went wrong it was hell's own job picking up again. The human body is a tough machine and I was convinced that starvation is a hard way to die.

At the end of March I got three more letters, Grandma's very nice letter of the 11 July, one from Jess, pretty mushy and both from Scotland, and Neil's. It was a great letter, all the boys read it and reckoned Neil to be a dag [someone special]. It made me so happy. I looked forward to having a lot of fun with Neil when I got going again. I missed him and to read about him being a scoutmaster, a write-up in the local rag, buying a 70s. rucksack and building a three-valve wireless, pleased me no end. I thought that if he kept mates with Ron I would be the happiest bastard to return from Changi. We were getting more letters and two more arrived for me from Mum, dated 2 and 6 June. The tenor of the letters amazed me as they were so confidently and cheerfully written, not knowing if I was dead or alive. My twenty-first birthday would have been a great day if we had been together but the coincidence of our thoughts on the day had to suffice. I was pleased that Mum wrote that friends far and near (and Dad I hoped) sympathised and consoled her until the first early shock was over. In Curly's letter from his wife, she told him of a nervous breakdown she had suffered that February and a consequent seven week holiday up the north coast. So it was with so many other thousands of homes and I thought then that these things, at these times, must be bravely borne. In the second letter Mum wrote that Betty Gibbs had been in touch with her, that Bill Freeman was in the AIF, that Betty Colebrooke, now Freeman, was expecting, that Ron had written and that Bertie Christie, from Wardie days in Scotland, was still alive. I looked forward to a letter from Ron and Betty. These letters completely changed the morale and outlook of the boys, home being so far away in time and distance. We were inclined to forget and be selfish, thinking that all the problems were our own. It brought home to us that others were as distressed, if not more so, at the fate that had befallen us.

Officer trailer parties were the latest. Of course they picked only medium-sized trailers on the wood parties and even then did not load them too much. But good for Jack Haig; he got all the worst bludgers on trailers too, the batmen, runners, even the orderly room corporal. It saved the boys from doing two trailers a day.

There was still a rumour of a big move soon but it was the sort of thing we had heard before.

Of an evening we played gramophone records, raking up a few good old tunes: 'You May not Be an Angel' and 'Peanut Vendor'. It was good to listen to some records as we had been a bit starved for music. Our favourites covered a good few years too. I went back to 1932, Curly to 1926 and Syd before that, 'You're the Kind of a Girl that Men Forget'. (Before my time.) Listening to 'Day Dream' with Johnnie Hodges and Barney Bigard et al., I still thought it as lovely as ever, even on an old portable and worn needles. I was the only Duke Ellington fan and was howled down, so to spite them I played it twice amid much verbal abuse. But even without the record I could hear all the Benny Goodman and Harry James solos in 'Sing Sing Sing', in my head.

An epidemic of food-poisoning went through the 2/29th Battalion, similar to that in the 2/30th previously. The boys spent the night at the latrines with acute stomach ache. Officially flies were blamed but we thought that the obvious cause was bad foodstuff (fish or prawns) passed by the quartermaster for the kitchen. Fresh food went off very quickly in the heat and humidity. We were lucky that in C Company we were separated from the main body of the battalion. We had to watch carefully what we ate, hungry as we were. We also had to look after what clothes we had as they were wearing out fast. I had two very tattered and torn pairs of shorts and expected to wear them until they were just waist-band and two pockets. It was hot working in the gardens and shorts were all we wore. What shirts we had we saved for parade.

Working in the gardens one day a sight that greatly amused me was of our big, bronzed, tough, he-man, fisherman, Curly Hardman, walking across the fields with a *watering can*. The man who belted up coppers in his youth, carried a gun and got damsels into distress: 'Mary, Mary quite contrary...' It really did look funny.

Standing Orders were that trading was prohibited of any kind, within or without the camp, and also the possession of any kind of stuff not normal issue. The two orders were hard to enforce but at least they had their good points. The trading that actually went on was a disgrace. But the worst example was an ex-staff Sergeant of the 2/26th Battalion, who feigned eye trouble, so going into hospital. There he stole god-knows how many M&B (sulphanilamide) tablets, for which a good price could be obtained. There were eleven men in the scheme altogether but he was remanded for five years. I always maintained that these affairs of stealing were infinitesimal compared with the legalised robbery of rations and pay that was going on at the same time by the officers, their formal dinners and a generally larger food distribution per man. The bulk of the officers' pay did go to the hospital but there was insufficient interest shown by them individually to the men there, whether hale or dying. When dead, a battalion parade was held to say what a good fellow he was. For all that though, I had no sympathy for the 2/26th man. In consequence of the orders we had regular kit inspections but no interest was taken of my bottle of vitamin tablets, which I had scrounged when at the Great World and was slowly getting through.

There was a new scheme to occupy us and we were given a plot of land to ourselves, early in April, to cultivate. This was from 'virgin jungle' and we enthusiastically cleared our area. I appointed myself a fireman but quickly got the reputation of being a firebug as twice the fires got out of control. It was hard work but fun and those from the bush went mad with the zeal. I thought that it was the closest they had ever been to owning their own land. The idea of private property, in addition to the communal gardens, was a good one. We could grow and tend our own plants; all we had to do was stay alive and stay in the one place long enough. It did however mean that I had less time to myself for reading and writing up the diary. What time off we did get was spent either on kit inspections, debugging our quarters or cleaning up generally.

For the first time I was on the right side of our sleeping quarters. Whenever it rained, as it did like blazes in Singapore, at the Great World, River Valley Road and on the square at Selerang I was always half-drowned. At last I could laugh and stay dry.

On 10 April we got definite news of a big move of 10 000 men, British, Dutch and Australian, starting from the following week. Until then I had not wished to leave the island but in changing my mind I looked forward to the change in scenery and routine. The moves were a big question mark as we never knew where anyone went or what they were in for. But I was tired of the monotony at Changi and thought that time would go faster, for a while at least at some new location. If some 3000 AIF were to go it would take all the fit men, leaving only the sick and the gardeners to look after them. I wondered if Jack Cressdee and Syd Grounds would be fit enough to go. We did not want to be split up but if it was decided that they were better off staying then that was OK with us. Both though, as too with Curly Hardman, wanted to go.

It was at this time that the 2/29th Battalion Association was being formed, with the 2/26th and the 2/30th Battalion Associations having already been constituted and under way. These associations had very ambitious objects in regard to the future and particularly the post-war years. The 2/29th Battalion Association was then in the preparatory stage with a proposal from the officers for nominations and the election of office-bearers from among the officers and men. The thought was to perpetuate the unit as a close-knit group, as we had so much in common, in experiences and outlook. Already at that stage the 2/30th Battalion Association was particularly strong. Pond, our CO, after having given us a pep talk about the forthcoming move, said that anyone not interested in the 2/29th Association could leave. Nearly half the men left, which disgusted me. When we did get down to business though, drastic alterations were made to the proposed constitution and then more nominations were put forward. We elected our privates into office and it finished up much more democratic. We had yet to finish the elections, refusing to hurry, when time ran out, so it was put off to another day.

Work around the camp went on and it seemed that it would do so up to the time to leave. I was on a demolition party pulling down an old workshop for the Japanese in the Southern Area. Flags had been placed on features around the camp. These were white, red, white, laterally and were possibly Geneva/POW flags. The camp motto on our gates was 'Cum gaudio haec omnia recordabimus', which was something like 'Be this happily recorded'. The significance escaped me. The three big guns at the naval base were near our gardening area and we were continually picking up pieces of the two which were blown right out of the ground. With the third gun, only the striker pin was blown off but altogether they made a pretty interesting sight.

I had received news that I was in neither of the advance parties on the draft but was to move, in a week, in train 6 to a camp strongly rumoured to be north of Bangkok, well into Thailand and possibly a railway job. Syddie Grounds had gone back into hospital with bad eyesight, so we were split up: from Singapore to Japan, Burma, Thailand and Borneo. Up north we expected malaria to be our main enemy as we had little or no quinine or proper clothing, nets or bedding. But for all that I was a bit sick of the garden, of digging and weeding and could not get away soon enough. I thought that when I got home I would never even mow the lawn.

We were given needles for cholera and plague, a vaccination against smallpox, a blood test for malaria and a dysentery test over two days. But really, the funniest sight of all was when we were lined up on the Selarang Square parade ground, in lines of about 60 abreast. The first line moved forward, the men dropped their pants to the ground and the medical orderly, with a paint brush and a bucket of mecurichrome solution (a deep purple colour), painted scrotum and crotch as if he was painting a picket fence. He went along the line, bucket and brush in each hand, slap...slosh...to the end. We stood there while it dried, brown, white and purple, then up with the pants and moved off. The next line came forward and the 'fence' painting was repeated. The orderly got through 600 of us in no time.

Insects, disease-carrying or otherwise, came in every conceivable shape, size and smell: half-inch long ants, flies the size of a five cent coin. Just drop a blot of ink on a piece of paper and there was an insect that shape too. A large praying mantis was one of the strangest insects that I had seen. There were mammoth mosquitoes, mammoth beetles, mammoth everything. There were lizards that changed colour, snakes (Curly reckoned that he had met up with a cobra) and squirrels but no monkeys as there were very few on the island. We did not know what to expect when we got up north except more of the same.

Jack Cressdee was also told that he would not be going because of his eyes. Between us we cooked a couple of cakes in a pineapple tin for me to take away. This had cost me nearly all my pay so I had no tobacco, not that that was any great loss. The 2/29th was to travel, 22 of us to a rice truck, some four days before the 2/30th so I did not expect to see Curly Hardman and the boys again for some time. Our last day, Sunday 18 April was a busy day. I visited the hospital and the 2/30th lines to say my goodbyes and after parade we had the deferred Association meeting. Two letters from Jessie Scott arrived just in time and that night, Sunday, we were each given five onion rissoles and seven biscuits to last us, we were told, until Wednesday breakfast. There was no sleep that night at all.

8
'Our Long March'

The big day—19 April 1943

Reveille in the morning was at 1 o'clock, breakfast at 1.15 and we were on the square at 2 a.m. After more goodbyes to Curly Hardman and the team we were trucked and moved out at 4.20 a.m. and then arrived at the station without it raining, thank the Lord. We were packed, 28 men, in an all steel rice truck, about 20 feet x 7 feet, with no ventilation except for the doors, and left at 6.50 a.m. It was not long before we were off the island.

We stretched our legs at Johore Bahru and I started to read *Try Anything Once*, which was somewhat appropriate. Rolling along with the doors open it was quite cool. Our team was made up of Tich Martin, McDonald, Murphy, Nagle and myself. Fortunately we were able to buy pineapples at one stop, which was very handy but by 12 o'clock, during a halt, the truck was turning into an oven. The guards, who had a truck to themselves, were turning out all right, allowing us to buy stuff along the way and at Kluang we bought some peanut toffee. Tom Pearsell gave me an ounce of tobacco and then the rain set in, which was very good in cooling the steel truck down. The villages went by—Segamet, Batu Annam and Gemas. At 6 we were given some rice concoction and tea at another stop and we thought 'so far so good'. Then we were on our way again and I finished up the day and all that night with Tich in my arms and my head on his shoulder. We were certainly cramped for room and lay on top of each other.

We made Kuala Lumpur at 3 a.m. for a breakfast of rice and curry and a stop for an hour. Then into the hills and back to sleep. At Panjang Milam we bought bananas. We had been travelling through rubber plantations all the way with very rare glimpses of jungle. Over the Slim River, on to Bidor where we got papaya and on to Ipoh where we had lunch of rice, salted fish and 'stew'. It was there that I wrote up my diary from notes made along the track. I also had a shower under the water pipe for the trains before we were 'kura-ed', [Japanese for hurry up or you will cop the lot] before getting back in our trucks again. It was very hot though mainly cloudy. We noticed in passing through the tin area that little of it was working. We bought papaya at Engor, where the town turned out to see us.

We were travelling about 20 miles per hour along a single track and the amount of traffic was surprising. We ate the food we had brought with us for tea at Kuala Kangsur and on again. It may have been a gorgeous sunset in the hills but we spent a simply terrible night, cramped and jostled with no sleep at all.

Breakfast next day was at Prai when we stopped for a while at 2 a.m. and then during the night conditions got even worse; though I must have got some sleep through sheer exhaustion.

On our third day we were at Alor Star and into the paddy fields. I had never seen land so flat before as the kampongs were really little islands. The countryside was dotted with huge peculiar rock formations, which stood up like towers and in the paddy fields the coolies looked just like their pictures on postcards. It was not long before we out of the rice fields, which were about 30 miles by 12 miles in area.

We had been suffering cramps in the stomach from all the unaccustomed fruit which we had been eating and this caused us more problems as we reached Padang Besar on the border at 11 a.m. All the stops on the way were toilet stops, with pants down and trying to ease the pain in the stomach as quickly as possible along the track before being hurried back into the trucks. The alternative was to hang out of the truck at the open doors, but this we tried to avoid.

The stop at the border was for eight hours and in that time we did some PT to stretch our muscles as well as try to catch up on some sleep. We also studied the form of the Thai girls, which was not too bad at all. And so we were off again and into Thailand.

The Thai railway station guards, who we saw at our first stop, looked very smart in their uniforms and with their own flag flying too. In the fields it looked all very natural with elephants and breasty maidens being new sights to us. Our Japanese/ Singapore money was not accepted so we could not buy anything at the many stops on the way. As it was we could not eat our tea (plain rice and fish) anyway because of the diarrhoea we were still suffering from as the result of all the fresh fruit we had eaten. And so we spent another miserable night on the train. By next day we were well into Thailand. We were still weak from our efforts, lack of sleep and cramped conditions in the rice truck. The countryside that we travelled through was interesting, with more elephants, water buffaloes, yellow-frocked priests and more breasty maids. The Thai officials everywhere certainly went for uniforms in a big way; from the police to engine drivers, they wore their smart peaked caps, jackets and trousers—but no boots.

By 2 p.m. we were getting hungry again and I had half a pastie. We were glad that we had brought some food with us. Later we pulled up for a meal of rice, grass gravy it seemed and a square inch of yak. But the continuous jolting along the track made our hunger worse.

We had been OK for the first two days but then the travelling was bad; cramped, jolted, no sleep and no food. That night it rained. With the doors closed you could have cut the air with a knife. We had started singing at one station stop but it was stopped and then disallowed. I did eventually get to sleep however, although at one stage my legs were extended up the side of the truck. Next morning, again at a station, food and cigarettes were thrown to us from an opposite train by some of the Thai people. We were passing quite a few temples and monasteries, Buddhist or Brahman we did not know but still thought them very interesting. It was maybe the dry season for we passed through an area of some 2000 square miles of dried-up paddy fields on this, our last day on the train. We noticed too that there seemed to be a different atmosphere and attitude among the Thais. There was not the same air of suppression as in Singapore and Malaya. While subject to the Japanese, they maintained an independence of sorts.

And so on Friday, 23 April, we reached our destination, Bampong, 40 miles short of Bangkok at 1.30 p.m. We had been on the train for four days and 6½ hours. We detrained, waited around and then marched to a camp a mile away.

There we were checked in individually, our gear and ourselves were searched and we got a meal of rice and vegetable stew at 7 p.m. It was my second meal in 52 hours. The camp was only a temporary affair and the biggest shemozzle imaginable. We were obviously going to move soon to God knows where. It took two trips back into the town to bring up the gear that had been brought on the train from Changi with us. I finished up the day, again with my glasses broken, dead beat and out on my feet.

Next day there was a lot more mucking around and I went on sick parade to see if anything could be done about my glasses and eyes. One of the lens had been trodden on when I had put them down on the ground beside me when having a wash. We soon learnt that on the next move everything had to be carried. Hence a helluva lot of rations and clothing came to light and the QM staff were eating and selling stuff for themselves. It was a bloody disgrace. What with the boys playing dice, meals, getting water and going on parades, getting counted and checked, it had been the maddest day in my life. Drinking water was scarce and I was still hungry; the previous night I had been so hungry that I could hardly eat my tea. Reserve rations were distributed and we packed up again, certainly travelling light. The day continued to be the biggest jumble of a day I had ever known. We were counted by the Japanese for the 999th time in five days and so we were ready to move on. I looked a wicked sight with a patch over one sore eye, no glasses and my hat set at a terrific angle to protect my face. We were on the road for our second stage at midnight.

We started off with 40 minutes of marching, pretty well in fives and 20 minutes rest, carrying besides our own gear, buckets, kitchen gear and, in turns, a large pannier of medical stuff on a long bamboo pole on the shoulders of two men. As time went on through the night we became a rabble with the pounding of feet on the road and the officer's voice calling out the numbers for the pannier. March and rests became half an hour and half an hour and finally we came to some huts at 9.40 a.m., myself again near dead beat. It was hard marching when both hungry and tired. Eggs and coffee were plentiful from the local Thais as the trading in goods, which boys wanted to sell, was good. I was too tired but had a swim. We revived. Later the day became a picnic, the meals were good and in the evening the boys had a burl at a bit of black velvet. Fortunately I had not the surplus sugar [money], even to be tempted. We were on the march again at 10.15 p.m.

There was little change in the routine of the march from the previous night, except that a cart was hired for the medical gear. By then there was not a man who did not have tired and aching blistered feet. I did allow that a lot was being done for us in that marching at night was better than in the heat of the day, that the lengthy spells gave us 40 minutes of marching and 20 minutes of rest, which became half and half as the night progressed, that we had been allowed to hire vehicles while we were still on a road but it was still pretty frightful that we should have been forced to march at all, considering our weakened state and health. After almost twelve hours we arrived at the next camp, again plain buggered.

Fortunately we rested for two days but in the sun. The first day was one of the hottest days I had known. I spent the afternoon guzzling coffee under a tree, selling my satchel and having continuous showers. Being financial I had three eggs with my stew and a beautiful cup of tea with limes and a nip of arrack. It made me sleep properly that night for the first time for nearly eight days.

It was not quite so hot next day so we took things easy. One of the boys was stood over during the previous night by a Thai with a knife for his watch and while we were away in the afternoon for dysentery and malaria tests (an extra three-mile walk) guards had to be posted over our gear. It was funny down at the well, though, where a dark girl charged five cents to wash anyone. Drinking water was scarce and what made it worse was that contamination of the water with dysentery was rife. A lot of trading was still going on but of course the natives exploited us. The Japs tried to control prices. It was a case of easy come, easy go as it was nearly all army stuff that could not be carried that was sold. A blind eye was turned. The packs and rolls were considerably lightened at a profit. My load was pretty manageable. The medical stuff to be carried was split up amongst us, making things easier. So far we had come 35 miles and we kicked off on our third leg at 10.45 p.m., the boys quickly bowling over from the effects of their day. They were collapsing all night from sickness and pains. Some then had to be carried on stretchers, which was a considerable handicap to the rest of us. Again at the half-way mark we got an hour's rest and after it my feet got worse in the early hours of the morning. The boys were great scouts in carrying some of my gear for a while. A yak cart was again hired for the heavy and bulky stuff, making things easier and we arrived at a river edge at about 9.30 a.m. It was another delightful spot. A couple of hours sleep and a good dinner and I was right again.

We were in the mountains by then, which was cooler. We had been mainly following the river and, until the previous day, a railway line. It was beautiful to have a swim in the afternoon and after rearranging my swag I was again ready for the track at 9.30 p.m. We loaded the yak carts and it was a bloody disgrace that men were refusing to discard their useless stuff and then us paying to have it transported for them—and then later having to carry *them*. One of them was even carrying a doormat!

Again we marched all night and morning, from 10.10 p.m. to 9.20 a.m., a distance of 17½ miles and bringing our total mileage to around 70. The going that night was worse than before as, after a while, we left the road. We then staggered, stumbled and fell along a jungle track in single file, one behind the other, in the dark. The stretchers were in constant use as men just could not be allowed to fall back because of attack by the natives. Wharton took a knife off the yak driver during the night when he started throwing bags off the cart for later collection. Any man who did fall back, we were ordered, must have a mate with him. The Thai bandits attacked stragglers in ones and twos. In the Japanese follow-up party one of their NCOs even lent one of the boys his sword. It all seemed like something out of a story book but we were right in the mountains and into tiger country. The tigers did not cause us any concern but the Thai natives would have cut our throats for a shirt. I had never dreamt that I would be another Frank Buck.

Next day we again rested and I took things quietly. Again we were near the river but I had found that swimming weakened the legs too much as the rivers were very swift. At least it saved the water position. The boys were still lightening their loads, profitably. Mal McDonald trying to sell a local trader a pair of long woollen underpants, in the mountains of Thailand, was one of the most amusing things I had ever seen. I was sure that my mother would forgive me for selling my portfolio as possibly saved my life. It was the eggs and limes we were marching on, not the rice. I did not believe in discarding my clothing unless I had to. Lieutenant Colonel Kappe, who was the senior officer in our party of 600, gave us a pep talk during the night too. He did his best and certainly spoke his mind. Lieutenant Colonel Pond was the big surprise; he was one of the men on the march and I meant a *man*. Capt Lloyd, 'A' Company CO was another who did a very good job as, like some of the officers, he did it tough and at the same time worked hard in getting us through.

The next night, 1 May, we were thirteen hours on the track, from 8 p.m. to 9.10 a.m. It was the worst leg so far. On the way over the mountains the going got tougher. We were virtually the pathfinders, being in the first two trains on the road and breaking new ground. I cracked up in the morning at about 3 a.m. In the last hours before daylight it was only willpower and determination that we were running on. I had fallen back to carry the stretcher and, after taking my turn, could not catch up again. It was dragging behind and missing half of the rest periods that got you down. But still I staggered in to the next camp with the mob. A swim in the river, a bit of sleep and poaching an egg just about filled in the day, with us still dead tired. We had reached a base depot at Tahso and thought that we might be there a few days but we pushed on again that night at 8 p.m., 71 of us from the original 100 in our lot. We had been dropping men off at every stop as we just could not carry all those who could not make it. Physically we were not able to do so, what with the nature of the track and the condition we were in.

On again, 45 minutes of marching and 15 minutes rest to our first real stop of the night at midnight. The going, during the morning hours of darkness, got easier for me as we had settled down by then, with our minds just concerned with plodding on, not knowing where we were or where we were going. We did fourteen miles during the night, scratched, blistered and weary, bringing us up to 96 miles. Certainly it was easier after dark than during the heat of the day, following the man in front of you in the pitch blackness, sleep being the main thing to fight against and falling over or walking off the track. Meals, now that we were unable to buy anything, were terrible; in fact we were on two meals a day. Even so the rice we had been given for breakfast at 1 a.m. was not eaten as it had gone sour. I wrote up my diary at a very smelly camp, with what sounded like ack-ack fire a few miles away. We only wished that it was fair dinkum. We were to be there, wherever 'there' was, for ten hours, being told that we would move on at 6 p.m. I boiled a bucket of water as never before had I appreciated a cup of tea so much: nor the solution of Condy's crystals either, in which I was able to soak my feet. Tempers were unfortunately getting short and a row was going on as I was writing. The COs had a job on their hands.

It was a very wet and sticky track on the next night, with quite a few of the boys going over and into the mud. Fortunately it was a short leg of 12½ miles but hard going. Another 'tiger' guard was put on while we marched, an hour at a time, until we made our next stop at 3 a.m. And *did* we sleep until daybreak! And again until lunch. I had another swim in the afternoon as we were still by the river, which at a bend was the very picture of a Tarzan scene from the movies. We stripped off and swam with some cattle that were there. We were all the same to the Japs. I had lost my mess gear and was eating out of a piece of hollowed-out bamboo. The jungle we were going through was thick with it. We were still in the mountains and the 'ack-ack' we had heard the previous day was thunder coming down the valleys. We rested that night, thank God, as were then down to 68 men.

It was a good night's sleep and a very quiet day before moving off again at 6.30 p.m. We had learnt that the scheme behind all this activity was a road and railway being constructed, connecting Moulmein and Bampong. The job just then was being rushed ahead. It had been started the previous October. Progress had been fast but we wondered how long the work would last before the rains came. We had been passing camps, which had been set up for the Burmese and Thai coolies (and never finished) all along the way and we thought that with us, there must be 40 000 native workers on the job. By then we were getting closer to the Burma border, right in the jungle and in the mountains between the two countries. A circle of fires had been lit around the camp at which we stayed on the previous night to keep away tigers, panthers, apes etc. That was the sort of country we were in. Presumably we were walking in more or less a straight line, north-west, while the river meandered around. We would go up the hill and down the other side to get to the next landing stage. The eggs we had been buying had come up the river in boats of the 'Sanders of the River' class. That day, however, we had another casualty, being a suspected malaria case, which brought the number down to 67 in our C Company. Already we realised what was ahead of us in the way of disease.

Another short leg during the night of 12½ miles, which brought us up to 120 miles. The road would have made the Big Dipper at Luna Park look like a foot rule. After four and a half hours in 'restos', during the period on the track, we reached the next stage at 7 a.m. By then we were hardened to it and we thought that the rest would be easy. But I still brought up another blister during the night from a screw in my boot, which caused me trouble. After a good wash in the creek, and work for the cooks, 'onion barbering', I was able to buy some tobacco. There was a lot of conjecture as to the distance we still had to do but I left that to the future. We still thought that we were getting close to the Burma border and I would have liked to have known our altitude, which must have been getting on for 2000 feet. Rain caught up on us a little during the day but it still looked as if our luck was going to continue. We had been missing the rain that threatened but it looked as if it would be slippery that night. Our force, F Force, was the first ever to do the trek on foot, others, to the lower camps which we had passed through, having had transport of some form or other. Our party was the first of the Australian troops on the march.

Thursday, 6 May and at 8 a.m., I wrote up my diary 'the last 24 hours have been just a bastard'. That night the column of us on the march was like a snake in convulsions and at midnight we had been huddled round fires on the track in the rain. On again after two hours, another halt for two hours at a water point, we staggered to a stop at 8 a.m., tired and bad-tempered. It had been bloody awful in the dark and the lightning. We were individually counted and checked in by the Japs and in no time Sergeant Rowe was being slapped in the face and later knocked out. Here the Japs were efficiency experts and certainly got things done. After 18½ hours without eating we had three meals in five and a half hours. But we were not allowed down to the river too often. After coming off another check parade, having boiled up water in an old bucket and made tea and written up my diary, I looked forward to more sleep. The Burma border was just a few miles to the west and in a pretty high mountain range, which looked forbidding. We expected to tackle it in the next few days, but just then I wanted to rest. Christ, I was tired.

Well our bad luck continued during the night. The rain came down again after we had lain down and soaked everyone. After getting wet we were allowed into some tents nearby, so it was not so bad after a change of clothing. All the way up we had been penned in cleared patches of scrub, like cattle. We would make humpies for ourselves when we stayed long enough, 36 hours, in any one spot. The Japs were forcibly moving us along, belting us up the backside to keep going and I believed that Major Wild (the interpreter) was done over, back down the track a bit. In Thailand no opportunity was given us to forget that we were prisoners of war. Curly Hardman was three days behind us and I would have liked to have left him some tobacco but did not take the risk. Later the main party of Japanese, who had been following us from Bampong, arrived at the same spot where we were. They were dead beat too, carrying full pack, rifle and dragging their gear.

Moving on, it was a short leg of 10½ miles (after 13¾ miles on the last leg) but stiff. Entering a pass, the marching had developed into a mountaineering exercise. Still we made fast time and even had four hours sleep on the 'road' before reaching the next camp. It was a case then of just dropping my gas cape, dropping on it and dropping off to sleep. After arriving we were soon annoyed by a couple of elephants for camping among their breakfast: and again later for using their bath. I slept and ate for most of the day. There was little to describe of our surroundings as we did not see much of it: most of the day we had just passed out.

It was on again early and the toughest going yet. We were going down the hills, which was harder than climbing up. It was easier to go down crabwise.

The Japanese, or us rather, had obviously taken on quite a job. Even the way it was tackled—with bamboo embankments, wooden bridges, the blasting to be done and the cuttings to dig—was awesome. We had heard that it was hoped to have it all finished in three months, which was just impossible. On the track the previous night we had been pleasantly surprised when our scheduled 15 miles was cut down to 10 miles. We knocked off, 65 strong having done 154 miles.

The food was still simply terrible, being rice and a meat extract, which should, however, have been called 'subtract'. There was nothing to buy, we were miles from anywhere and tea was a thing of the past.

We were told that six miles was the distance to be done the next night. We were nearing our working area. Two trucks were provided for the heavy stuff being carried as well as for the crippled. But the distance being short, most of the lame were too proud to take advantage of the trucks. So we set off at a helluva pace, hoping to end the journey soon. But at midnight we had covered eight miles and were still going.

On Monday morning, 10 May, we reached our destination, Konkoita, at 8 a.m. having done a leg of 15 miles and making the trip 160 miles in 14 days. We had slithered, stumbled, fallen, been scratched and bruised, weary, hungry, sick and sore, in dogged determination, for the whole of the 14 days. We had walked along what was once an elephant track from Thailand into Burma, with Jap guards in the rear hurrying up the stragglers. It had been one step after another in the dark, not knowing where we were, where we were going or what was in front of us. We had carried on sore shoulders and aching feet everything that we had in the way of personal belongings as well as the battalion gear, the medical and kitchen stuff and our mates as well, when they could not walk. We were still an AIF unit. If the stopping places we had reached on the way up had names, we did not know them for they were simply clearings in the jungle to us; some with shade, some without.

The day we arrived was a bigger shemozzle than the first day at Bampong. For about four hours in the morning we were left in the sun on a strip of sand with very little water, as we were told that the river water was impure. Later we came into the camp and we set about fixing up huts and tents. We in C Company were in tents, 25 to each tent. We got two meals that day of rice and onion water and after the second meal things settled down as it got a bit cooler. But the heat that day had been terrific. We did not know when we were expected to start work but I was not looking forward to it without my glasses and the jungle so thick. We were right on the Burma border at Three Pagoda Pass—possibly, we thought, just inside it. I was glad to have made it; just to get there, no matter what the future held. That evening there was a check parade, a swim in the river and 'goodnights' all round, in the Thai jungle. [We were actually some miles short of the border.]

We were mucked around some more in the morning, shifting quarters, as we moved into huts with about 18 inches per man. But we were off the ground. I made some new mess gear out of thick bamboo and went on sick parade. The piles were again troubling me besides all the corners knocked off my feet. Nothing could be done for my eyes, which were sore and swollen. I had just about knocked off the smoking, saving what I had for Curly when I got the chance.

Our arrival at Konkoita was premature as no local administration had been set up for the establishment of proper facilities or amenities in setting up a camp. No provision had been made by the Japanese to issue medical supplies or care for the sick. We expected that it would be the same all the way up the railway.

We started work at 1 p.m. next day. All the men had to go out to work on the road-building and bridge construction. This took priority over establishing proper sanitary conditions, cleaning up the area of excreta left by the native labour and making a reasonable cookhouse. Carrying our tools we went to a rough section of road, widening it and levelling it off. I was on a shovel all afternoon. British, Australian and Dutch POWs, Chinese, Tamil, Thai and Burmese coolies and the Japanese troops were all working on the road and railway. Camps were set up all along the track. As we finished one sector we moved on. But, Christ, it was hot. That afternoon, thank the Lord, boiled water was handy and kept up to us. It was to be our greatest concern at the time we thought. Meals were still something terrible being rice, onion water and whitebait. This was exactly the same as the coolies but they got chillis and more rice. I thought of myself as a man, for we were all boys really, and felt that I had earned it.

A routine settled in. We were up at sunrise, 8 a.m., breakfast, on parade for work at 9 a.m., lunch from 1 to 3 p.m., knock off at sundown between 7 and 8 p.m. Then we would have tea, a wash, check parade and get our bottles filled by 10 p.m. The only time we had to ourselves was about an hour after dark, while waiting for the boiled water. After that we just went to bed and died. The job at first was not too hard as we were in a crowd of 500 or so but we were still weary from the march. Hunger was just taken as a matter of course.

All along the track we had hoped and prayed that we would not be camped with the native coolies. But we struck worse—filthy bloody Tamils, who defecated and urinated all over the place and made the camp, more especially their end, simply disgusting. Dysentery was not a possibility, it was a certainty. They made no attempt at digging latrines and left their mess anywhere and everywhere as a breeding ground for millions of flies.

Quite a few were already sick, spewing up their food and with diarrhoea. It was thought that Dick Trew had beri-beri. If vitamin deficiency had caused sickness at Changi, it was obvious that it would kill us in Thailand unless there was a very big improvement in our diet soon. A little pumpkin appeared and more onion but still the meals were the same day after day. Already seven of our C Company had gone in to hospital with dysentery. We had the water problem licked though and I was able to keep my bottle full. I thought that once we got used to the job that it would not be too bad. The Japanese guards were camped with us, right on the job and one was allotted to each company. I did not think at first that, as far as the ordinary Japanese private soldiers on the job were concerned, we had struck too bad a crowd.

I met up with Curly Hardman as the 2/30th passed through. He told me that he had done the trip OK so far and had sold everything, so was travelling light. I left some tobacco with him but I could not get into his crowd as we were not allowed to swap over. The 2/30th had certainly struck the toughest of luck along the track. After arriving at Bampong late and being bundled straight out on to the road, they had five wet nights to our two. They had only one stretcher and men had to be carried on the shoulder.

Two or three natives died in the two days we had been in the new camp and, with all their other refuse, were supposed to be in the river. They were the filthiest lot I had ever struck in my life. A major cause of the high death rate already among the civilian labourers and the spread of disease and the suffering borne by the men of F Force, was the failure of the Japanese and Korean guards to make the natives clean up their areas of excreta and vomit. No attempt was made by the natives themselves to get clean and stay clean. They simply worked, ate and died. On the job the work was very rough but I came across a cascara tree and ate a fair bit of the seeds with the idea that it would fix up the constipation, which alternated with the diarrhoea.

Work next day was about two and a half miles from the camp. We were still road-making and building embankments. With chunkels and baskets we dug and carried dirt under the direction of the Japanese guards. The chunkels were the main digging tool. They were heavy, wide-bladed hoes, which we swung into the ground and hauled up the dirt, pulling it back towards us. That day we did not get back until 8.30 p.m., which was after dark. A swim, tea and a smoke fixed me up. By the 15 May most of the natives had moved on for which we were very grateful. In the corner of hell which we occupied, there was every kind of fever and sickness known to God and man. Malaria, dengue fever, cholera, typhoid, dysentery, scabies, hookworm and tinea. That was 1% of them. The boys were keeling over and the sickness in the camp was about 12½ % already. We were all very weary still. I did not know if it was the intention to make us sorry for the day we were born but the Japs made a very good try.

It was funny one day as twelve men in our work party were struggling with a large tree stump. We hailed a passing elephant and it just tested the stump with his foot and then pushed it over with his trunk. It was as easy as winking. That night we had a needle for cholera, which we hoped would be effective. Later there was another death among the natives and one of them, screaming at about 1.30a.m., resulted in us shifting to another camp four and a half miles away later that morning: without the loss of a day's work of course. We took our swags with us on the job.

It was a Sunday and I was working in the rain with a singlet around my waist, shovelling mud and thinking of cosy fireplaces and a light tea at tea time. That evening, work done, I plodded on to the new camp at Upper Konkoita with all my possessions under one arm and a pick on my shoulder. But on Sunday night they could not stop me from dreaming of better things. The new camp was a lot cleaner and with no bloody natives. A stream was at hand (which by 10 June was a river) and we had more sleeping room. It was further to walk to the job but that was nothing compared with getting out of the last place.

F Force seemed to be split into three groups:
  • 600/700 of us (mainly 2/29th) at Upper Konkoita;
  • The main AIF camp at Songkurai; and
  • The main British camp at Neike. [The Dutch later moved to Neike too.]
Our pay was to be 25 cents a day or the equivalent at the canteen, when and if we ever got it. We did not look like getting anything for some time. I hoped that we would be successful in having a canteen set up but transport, either by road or river was a problem. Rupees or ticals were all the natives seemed to use.

We learnt that cholera had broken out among the 2/30th, who were about ten miles away from us and further up the road. Their conditions were worse than ours. We were told that there were eleven cases already, including one death. It was carried by water and flies and I could not see anything but that it would spread right throughout the area. Every man was battling to look after his own health and that of the whole camp. That way we thought that we could win. We had to watch what we ate and keep it free from flies. George Boulton was one of the first in our crowd to go down by eating contaminated food. I was glad that I had forced myself to eat the terrible rice as I thought that there must be some good in it, otherwise we would have been dead long before. I made myself eat the disgraceful mess which was put in front of us as it was a case of have to or starve. Gradually I was picking up again and feeling a lot fresher. We still had a lot of sleep to catch up on though. We were on the go from 8 a.m. to 10 p.m. every day, which was *every* day.

I was working on one of the jungle bridges. Everything but the tools was obtained from the side of the road—bamboo abutments, dirt embankments, tree-trunk piles and decking. They were beauties all right, for they rocked fully a foot when a truck passed over them. That day they would not trust an elephant on the one we were working on. Bamboo up in the area where we were was like rubber and attap in Malaya. It was used for everything from water bottles to huts to cigarette papers.

Back in the camp, when we got there, there was water to boil for our water bottles and on alternate nights I washed my clothes. I had two sets only and they got very dirty on the job.

In embedding the piles in the bed of the river we would build a high tower above the spot where the pile was to go down. We would haul a thick teak tree out of the jungle, trim it and haul it to the site and attach a rope to it through a pulley at the top of the tower. Twenty five or so of us would then haul on the rope, pulling it up to the top of the tower and then letting it go. Pulling on the rope was the easy part. Letting it go on the order to do so was a killer. If you all didn't let the weight off at the same time you got snatched forward with a jerk and when you did let go your stomach muscles were wrenched upon releasing the strain. It was about the hardest work I ever did.

On Wednesday, 19 May we worked only half a day. I hoped that it would become a regular thing, Wednesday being their Sunday. It came as a surprise as on the previous day we had been told 'though Australians die, English die, Nippons die, the road must go through'. Beautiful.

We could not get in touch with any of the Burma POWs. I was thinking of Alan Pendrick and others, but we kept on trying as we thought that they were on the same road as us, at the other end.

Attempts were made to do something for the men with no boots but really there was nothing that could be done. Those who had no boots made wooden clogs or whatever they could make of any material to cover their feet. When we were at Bampong and the reserve rations were distributed among us, tins of margarine were even used to clean and soften our boots, like Dubbin. Certainly we tried to look after them as best we could as they were more important to us than anything we had. The Red Cross shorts, which I got at River Valley Road and were then much too small for anyone, fitted me on the railway as we were really very thin.

We were doing it hard in Thailand but the hardest thing of all, I found, was having to put up with everybody's bad temper from daybreak to dark. As, too, in the early days, when things got tough, tempers got short, so there were rows going on all day long. It got that way that I was getting as bad myself. But I never thought that I would scab on an elephant. One day we were hauling logs all day out of the bush, thirty or so of us to a log, doing a good elephant out of a day's work. 'Britons never shall be slaves' ?!

Apart from the few chillies which appeared, the first variation we had in 32 meals was when the onions were fried and some burnt rice added. There was not any change in the ingredients, still only rice, onions and whitebait but the change bucked us up. It was little compensation to be told by the Japanese that they were sorry that the meals are poor, work is hard, hours are long, sickness is bad and huts are terrible.

Of the 73 ORs in our C Company, 46 of us went out to work, which was indicative of the state we were in. It had rained each of the last seven days and although elaborate huts had been half-built, there were as yet no roofs on the huts. We were in tents which were erected in the framework. I got soaked through at night even though we tried to fix the tents up as best we could to improve things a little. But I got a small piece of yak in the stew one night, which was good and I was eating my rice like 'Fu Manchu'. I could not get enough of it.

With the conditions and my spirit so low, I had been doing a fair bit of dreaming of Australia and home. I surprised myself thinking of friends like Alec Nicholson from the office, who had slipped my mind for the past fifteen months. And on the job at lunchtime I would talk to Captain Jessop, who had been an island trader in the Netherlands East Indies. It was all very interesting discussing sailing in the 50 to 75-foot class of boat. Still *Virginia,* at 25 feet, would do me. I was determined to have her one day. One of the easier jobs I got was to take the mess tins back to the camp at lunchtime. It gave me a short break and I would write up my diary. Then back to work, standing and working in the rain getting freezing cold. Although it was cold where we were we still only wore boots and shorts, if we had them. Back at camp I would dry off and get into the heavy Pommie giggle suit, which I had acquired and still clung to. It came in very handy.

Sunday 23 May, was a repetition of the previous day, as I expected every day for the next two to three months to be now that the monsoon had set in. Working in the rain, we would dig mud, carry mud, place our baskets of mud on the banks and mounds of more mud, until we looked that miserable that the Jap guards recognised that we, and they, were not getting anywhere and took pity on us. It was all so stupid that at times we even came back to camp early. One of the first things that we were told on arrival was that the Japanese Commanding Officer in Charge of the project was a very humane man. I did not know how many of us it would take to die of pneumonia before that opinion was revised. The Japanese Chief Engineer had earlier addressed us as Australians and good soldiers but in fact he had no other interest in us other than as an expendable work force. It was said that the cholera outbreak was under control after there being four deaths amongst our lot.

The boys were eating anything and everything, wild yams, banana shoots, lily roots and a lot of stuff without names, vines, leaves etc., growing in the jungle. I did not touch the native stuff myself so just went hungry. I did try to get dry at night though and when I could got right under the tent. We got one quinine tablet each at that stage with the understanding that it would be a nightly issue.

Walking up to 4 miles to the job, we often had to carry logs on the way. With three to five men to each 14-foot log, it was always hard work before we even got started on the road. Being belted to push us along did not help. Yet for some unaccountable reason, certainly not for Empire Day, on the 24 May we did not start work until after lunch. It gave me the first opportunity for a couple of days to get all my clothes dry, as it turned out fine. It rained in the afternoon on the job, Curly Avard working in the nude and me in boots and a rag between my legs. We must have gone tropical. What had previously been a jungle track, we were widening, levelling and making a road for trucks to travel up to and into Burma. It was mountainous country, which meant a lot of cuttings and filling-in of gullies to even out the road. With primitive tools it was just hard heavy work, felling trees, clearing the jungle, digging and carrying dirt and rocks in the baskets. The previous day the Japs in our camp bought a passing yak just before it died of starvation I thought. They gave us about 8 lbs of bone and fat, which hardly made up for all the talk amongst us of sizzling sausages, grilled chops, rump steak, apple pie, cream puffs, chocolates and pots of amber fluid.

Diarrhoea caught up with me during the night and continued all day. There were so many of us with the same thing that our MO was dubious of giving us the day off. The Japanese demanded that all fit men go out and our doctors had the unenviable task of deciding who had to go out, to keep up the number required every day. No one was fit so we went out sick or not. If you could stand up and stay on your feet, you were fit enough to go out to work. In this way, to comply with the numbers of men demanded, we thought that those even more seriously hospitalised would not be made to go out and labour on the road and bridges. I stayed in that day and, apart from a couple of duties around the camp, spent most of the day trying to go to sleep. The hardest part of all was to have to use the maggot-infested latrines. They almost made you spew, just to go near them.

'Buckley's was one of the main topics of conversation. There was just no point in trying to escape. It was all too easy to walk out of the camp or from the job but there was simply nowhere to go that we had any hope of reaching. The jungle, the wildlife, infection and disease were more effective than any wire, walls or fences to keep us contained.

The Japs had a novel solution to the problem that we did not have sufficient food to work on and maintain our health. They suggested that those men who go out to work receive twice as much to eat as those who were sick and stayed in camp. Apparently it was their idea to kill us off and start afresh. It was hopeless telling them that it was quality not quantity that was lacking.

Wednesday, 26 May 1943 and the previous night had been a living nightmare. After waking up, making a terrible mess in my trousers at midnight and washing myself and clothes down at the river, I was up most of the night by the fire. There was a continuous procession of men to and from the latrines. There were the sounds of the men who did not reach them in time, coughing, spewing and cursing in the mud throughout the night. The RAP orderlies were running around boiling water and the Japanese guards with fixed bayonets were questioning everyone who was up: 'Benjo'... 'Urossi'. At Reveille we were told that we were quarantined and put in a small area of the camp. On no account were we to go near the Japanese. There was no work that day but a parade was held by the Jap MO of all the dysentery and diarrhoea cases, approximately 125 of us all together. Nothing was done. Young Tich O'Shea died very early in the morning. Never before had white people been treated the way we were at that time. It was the same among all of F Force at the other camps, on our part of the railway. Undoubtedly, to that stage, [it was to get worse] that day had been the blackest since we had been made prisoners. Of the 696 men in our camp, 206 were sick: 55% dysentery, 10% beri-beri, 10% malaria, 10% with other fevers and 15% from miscellaneous complaints. Because we were not working our rice ration was halved. However, the stew that day was the thickest so far. I thought that the Japs had released some of our rations, which they had previously taken for themselves. Our MO, Captain Mills, seemed too young for so big a job but had an enormous task before him. Just at the time I was writing up my diary that evening we were stood at attention as the cremation party passed through our camp.

Next day was much the same. We were still quarantined; no work, so 'no chunkel—no makan'. We were still on half rations and there was another death from dysentery, this time Keith Cattamana. By then Captain Mills was doing a tremendous job attending to the sick and partially fit men. He stood up to the Japs fearlessly and although he was not much older than most of us, his experience and judgment played a big part in keeping us going. And all the time he was working in soaking rain. Some of the boys, who were out, met up with a burial party who were cremating bodies between our camp and another, ten miles up the line. Ten Australians were being cremated. Large teak logs were used in the funeral pyres, fires that burnt bodies every day and were not to go out for many, many months. A day was not to pass that I did not hear the Last Post echo between the hills as the bugler played and the bodies were committed to the ashes. That day too our quinine tablets for general issue gave out.

One day the Japanese guards saw a man with a bag of about 10 lbs of rice, who then threw it away and ran off. A muster parade was immediately called and as the man did not step forward we were told that we would not get anything to eat at all until the thief was produced. Our officers were given the responsibility of finding him. Our breakfast had been cooked. We did not know for how long the situation would last but of course we were hungry. The meals were 80% water, 16% rice and 4% whitebait, so of little real nourishment. Most of us were out of tobacco too and no one was happy. There was not anyone working harder than Captain Mills, who was doing his best and more to keep us alive. The added withdrawal of food was not helping his seriously ill cases. At 2.30 p.m. the man gave himself up and we had our breakfast rice at 3 p.m. We then had lunch at 6.40 and tea at 9 p.m. You could never tell what the Japs were going to do.

It rained as usual all that afternoon and on the previous day one of our C Company tents was taken away, reducing us to the average of the rest of the camp (excluding officers of course) of two tents for 70 men. They were not waterproof and there were no mosquito nets, not even in the hospital. On the 29 May there was another cholera death—a Sapper Haywood of the Engineers. All preparations possible, hopeless as they were, had been made against an outbreak of the cholera epidemic, which was going through the whole area. We were due for yet another needle that afternoon but they ran out of serum before we were all done. It was the last of what we had been able to carry up from Bampong. There had still been no issues from the Japanese and they did not allow further supplies to come up from Bampong, where stores that could not be carried, had been left.

The man who stole the rice was made to apologise to us. Again I asked myself what about the legalised robbery, formal dinners and even more direct misappropriation of rations by officers and QM staff that had been going on all along?

There was still no sign of us going out to work or ending our quarantine. It was an 'ill wind, which blows no good' for it had given us a much-needed rest up. I was still on 'no duties' but had improved. I only hoped that this 'long road had an early turning'.

In the onion water we were getting a little beans, towgay and whale meat, which was something. Salt had given out at the kitchen, making the food even more unpalatable. After giving some of the salt that I had taken in my trading activities to the RAP, I still had a little left. The river was placed outside the fence. I did not know whether it was thought that we would pollute it or it pollute us but we were only allowed to draw water for boiling. It was a wise precaution. There were two cases of diphtheria that day and on top of all our other strife I prayed that it would not become an epidemic. That day those of us who had chronic diarrhoea and dysentery were even more isolated from the rest of the lines in the camp.

We were told that the few Japanese in the camp and ourselves would go on to two meals a day from the next day. The position was, that at Changi a letter had been received from the Japanese Malayan Command stating that as food was scarce around Singapore, 10 000 men would be shifted to a place where it was more plentiful. This was believed when we left Changi. The truth was that we had been pushed along the road in Thailand, which was purely a military affair for facilitating supplies and the movement of troops to Burma, long before any preparations had been made for receiving us. The road then was blocked at both ends by the monsoon. Only yak-drawn carts were getting through and their maximum load was one bag of rice. We would not die of starvation but the lack of food would be a contributing factor to the effects of other diseases.

That night we had our fourth death in five days, Curly Hamilton of A Company and again of cholera. The news was that three camps up, of 146 cases, 49 of them had died, 23 of them out of the 2/30th. The figures were second or third-hand but I believed them to be right. Our camp, being isolated by the rain, was the worst fed of all as little or nothing was getting along the rain sodden road. The two meals we had were at 12.15 and 7 p.m., being rice and boiled banana shoots, which the boys had gathered from the scrub that morning. We took heart though in the hope that this was to be our 'darkest hour before the dawn'. We had no idea really what was going on in the outside world. We did not know it but our isolation had also kept us from the worst of the contagious cases in the other camps. Meanwhile I spent the day playing cards, five hundred and patience, yarning a bit and, for most of the time, on the broad of my back trying to sleep. I was in an isolated part of the camp as a risk with chronic dysentery.

After doing light duties for a couple of days I was discharged from the isolation area. I was a bit more comfortable in my inside. We were all pretty weak and had lost weight in front of each other. Tactics by Colonel Pond and Captain Bowering, in trying to bounce and stand over the Japanese had come to nothing. Pond had made a trip up the road to Jap HQ to see what could be done to alleviate the situation but to no avail. The way it was, we hoped that a passive and unsuspecting yak would enter our camp.

Thais or Burmese were still hanging around the camp and trade was mostly on the bartering system and operated all day. Personal items and gear were swapped for food and tobacco. If Javanese and Malayan tobaccos were wicked the Burmese was simply awful.

The rain continued and we had not missed a day since it had started two weeks before, on 14 May. Actually we saw the sun for a couple of hours at times and tried to dry our stuff. I would get up at 12 o'clock, noon, breakfast at 1 p.m., more sleep until 5 p.m.: go back to the lines for tea at 7 p.m., make up my bunk and write up my diary; it would be getting dark at 9 p.m. and back to sleep. Those were my days: ill, weak and lethargic.

I spent my twenty-second birthday on 2 June very quietly. I got up at 1 o'clock and put most of the day in reading my diaries and letters from Mum and Neil, over and over. I especially read the letter from Mum dated the 2 June of the previous year, a simply wonderful birthday present. That morning, lying half-awake and half-asleep, naturally I reminisced a lot more than usual. I enumerated in my mind, one by one, all the friends I had ever made and imagined the circumstances and surroundings that they may be in and whether they might be thinking of me at the same time. I especially hoped that my mother, Dad, Neil and Ron had unshakeable confidence in my return. I had no doubts myself. So closed my twenty-second birthday, unique but I prayed, never to be repeated.

The days changed little: watches for some unaccountable reason were put back 20 minutes. The boys in A Company had quietly cut a yak's throat during the night, cut it up, cooked it, buried what was left and distributed it among themselves and the hospital: all in the dark. The risk was considerable as the Japanese prized the working animals much more than the prisoners. There was not much meat on the yaks, which were as underfed as we were and what there was did not go far. That Lloyd in A Company and others on other nights (but not too often) knocked off a yak to share with his mates was typical. Those at work, getting a bigger food issue shared what they got with those of their friends in camp who got less. As and if, the sick got better and went out to work so they too did the same thing. It meant that, by sharing what we had, fewer died than those who went along on their own. We were not heroes and not fighting a tangible enemy, but the fortitude and sacrifice fighting the horrors and suffering of starvation and disease to save lives among our mates was the equal of any AIF soldier at war. Shirts, shorts and pyjamas were traded for very small chickens and tobacco and these too would be split among a group of close mates. Eventually a convoy of yak carts passed through the camp and our rice ration was increased from one to one and a half bags of rice per day. This was about 335 lbs to 700 men. Actually our two meals a day worked out at a little over a pint of watery rice gruel and third of a pint of the water (the grains went to the hospital) of boiled banana shoots and a small amount of towgay and chillies. This was flavoured with some oil at each meal. It was however a variation from the 90% onion water that had been all that we were given. Although we were at our lowest ebb since being prisoners I hoped in some ways that the rain never stopped, making the road just a river of swamp and absolutely useless to the Japanese. Trucks were bogged along the track; one within hearing distance had been vainly screaming for three days.

On 4 June we were sent out to work. It was something pitiful—we were weaker then and quite a few of us were having continual blackouts. In my case everything would dazzle and shine for a minute or so and then go black. Colonel Pond told us not to work too hard and to put on an act or two. But it was quite unnecessary as it was only too genuine. After getting back to camp at 3 p.m., moving around a bit and getting three meals as a worker, I picked up a little.

The Japs had let the boys catch two yaks during the night, a big one and a little one, from the mob sent down as part of their food supply. They killed the big one themselves and later gave us 6 lbs of it. They told us to let the other one go. It went all right; west. It was gorgeous, the freshest, tenderest piece of meat that I had ever tasted. With the broth for next morning, undoubtedly a yak a day would have kept the doctor away.

Work next day was again shovelling mud off the surface of the road. We had to go out to work, if we could stand up, to fill the numbers and in order to get three meals of rice (while those in the camp still only got gruel and stew, twice a day) and to get a bit of exercise to build ourselves up again as much as possible. I would have hated to have had to move very far carrying my gear, as like the majority of us in the camp, I just could not have done it. We were still at about the 160-mile camp. There was a new cholera case in the hospital. Nothing frightened the Japanese more than cholera. The only time that we got any real cooperation or involvement in attempting to alleviate the risk and spread of cholera was when the guards felt themselves threatened. They would then panic. On the road work we had quarter-hour smokos every hour, a two-hour lunch break and we were not pushed that much. I thought that the Japs, who were working then alongside us, were as fed up with it all as we were. If that was possible.

On the job I had a word or two with Ben Barnett, the Australian wicket-keeper. His international cricketing days were over but there, on the railroad, he was just another captain, working for the Japanese. Colonel Pond was still the biggest surprise packet and continued to stand up to the Japanese on our behalf.

For three weeks it had been raining and I thought that I would not write in my diary that it was raining every day but would wait for a fine day and mark it with a big cross.

Work went on every day, seven days a week as long as you were on your feet. We were brought back to camp one day at 12 o'clock for yet another dysentery and cholera test. We were old hands at it by then. I had been talking to an Indian doctor who had been further up the road. He had heard that deaths in the 2/30th had reached 49 in number. I hoped that this was not true. The doctor proved invaluable in advising us as to what and what not to eat out of the jungle. Wild peanut tops he said were good and these went into our stew, along with vines of some sort and banana shoots. We also went on to some kind of berry but I was very dubious of them all.

Three events in quick succession on Sunday 6 June:
- The officers did not like the idea of some of the men holding a formal dinner.
- A cholera needle.
- An extra rice meal, the culmination of a row between the Japs, our MO and the QM.

A Sapper Price was another victim of cholera in the early hours of the morning: our sixth. Later in the day, when out on the road, I slipped, arse over head in the mud, just after drawing my lunch. This prompted quite a few caustic comments from the boys. I had a reputation for clumsiness, not entirely unearned and I missed my glasses. That night I reported sick again with a temperature of 102°. A milder form of malaria had caught up on me. Fever was very prevalent and no wonder for we were never really dry or warm (neither ourselves nor our gear). This was especially so at night when we had to get undressed to go to the latrines in the rain.

All the 'fit' and quite a few of the sick to make up the number moved up the road a further six miles to Lower Neike as our part of the road was completed. I wondered how some of the boys would make it for they could do only one mile an hour. Left in the camp were some pitiful cases, e.g., two men assisting one of the boys to the latrines as he could not walk. We tried so hard to avoid making a mess where we slept alongside each other. I was still down with malaria when the others left. For all the talk of long looked-forward-to meals, when we did get one decent meal, including a little yak meat, it stopped most of us. We just could not digest anything solid. It was apparent that something would have to be done in the way of convalescence on our release.

Lower Neike and Neike camps were the headquarters of the Japanese and F.Force commanders. Neike was a small village on the river and barges came up to supply the shopkeepers and the Japanese camps and engineers' stores. It was a concentration point of the railway system, with branch lines and shunting yards being constructed. The railway lines were not yet laid but a lot of work was being done in levelling the track and laying down the foundation for the lines.

The oft-repeated rumour of an H Force (G Force went to Japan), following us up to Thailand was substantiated when some of them reached our camp. They too were very sick and very weak. It was bloody murder to send them as there were very few who were fit at Changi when we left.

I was marked 'fit' after a couple of days and spent the day digging a latrine trench, which made me worse than ever. Tempers were all too short all round and I would get into strife, pride and independence getting the better of me. I missed my closest mates, like Curly Hardman and Syd Grounds and the others. 'Panto', Kevin Panton, died of malaria and dysentery. We thought that we were the worst fed in the area, being the furthest from the Jap base (from both ends, the Thailand end and the Burma end of the railroad). We knew that we were not getting the full ration of what did arrive. At the same time in our camp, being in more or less isolation on the road, the number of deaths was comparatively small. We thought it would be a shame to die at that stage, as we believed, foolishly, that the end of the job was in sight.

I was in the Price cremation party for nearly twelve hours, from 10.30 in the morning until 9.30 at night. It was an interesting though unfortunate job. After building a square pyre, 6' x 6' x 6' (with a platform at 3' in the middle) of teak logs and the centre filled with light bamboo, the body was placed on the platform, stripped and covered with leaves. As it was in a clearing in the scrub, nearby cicadas were the organ to Colonel Pond's short service (the 23rd Psalm and the

Lord's Prayer) after which the pyre was lit. It took six hours to burn out and it was after dark before the fire and body were reduced to ashes, which we then had to bury completely. A little of the ashes were saved in a small bamboo container I had made for burial in the miniature cemetery we had formed in the camp.

The boys, who had moved out of our camp, finished up doing about fifteen miles but at least had had one good meal up there. We were soon to follow. They sent back news that there had been nine 2/29th deaths, including our first C Company man, Alex Cameron.

On Friday 11 June we were in the middle of a drought, as it had not rained since 3 a.m. the previous day. The sunshine, with a little yak meat in our meal had noticeably brightened up everyone. At 4.00 in the afternoon the drought broke. It was just as well for I felt that I would rather it rain every day than be as hot as it had been at midday. Surprisingly it was not humid but a dry heat, the air being like the inside of an oven. It dried things up, thank God, for rumour had it that we would be moving up next day.

I was speaking that day to the first audit clerk I had met in the AIF. They were certainly scarce; as were law clerks, solicitors, etc. In fact I felt that, on the whole, our kind were not too patriotic. Most professional people in the army were officers and I had thrown that away in volunteering for the draft back at Liverpool. I still had no regrets.

We were getting more yak in our stew, the difference being noticeable when it was going through the centralised camp kitchen instead of a number of separate kitchens attached to each company, as had been the case before most of the camp moved out. We were getting two or three cubic inches of yak a day each and the broth, with the bones, was good for us. It was an improvement, but only a temporary one, for we could not expect that there were enough yaks to keep knocking them over indefinitely. The alternating meals were still gruel and dry rice.

9

'*We Died in Singapore and this is Hell*'

On the 'Road to Rangoon', 70 of us, a pathetic bunch, set out to catch up with the boys. Carrying all we possessed, as well as a chunkel or a shovel each, we had three tents and buckets to carry as well between us. We started off perfectly, the road being as dry as it ever would be in the monsoon season and the sky cloudy. From 10.20 a.m. to 12.40 p.m. we had covered a distance of three miles, which the battalion in the previous week had taken all day to do in the rain and pushing the yak carts carrying their tents and tools. We set off again, shuffling along at a bit quicker pace but rain, the solid lump of water variety, caught up on us very quickly. We did the next step non-stop in another two hours, 'marching' most of the time ankle and calf-deep in mud. With my wallet and diaries in my pocket, wrapped in oilcloth, I was concerned more with keeping them dry than anything else. When we did reach the next stop it was another instance of God opening a window (as a door was closed) as that night we found ourselves in a hut with a roof. It gave us a chance to sleep and dry our gear. We had saved some rice and whitebait from our previous night's meal so at least we were fed. I thought of Neil and his 70s. rucksack and fancy frame but for convenience the old 'bluey' was on its own. The old-timers had shown us how to wrap our swag and I had lumped mine, wrapped over my shoulder, for 165 miles up the track. I would carry it no other way. I supposed that around Blackheath or Wattamolla I would have to conform to fashion.

We were at a camp set up a little to the south of the base camp at Neike. This was the base for the railway and was mainly occupied by British troops after the Australians had moved out.

It was a bastard of a day marching next morning, the worst that I had put in the army since the march from the railway line at Johore to the GBD [General Base Depot] with full kit. I had gone in the back and in the calves of my legs from the long stretch in the rain and the mud on the previous day. It was as hot as Hades, weakening us even more. In fact Dizzy Dean summed up the position adequately by reckoning that we were all killed in action on Singapore Island and that this was Hell, although we did not know it. It was mud all the way. The road, at that time of the year at least, was just plain bloody ridiculous. The rain came again just before we arrived at our next camp. We then put up our tents and lit our fires with everything soaking wet. The 12½ mile trip had brought the total distance that I had marched since leaving Bampong up to 186 miles; wet, sick, beaten and starved.

With mountains on three sides of us, between the road and the river, the camp was a collection of dilapidated bamboo huts, some among the trees and some on the river flat. It would look for all the world like an idyllic scene from *Sanders of the River*. From a picturesque point of view it was a real jungle picture of tropical vegetation, pathways among the very tall teak trees, rain-soaked huts, the odd elephant and the barges on the river.

It was, however, the same old story, in that the camp had been, and still was, occupied by Burmese natives. Sanitation was nonexistent. Human and ox dung lay everywhere and flies bred in millions. It was always a fear that we would pick up infected maggots on our boots and bring them into the lines and near our food.

We were eighteen miles from the Burma border. A Force, which had left Changi back in May 1942, was over on the other side and, we understood, were doing well. The 2/30th was in a big AIF camp five and a half miles further up and there had been 22 deaths up to then in the battalion, including Clem Everingham and Billy Keighly. The 2/26th had been hit hard by cholera too but the Pommies were even worse. Our party (F Force) had struck it unlucky by being loaned to the Japanese Survey-Engineering Unit, who were working Christ out of us in a mad rush to get the bridges finished. The barbarism to which we were subjected had no equal in ferociousness in the history of any other AIF workforce, anywhere. We were not under the direct control of a Japanese Colonel who, it was believed, had been trying to do everything possible for the prisoners.

I went on sick parade just to be sent out to work, however. Later a full parade was held, when every man sick in camp was interviewed by a Japanese lance-corporal who would not and did not believe that any men were too sick to work. In their army a casualty was a liability and written off as such. Consequently the Japanese engineer in charge of us had no sympathy at all for anyone not fit to go out to work. Our own Commanding Officer, Lieutenant Colonel Kappe, was trying to help us but was met with complete indifference.

On Tuesday 15 June I was too dopey to write up my diary properly. I was belted to leg by another attack of malaria. I started then to get a regular recurrence of it and in fact did not get free of it for some considerable time, some years in fact. It was the same with us all. Never in my life had I felt worse than I did that morning. Fainting twice in the sun, then having cold shivers, it made me weaker than a new-born babe. With little or no resistance, hunger and with sleeping accommodation being just a leaky fly over twenty-two of us, my situation was only too serious. We had quinine and I took four of the six tablets given to me that day. They made my head feel like a goods train going from Town Hall station to Wynyard. The main cure was in ourselves, to look after ourselves and maintain a positive attitude. I tried to play patience so that the fever would not get me down. I did not know if it was the Japanese captain's intention to see us all die with a chunkel in our hands but he had a good go at it. He was ruthless and cruel and made life hell for us with contradictory orders and withholding rations. The Japanese medical officer, who had started to interview all the sick pretty thoroughly, had gone off when it rained. We had only Clive Brown as MO in our camp.

Next day there was no other way to express concisely, adequately and correctly, but that I was fucked—in fact I felt that I was like a clock about to stop. Just about every bit of strength and energy had been wrung out of me. I was practically in a semi-coma for 48 hours and knew nothing of what was going on around me.

There were rumours of us moving:
- Across the border.
- To work back along the road to Bampong.
- To Changi.

Bampong or Changi would have been heaven compared with where we were then. Home would have been paradise. As for getting anywhere, I wondered... We were right on the river again. Neike was half a mile up the road and had a canteen, but only for tobacco. Every type of mosquito bred around the river; some were like dragon flies. The officers and professional bludgers, those who crawled to the Japs for attention and favours, were still a bloody disgrace and pay seemed as far away as Timbuctoo.

The road seemed almost strictly one-way traffic; movement down the road was negligible. Suddenly in the morning of 17 June we were told that work was off, to pack our gear, we were moving back 45 kms. [By then we had got used to measuring distances in kilometres, which was generally in use.] I went on sick parade for my quinine as I could no more walk 45 kms than fly. Then the Japs, according to form changed their minds. The boys went out to work and we did not know what was going on. Rumour had it that our supplies were cut between Moulmein and our sector of the railway and it was to be a big move back. After those of us who were unable to walk were packed up and ready to go on the road to Neike, it too was called off. Later we were reclassified, our party of sick men cut down in numbers and we were again waiting to move on. That day too, 90 men from our last camp arrived but were expected to move back again with the rest later.

Our party of sick men (mainly dysentery, malaria and cholera) moved out, just before dark, another mile up the road. Again we were in roofless huts and wet too. This was the Neike Base Hospital Camp. Undoubtedly there had been a panic among the Japanese that day. We did not know what had caused the commotion but hoped it was from an air raid up the line or some otherwise bad news for them.

After working out that I had £212 1s.9d. in my paybook to 15 June, I thought that I was going to need a lot more than that to set myself up when I got back. I met up with some of the 2/30th boys and got news of Mark Wilson and McGregor. Goldy Golding and Frank Nokes, whom I knew at the Great World, had died. These sudden deaths of men with whom we had been mates made us think. I was worried about Mark though and he later died too. Of all things though, I would have liked to have got through to Curly Hardman at the next camp. It would have cured me and bucked me up but the chance was slender and was not to be. The rumour remained persistent that we would all be moving back to Changi.

At the cookhouse I had been winning the yak lottery, getting a couple of pieces in the last few meals. One yak a day was killed for 900 men. The 'stew' was stirred and ladled into our bamboo mess bowls: if you were lucky you got a piece of meat; if you were not you missed out. Rice was a two-thirds of a pint each meal per man.

In shifting quarters again I moved in to a hut with a roof and walls. For the first time since leaving Changi I had a chance to keep dry. Australians were in the minority in the camp and on one side of me I had a Malay Volunteer, on the other a Digger and next to him a Scotty and then a Pommie.

Altogether cholera, malaria and dysentery had killed 500 British and Australians on our draft since having been in Thailand for just over a month. At the crisis stage up to then, deaths were at a faster rate than during the campaign. That summed up the disgrace of us being brought to such an unhealthy, inaccessible part of the world, with little or no preparations being made except to work. I believed that the same railway scheme was turned down by the British as impossible. It did seem just then that the Japanese would abandon the railway half of the total project but this was not so.

I played patience, practised my knots, went over my sailing books, yarned with the boys and did anything to keep awake. I had learnt that it was definitely no good to sleep during the day when you were weak and ill. Consequently, although I had gone in the legs a lot I felt quite a bit better. The fever had gone down and the dysentery had eased. We looked like living skeletons and in fact it was to get worse. The boys even had a stab at a concert, which was not too bad. Many of us, particularly the Australians, would do anything to keep alert and as clean as possible. It was a matter of willpower. I did not want my diary to read like an Honour Roll but Ivan Bancroft, another mate on the Delivery Party at the Great World, died of peritonitis after an operation for appendicitis. The doctors did not have the facilities, not even a decent table, for surgical operations.

We were warned against trading with the coolies in case cholera had infected the stuff we bought and brought in to the camp. As it was, using a $1 dollar as a unit of currency, one of the native traders:

Buys a shirt from us for $2.
He sells the shirt for $6.
With the $6 he buys some of our rice from the Japs.
He then sells our rice back to us at a profit or trades it for more clothing which he can then sell.

He probably does this many times a day. The Japs finished up with the money, the native trader with the clothing and us still cold and hungry. We finally got square by knocking over a yak or three of the native working stock. Meanwhile, pay was possibly winding its way to us. We were told that the Japs had gone to get it and I signed some form. I wondered if anyone at home would have recognised me. I had aged a fair bit in the last year, besides being quite a bit thinner. I hardly recognised one of my own 'choco' photos, taken when in the CMF and which were the only ones I still had.

My temperature having gone down I was put on 'light' duties. There was no such thing as convalescence, even if we were called a Convalescent Depot. I was out on a truck for most of the day, loading and unloading bloody big logs. After that, till dark, I was shovelling and carrying sand and dirt. That was what the Japs thought of sick men. The little extra rice we got (1½ cups instead of ¾ cup) was no compensation. We shared our food with each other anyway. As at the camps all along the way, the Japs believed in feeding the workers and starving the rest. The food was better than we had previously been getting but was still something wicked. The yaks that came down the road for food were thin half-starved beasts, of which some were killed each day. I thought that if I had to keep going out to work on the road, too frequently in addition to the way we were being driven, it would affect me pretty seriously. I was just not strong enough for it. I was not thinking of bludging but it caused me some concern as I did not want to rupture or kill myself. As it was, when we had to break up rock I was usually the one to hold the gad while a bigger bloke swung the hammer. It was still hard physical work. This was especially so on cuttings. Having broken the rock face up by hand a three or four-man team would pick away, one with a shovel and two men carrying away the dirt and rock in long baskets made of bamboo. We would carry the stuff anything up to 75 yards away through mud and sodden clay. God help you if the basket broke or a man slipped and spilt any of the load. This would go on from about 9 in the morning to 9 at night. Before that we had to get to the job and be checked and issued with tools. After work we and the tools were checked again before getting back to the camp at 10 p.m. for a wash, meal and sleep. We got two breaks during the day, a morning smoko and a lunch break of about an hour. Having slept at night, if you were lucky, the next day would start again, before light. At first light the MO would commence his sick parade for the dressing of injuries, cuts and ulcers; he would classify us to fill the numbers demanded and if we were 'fit' or 'light duties', the day would repeat itself all over again.

The Japanese Engineer Commander continued to be maniacal in demanding men to go out to work. It was made known that if Japanese engineers were prepared to die then prisoners also must sacrifice their lives for the railway. They were becoming frantic. It had to be finished within a certain time at all costs and certainly irrespective of the lives of the native labourers and the prisoners of war. The main working parties from Neike were occupied at this time on pile-driving for the railway bridges and corduroying the road. This entailed laying tree trunks transversely and staking them on the road. Pile-driving was always heavy work and wrenched the stomach muscles every time a pile was driven in. The corduroy work on the road also continued to be brutal, with fewer and fewer men allocated to carry each 15-foot log to the worksite as less and less men were physically able to go out. Having got to the job it involved removing all the surface mud to lay the logs on relatively dry ground and then draining and reinforcing the track with earth and stones. If you were not on those jobs you broke rock.

In the camp the cookhouse was the usual rort and a bludger's paradise. The Pommy officers were the main garbage rats, hanging around for an extra mug of rice and stew halfway through the morning. There was a big 'blue' one morning when the Japanese guard was not satisfied with our rice issue. Some of the English officers were very autocratic in their attitude to the men although Lieutenant Colonel Dillon would speak up for them with the Japanese guards and tried for some improvement. I had a quiet day as the only job I was on was carrying rice to the place on the road where we were working. I hoped to continue to be as lucky. I even got in a little bit of reading, being early back to camp—an abridged version of *Peer Gynt* and *Das Kapital*. I had shifted around and was sleeping next to a couple of good mates from the 2/30th. It made all the difference in the world to me, with none of the everlasting Pommies' bickering going on around me. It was a change to talk about Sydney instead of Melbourne all the time too, as was the case most times with the 2/29th.

There were rumours of an I Force, with Black Jack in charge but that seemed a trifle far-fetched. Although I would have put nothing past the old bastard, I did not think that he would ever leave Changi unless forced to. He was too anxious to get home.

We completed the 'forty days and forty nights' of rain without floods. By the look of the weather pattern we were experiencing, we certainly would have another forty.

The hospital orderlies put on a pretty disgraceful performance at times and their reputations as a whole were not good. Admittedly they had an unenviable job as they were exposed to infection and contagious diseases at all times. In addition, as patients, we just stank. The job of cleaning up maggot-infested bodies was not a pretty one. At times though they clearly shirked their duties. Many of the medical orderlies were untrained volunteers. Some volunteered for the wrong reason, not to care for the sick but to escape going out to work and so bludge on the system. It was to be expected as there are always all sorts in the army. Many in the AAMC [Australian Army Medical Corps] did an herculean job.

I was carrying logs again on the job but shot through after the lunch break. It was a risky thing to do but I could hardly see and stand up. I gauged the mood of the Jap in charge of us and saw our Sergeant, who probably got me off and I reported sick again. The MO put me on three days 'very light duties'. The heavy lifting still made my head swim. Looking at my sketch of *Virginia* and thinking of Neil, I was determined to have her built to compensate me for all the ill-health and discomfort I was going through. I thought that then I would have no regrets.

I was in a sort of midway section between the hospital and the main lines and did not miss the main body of the 2/29th at all. The longer I was away the more I was pleased. Bowering and his cub-leader officers, his domineering sergeants and the original unit members were getting on my nerves. I went across to see some of the boys in the hospital, Curly Avard, Dizzy Dean and Curly McGrath. Curly Avard was not too good with dysentery and had not been for a day or so. Certainly he was a different Curly from the days as mates at the Great World.

Ted Watt came down from No. 1 camp, which was much larger than ours. I learnt all their news including that of the 2/30th. Curly Hardman was presently in hospital with malaria and had been there for fifteen days. That was a long time and I only hoped that the worst was over for him. There were 1300 in the hospital and 300 going out to work. Hardly a man had not had dysentery or fever. It seemed that their rations were even worse than ours, both workers and non-workers. The Japs were driving them hard too, especially as their sector was nearly finished. Ted was going back so I washed one of my two shirts and sent it to Curly Hardman. I knew that he was out of everything as he was travelling light enough when I had last seen him, six weeks previously. It was good to be able to repay him a little for all he had done for me. I hoped that he would receive the shirt OK, for he would be able to trade it and get some bananas and tobacco into him.

Like the relief of Mafeking, news of the sight of ration trucks arriving down the partially dried up road spread like a bushfire. I was sceptical that there would be much improvement though. It was a pretty busy day: a wash down at the

river, breakfast, parade, cleaning up the hut, collecting firewood, cooking with
Bridgy [Graham Bridgewater] some meat he had bought, a good lunch (with an
increase in our rice ration too as the result of the Jap inspection), on parade
again for a glass rod up the backside (my fourth on the road and seventh
altogether), arranging with Dizzy Dean how we may do over a yak, which was
not really on, tea in the evening, the daily check parade when we were counted
and identified, seeing the boys in hospital and so to bed after dark. It was plenty
too for my head swam from sheer weakness whenever I exerted myself. I could
not read very much at a time for I missed my glasses. It was a pity that they had
been broken. We were told that night on parade:

- That our rations *had* increased.
- Because some of the yaks sent down for food had got out during the
  previous night and because the Japs found a carcase which some mad
  bastard had not got rid of, we would not get any meat in our stew for
  two days.

The Japs were very strong on punishment and always of the whole camp.

I was glad that those at home could not turn a television set on me, or all of us
come to that. Digging drains and 'turning over' in the Jap garden (very light
duties) had sapped all the strength I had. At that stage I probably weighed about
80 lbs. It would make you weep. And on top of that, at tea, squatting on my
'hunkers', with my bamboo bowl between my knees, I was tearing at a big lump
of gristle like a dog to get every bit of meat and fat off it. It was not a pretty sight.
But I was very lucky and thankful to get the lump of gristle in my 'stew'.

I was smoking very little, being out of tobacco and disinclined to trade my
clothing. I did not 'bite' any of the boys and so was all the more grateful when I
was offered a smoke or a banana. Pay seemed as remote as ever. The rice and
stew-water still passed straight through me and it was annoying to get up to use
the latrines, more during the night than during the day. This was always a long
walk in the dark, first disturbing everyone around you as we were packed like
sardines, then crouched on the bamboo poles over the latrine pits with the fear of
slipping in; the long walk back, soaking wet and disturbing everyone
again...numerous times every night.

I felt that if only I had a crystal ball or even a cup of tea so that I could read the
leaves. It would have been a helluva comfort to know what the future held for us.
Or would it? Deaths being at 1 in 14 at that stage, the immediate future promised
nothing but sickness and hard work. A year previously I had written '18 months?
2 years?', which took us to February 1944. It was possible but not likely. Six
months previously I had expected that it would be December 1944 when we may
get home and I still stuck to that. I had annoyed an engineering officer a month
back by saying that all his hot stuff about being home soon was all pep talk. But
I was always able to look at the present more or less from the outlook of the future
and this helped make things that seemed pretty important at the time a lot less
significant. I thought that next year, Neike camp and the low conditions there
would be just a passing scene in the kaleidoscope of life; in three to five year's
time all that we were going through would seem a bad dream and that we would
be fit and well again.

It did not seem six months since Christmas. To me time still continued to fly although the campaign seemed years ago, ages before. It had been a year and a half since my final leave and two years since I had joined the UTs and the army. Memories of those times were as fresh as ever. I always held an affection for the old Liverpool camp. They were good easy-going times.

I was growing a moustache again and if I thought Neil a bit of a lair in his letter then I was something of a 'teddy bear' also. I had my first shave for a fortnight and cleaned my teeth for I still had some of the Gibb's Dentrifice left. I even greased my hair. So I felt considerably freshened up and it made all the difference as far as mental attitude was concerned and my outlook and acceptance of things as they were. Nervous disorders were becoming common and there had been the odd suicide or two. It was thought that the strain, continuous anxiety and the quite abnormal experiences, good and bad, that we endured may even have a long term effect on us. I knew that I would never be the same again.

There were two further orders that night. We would be shot in future:

- For being outside the boundaries of the camp.
- For breaking into the Japanese ration and motor transport stores.

We had learnt that A Force men (in Burma) had been shot for being outside the fence and this added weight to the orders. Not having tried out this crowd's form, we did not know whether they were bluffing or not. A considerable amount of bloody stealing was going on within the camp of boots, shirts, shorts, wallets etc. The bastards had sold all their own stuff and then were pinching from others for a bit more tobacco. I had lost a singlet and a pair of socks but boots were the most precious things we had. We even slept in them.

If we were obsessed with food, we had good reason to be. Obsessed we were. We put on a bit of a blue again at the cookhouse at lunchtime one day, after we were given a very small pint issue of rice. We had had quite a bit to complain about in regard to the meals. That afternoon a Japanese sergeant went through the hospital as half a mug of rice was being issued to each man. He went mad and straight to the kitchen, finding two bags of rice which should have been cooked. They were their beloved reserve. But why was it that the privates always had to fight for their full ration? It all proved effective for we got a good issue that night. I hoped that it would be consistent for we were getting four to five bags of rice for the 900 odd men that then made up our whole camp.

Wednesday 30 June and on the previous evening I had felt very pleased with myself: a good tea and later Arch, who I was alongside in the tent, gave me a cigar and Denny and Diz presented me with a cup of tea. It was all very beautiful.

Then in the morning I found myself under open arrest. As it was the first time, it was an interesting experience. I was on yak picket at night and the sergeant had failed to wake me and post me on duty. I was charged with not doing my shift. On the surface they did not have a leg to stand on but ever since we had been POWs this sort of thing had gone on. Technical points or a sane outlook had been often ignored. I had yet to find out how I would go.

I was back on light duties, taking rations down to Lower Neike, three and a half miles away and bringing back paniers of medical supplies on bamboo poles between two of us. The road was still just mud. Next day I was made to go out and work on the road. Luckily I struck the best of a bad lot. Other parties were being bashed by the Japs with their fists, bamboo sticks and *axes*. We were made to keep going all day and unfortunately I had pains in the stomach even before I left the camp in the morning. I was doubled up by the time I got back home again. The last two days had set me back again, just as I was definitely starting to come good.

Although the figures may not be exactly accurate they were near enough to be a pretty good guide to the state of things at the end of June. After being brought the best part of 2000 miles to Thailand, of the 7000 men, in the two months we had been there, 7% were dead, 60% were sick and in hospital, 18% were convalescent and recuperating from illness and *15% only* were working on the road and railway which we had been brought up to build. All that in two months and a long way to go yet.

Friday 2 July was not too good a day. The cramped pains in my stomach and the diarrhoea had eased off though. Curly Avard was still very ill. For over a month he had had dysentery and the same pains in the stomach I had, which meant that he could get little sleep at night. I had given him some of my vitamin tablets but I did not have enough left to be effective. Graham Bridgewater, Curly McGrath and Dizzy Dean were coming good but I did not like things with Curly Avard at all. It seemed pretty definite that a proper hospital was being established in Burma and that the worst cases from the various camps were to be sent there soon. We were in the middle of a God, man and beast forsaken area where no one had a hope of ever getting fit. Just five yards off the road, into the scrub, mosquitoes were as thick as snow in Siberia, the maggot-infected latrines were thick with blowflies and the cholera ridden river was our only water supply.

I was still classified light duties and yet put in the hardest day's work since being up on the road. I was felling timber and sawing it up in five metre lengths, 1½ to 2 inches through. Four of us then had to lift and carry the pieces wherever they had to go. I, with the others, was bashed up because we could not lift them onto our shoulders. We finally shifted them with poles but the beatings went on all day, being hit wherever the blows landed. I did not see the day out. I passed out, unconscious, and was left where I lay on the ground. There was no other way to describe how I felt when I got myself back to camp that night but that again I was just fucked.

The workers were still supposed to be compensated by getting about five pints of rice a day, which was more than I could eat. It had to be forced down for it was near enough to all we got. That night though we did get a cup of tea. The officers received their pay of $90, less $20 taken back, and a buying party was organised to go to Neike village for tobacco, gula malacca, soap and tea.

I had been up before the Company Commander in regard to the yak business as though I was being court-martialled. After telling my story I was remanded to go before the CO [Anderson of the 2/15th Artillery] but I decided to go on asking for remands until I got to see Lieutenant Colonel Andy Dillon, who was the top officer in the camp at Neike. I did not hear any more on the matter. That Sunday, 4 July, I came over with cold shivers in the afternoon and a blood slide was taken. In the evening, on sick parade, I was put back in hospital with a temperature of 100°.

I had BT malaria and when it hit me again next morning it 'put me down for seven'. It certainly hit solid. Wearing long trousers, shirt and heavy jacket, a big towel and a double blanket wrapped around me I still felt cold. Then when the shivering passed off I felt on fire and was bathed in perspiration. For two hours the attack lasted and left me with a head like an elephant. Just at that time a cup of tea arrived and it was the most beautiful, gorgeous cup of tea that I had ever had in my life. I brightened up in the afternoon, though still thick in the head. Malaria hit us in waves, I was as good as gold one moment and yet half an hour later would be as feverish as hell, shivering under my blanket. I did appreciate the warm clothing, which I had lumped up from Bampong and had not sold.

July 6 and it was announced that from a camp up the road, eight officers (including five divisional officers, one of them a colonel) and a batman had escaped and that a search was likely of our gear for arms, ammunition, maps, etc. It was a British party and, it seemed, a long-organised affair for being caught meant getting shot. It would be a bloody hard job to get away. I believed that one development that day was the calling in of officers' pay.

I was not feeling so bad, just very dull and dense. The effects of the quinine were almost as bad as the malaria itself. Besides being off my food, I was starving myself a bit to try and relieve the cramped pains in my stomach, which I had had for the last week. The officers in the camp set up their own separate mess with the objective of improving their own meals. This could only be done by increasing their individual ration by a fraction of an ounce of meat, a fraction of an ounce of beans, etc. per man per day. To get anything besides rice to cook made an appreciable difference to appetite and health. A little oil and flour had come into the camp (not enough for 1000 men) and it was apparently things like that, which the officers intended to get down on. I did not moan or complain about them increasing their own rations above that of the men, although it was incredible at that time. I was disgusted that, ever since the surrender, the officers had not had the *guts* to do it as hard as the men had had to. It was an underlying greed, selfishness and fear that caused them to be frightened to remain on the three to four pints of rice and three ounces of vegetables (cooked), the rest water, per man per day, that we were on. Of course it would never be admitted but I claimed to be intelligent enough to form a pretty definite opinion. They had even taken more than their allotment of space. The whole move was clearly to increase their survival odds, which among the men, were decreasing rapidly.

The Japanese were pretty concerned over the escape business. The 'lolly loppers' [Japanese officers, who beheaded men with the swords they carried] ran around all day and a check parade was held but as yet none of us had been shot or our rations cut as a punishment. [Four of the officers, who survived were found by the end of August and executed.]

We learnt some more general news:

- Things were still pretty bad up at Sonkurai (AIF) No. 1 camp. Their Japanese commander was mad but he in turn was being pushed to provide more and more men on the job, for longer hours, by the Jap engineers.
- Some AIF men had been killed recently in allied bombing in Burma.

- A POW ship was sunk, with mainly Dutchmen aboard.
- A Force drivers from the Burma end were through our camp but we were not allowed to contact them at all.

There were now armed guards patrolling our lines. Also a Japanese colonel, who was on our side in the last war, inspected our camp. He went through the hospital and demanded that more men go out to work. That day another man died in the adjacent dysentery ward to me and our quinine issue was cut down to five tablets a day, supplies being light and uncertain. In cases of BT malaria it should have been ten tablets a day, not to mention atebrin tablets. The three meals were something terrible, bloody awful in fact, and yet more men were taken from the hospital to go out to work.

We were innovative at least. Besides the 1001 uses of bamboo we had:
- Tent canvas shorts.
- Kitbag jackets.
- Rubber tyre boots.
- Banana-leaves socks.

There was no sign of our pay, yet rations were again cut down. The Japs must have expected miraculous healing properties from the last extra rice given to us and were disappointed. Work duties in the camp and on the road were thick and fast. However, the Japs had no difficulties getting flunkies for themselves, even a corporal had taken on a job working for them. Some had no pride at all. Our common saying at the time was 'Christ, we must have done some terrible things to be doing penance like this'. And as if our penance was not bad enough, body lice started to spread throughout the camp and in no time we expected to be driven mad. The two men to the right of me had it on them and I supposed that it would not be long before they were on me, too, no matter how hard I tried. I had a cold on top of the fever, with my nose clogged up and a head like a lump of cheese. At the same time I was deaf from the quinine and was going blind too. My eyes were worrying me. I found it difficult to recognise people at 35 feet and at 2 feet, with my right eye, the outline of objects were blurred. With headaches and aching behind my eyes I was by no means happy about the situation. All that remained, I thought was to get toothache, which was not unlikely as I already had broken a big bit off one a short while before.

The rain was even heavier in July than in June. In May and June we *did* get an hour or two of sunshine each day but in mid-July it hardly stopped except for occasional half-hour lapses. I did not think that I had seen the moon and stars for two months. I had lent my pullover to Dizzy Dean two weeks previously when he had had to go out and I was in. The first time I got it back it stank and was covered in mud. Another of his mates had been working in it. I gave it back to them to wash and then I was told that it had gone off. That was what you got for lending your clothing to men who had sold all theirs. I determined not to part with much more as I only had a shirt, giggle suit, two pair of shorts, one pair of socks, boots, puttees, hat and a gas cape.

The yak herd was exhausted. Two weeks before there had been 31 in stock but hardly half of them saw the cookhouse, what with deaths and losing a few. We were only allowed to kill one a day but not one of them could have lived the month out. Possibly, we hoped, we would get some more. Actually a case of dried meat came to the camp and I even struck a piece in my stew. That the cases of dried meat were covered in flies and maggots did not worry us. We scooped off whatever was floating on top and ate the rest.

We thought that we had the cholera outbreak under control, thanks to the Lord, to the Indian doctor in charge of the epidemic and to the hygiene that had been vigorously carried out since it started. The Indian doctor, the same one who had advised as to what we could eat out of the jungle, had done excellent work, not only in attending to the sick but in advising the other camp MOs about the diseases. We did not know how many of us owed our lives to him. Like Major Wild he deserved a special award for the job he did. Dysentery was still rife but not nearly as deadly as cholera.

I met a Tommy Morrison of Bellevue Hill. He was a buyer for Angus & Coote and we had a good yarn about H.H. Halls, the wholesalers in York Street where I went on audits. We talked of Mr. West and Mr. Clift. He was good to yarn to but was pretty sick. He was only the fourth man I had met, with whom there were people we knew in common. I had never ceased to wonder about Bob Logan knowing my cousin Gertie in Glasgow and Curly Hardman, who knew the McPhee girls and the Calders at Ryde.

The BT malaria treatment was extended from ten to fourteen days. The Japs took blood slides in the camp and the results shocked even them. Extra medical supplies were issued but still no atebrin.

Joe Pearce, Joe Vievers and Ernie Gayford of the 2/30th were down working in our camp from No. 1 camp. Curly Hardman was still in hospital up there but I only had time to send up a message. That day also we got on to some wild custard apples, which were not nearly as tasty as the cultivated variety. However, they went well with the rice and made a variation at least. Our minds dwelt all the time on food and it dominated our conversation.

Daily check parades were again ordered. Some of the Japs, especially those who had been with us all along, told us that we would be going back to Changi in six weeks; by the end of August.

We still quite often heard monkeys whining away from the scrub up in the hills but I had not sighted any. What I did see were some of the most beautiful butterflies in the world: they were in all sizes and colours. Really lovely.

The 2/30th boys were working in our camp at Neike on an air-raid shelter and an ammunition store. We were then told that Reveille and breakfast would be in the dark in order to get the check parade over 25 minutes after daybreak and the workers out earlier. With the panic to finish the railway, the working day on the job was extended to 10 at night, necessitating the march back to camp to be carried out in the dark. At worst the boys went through to 2 a.m., working by flares and firelight. At times they would have gone even longer except that the incessant rain put out the flares. In the morning the bugler would sound Reveille and as a variation would blow what sounded like something by Raymond Scott and his Orchestra [a jazz band with very syncopated and unusual rhythms]. As it was I continued to hear the bugler blow the 'Last Post' every day and would continue to hear it every day for months to come.

Things were quiet in the hospital; we did not learn very much of what was going on. It never ceased to amaze me how secretive a soldier was; information had to be dragged out of him like a stubborn molar. I was moved from one overcrowded hut to another, where fourteen of us and our gear had to sleep in an area 12 feet by 12 feet. In some of the sections of the long bamboo huts, private fires for boiling water and drying clothes were lit about every two feet or so up the centre. The smoke made my eyes ache even more. The cooking at the kitchen improved though, after long overdue changes. I was getting the rest I long needed and was on 'sufficient' meals for the lack of activity. Malaria, I even thought, was a much exaggerated complaint as we were getting very blase. Undoubtedly it made you very weak and the first belt was not nice but the quinine deadened you and then did all the work. I had learnt to live with it. I would not have liked to get malaria though without the quinine.

It was mid-July and I went down to the river for a good bath for the first time since the fever had got hold of me. I noticed that the water was so hard that without soap I could not get all the dirt off properly. It took three or four days to get my legs really clean. Incidentally, although it was only a simple thing, I had washed my face in hot water a few days previously; this was the first time that I had done so since being on the *Aquitania*. The river had risen quite a few feet since we had arrived at the camp and flowed west. I had a good dip, even though we could not swim for fear of getting water in our mouths because of the cholera. A dip in the river was one of the few (more properly *rare*) pleasures that we had. I remembered that back in Edinburgh some of the kids were none too clean. They did not improve as they grew up and quite a few of the Poms were simply frightened of good clean water. They stayed filthy. I often yarned to some of them and it was interesting talking about places like Edinburgh, Glasgow, Harrow, Edmonton, Birmingham etc.

There was an alarming increase in the number of deaths from dysentery in the camp. They were almost a nightly affair; five in a week. Our conditions were purely and simply murder. As was the case with the cholera patients, the boys had the strength to overcome the disease but not recover as well. Young Curly Evans who died, had been lingering on, like quite a few others, until his heart just stopped. Most of the boys died peacefully in their sleep. They were on the lowest rations of us all, being a liquid diet of the water the greens were boiled in and rice water; about one and a half pints altogether, each meal. Lying in bed, continuously bogging where they lay and among equally distasteful company, every day for a month, six weeks or even for two months, you must indeed be heroic not to drop your bundle. It was not as bad as cholera but after that nothing weakened you or got you down more, than prolonged dysentery. This was not going to improve until there was an all-round improvement in the *meals*, not just an increase in the rice ration, the *weather*, our *outlook* on the future and a consequent improvement in *morale*. The hospital staff were not entirely free from blame. Little as they had in the way of instruments and drugs, inattention and lack of sympathy by some had its effect in not helping the patients get out of the feeling of depression, of which most were victims. The MOs and the orderlies were simply overwhelmed.

We were into our third month and it was still raining every day. It had got into my letters, my wallet, my cards (you never saw a more dilapidated pack and me a rabid Patience player), *Sea Boats, Oars and Sails*, even my toothpaste. Everything was more or less permanently damp. I continued to carefully nurse my diaries and pay book wrapped in oilcloth. I finished the fourteen day quinine treatment. It was undoubtedly marvellous stuff and I felt much better, though still a bit dense from its effects. I hoped to get a day or two off to clear my head and try to get rid of the cold that I still had.

Unbelievably, the working day was extended even further and Reveille was even half an hour earlier still, at 6.30 a.m. (or 4.30 in normal times), so that breakfast and check parade could be held right on daybreak. One day there was another check parade later in the morning because some stupid bastard, to dodge work, decided to hide himself under his blanket in the half dark. I did not think it right that our officers should have put him on short rations for the day, stood him on the parade ground and fine him a month's Japanese pay. Actual cowardice was rare. There were English officers who never came out of their mosquito-netted tents and had their batmen bring them their food. Fear affected officers and men in different ways. I never knew any of us who actually cowered before the Japanese.

One of the doctors, a Captain Barbour of the British 18th Division, was excellent and gave us a real examination. To describe the treatment our MO and others gave us as cursory would be a terrific exaggeration. But the doctors had a hard job, to do their work properly and sympathetically and at the same time to satisfy the Japs, who demanded that men go out to work. They continued to decide on men's lives in selecting which of the sick had to go out each day. We could be critical of the MOs and orderlies, as we were on the receiving end but the sheer size of the task and the number of sick involved were beyond the human resources and physical ability of the staff to cope.

More canteen stuff arrived, some of it even by elephant and included gula malacca (a sweetener), tobacco, peanuts and soap. Thanks to Colonel Harris we received 50 cents as an advance on our pay from the officers generally.

Monday, 19 July and it was three months since we had left Changi. It seemed incredible, so much had happened, history-making events, to make the time seem so short; like proverbial lightning in fact. The quarter had been such a rapid succession of experiences—the train, the track, the roadwork; cholera and starvation, the loss of weight and strength and then malaria. It had been a lifetime in experience for me and a reality for others, no doubt about that. My only prayer was that succeeding quarters on the railway job would be no harder. I had lost so many mates since April.

And yet the Pommies and the Scots never ceased to amaze me. One of the British units had brought Henry all the way up from Changi. He was a pet dachshund and had his likes and dislikes, as did all the other local dogs in the camp. It was funny when he made an attempt to bark on check parade at night. But with all their different broad accents, when the Poms and the Scotties shouted out across the camp, like the rest of the boys, I sometimes could not tell them from the Japs.

Before even touching the canteen stuff I came down with diarrhoea again, bringing me in line with the rest of the camp. Hygiene in the camp was nearly an impossible job. The latrines had to be close enough to the lines to use and at the same time well away from the kitchens. At night, unfortunately, indiscriminate bogging did go on. The lines had to be cleaned up every morning.

The sun came out beautifully for a few hours one evening and it was a pleasure to swim and be out in it. Even so a Japanese officer had to drive *all* the men outside. The canteen stuff, combined with our normal rations, provided us with our best meals for some time. I was mates with Jim Clarke of Western Australia and Bert Franklin of Queensland and we had done well, combining our resources.

I had not written of it at the time, in my diary, but a month previously, when out on the road, I was so starving before lunch that when a dixie of rice was spilled in the mud I ran to scoop some of it up before the dirty water went right through it. It was dry rice and tasted good, like fresh bread. I was not proud of the event or myself but at the time I *was* hungry, the greatest demoraliser of all.

The working parties out on the road were still having hell worked out of them. They were on the bridges, making the road, putting down the bedding for the railway, building up embankments, making cuttings, breaking rock, felling trees, sawing timber, carrying dirt—all by hand, with baskets, chunkels, axes, shovels and hammers. In the camp we dug trenches, pits, felled timber for the cremations, repaired the huts, cleaned up the lines and buried the dead. It was a lucky crowd who got in before dark, most arriving back between 10 p.m. and midnight. It was a long day from 8 and 8.30 in the morning. I was still losing weight: all of us had our ribs and hip bones sticking out. I saw Captain Barbour about the malaria, diarrhoea, piles, headaches, dizziness and weak eyesight I had then. I went on to a liquid diet, including three-quarters of a pint of peanut-top water a day for my eyesight. This was a common vitamin deficiency complaint which affected our vision. I was on five pints of liquids, three-quarters of a pint of rice and some peanuts and gula malacca of my own from the canteen, daily. It had quite an effect on my bladder. I was certainly not the young man I used to be. The boys were still dying pretty regularly and quietly. No fuss or talk was made to prevent upsetting those of the very ill, who would likely be disheartened; also for the general morale of the camp. It really was something terrible.

Rumours were getting prevalent of us moving into or towards Burma. These were backed up by the appearance of elephant teams, large mobs of natives moving up the track and new Japanese officers at their HQ in Neike.

An engineering officer, Downes, was found on Friday 23 July. He had brought us to our present camp on the 17 June. Delirious with malaria, he was missing from the previous night but was dragged out of the river, drowned in the morning. A pathetic way to die, especially to have come so far in seventeen months.

One of the boys near me had to take Epsom Salts to clean him up and I gave him some of my peanuts to take the taste away. Big oaks from little acorns grow: he filled my tobacco tin. It was pretty well like that all the way through among the men. You shared what you had when you had it.

Mud! It was ankle-deep over the whole camp. It was terrible getting around at night, with no moon. It was 300 yards up hill to the latrines. At each step of the way I had to pull my boots out of the mud with my hands. Getting back to the hut our feet were almost as muddy and then we had to walk over men to get to our sleeping place. I hoped that typhus did not break out as, with the lice through the camp, it would have affected us all.

Food was the dominant topic of conversation around me. I was with a Scotsman, a Welshman, an Englishman, an Australian, a New Zealander and an Irishman. I learnt about haggis, rarebit, Yorkshire pudding, damper and ice cream from a Yank, all from experts, recipes and all.

My gula malacca gave out but it remained important to me to eat as well as I could. The first sign that one of the boys alongside was going to die was when he stopped eating; when he could not force the stuff down any more. When they gave up they died very quickly. It was common for men to simply not have the will to carry on any longer. Without the will to live they died within 24 hours.

The MO gave an orderly a dollar for a fly-catching competition among the patients. We caught flies but the result was put off and off and the orderly finished up with the dollar. There were none with a lower reputation than many of the AIF hospital staff. Nevertheless I had been lucky.

Like the day on 23 February 1942 when, by a fair amount of luck, I went to Singapore and escaped the terrible conditions in the early days; also the move on 17 June 1943, when I left the main body of the battalion to go up to Neike, which probably saved my life. One of the drivers described some of the boys he saw as they moved back as just skeletons, lying on the side of the road. They had to cover two and three times the distance (about 39 miles) to Takunen, going backwards and forwards at each stage, carrying their own gear and tents, then the gear of the sick and then the sick themselves. Individually they also carried their rice ration, eight lbs to last nine days, although at times they had nothing to eat at all but plain salt. Christ knows how I would have gone. Christ knows how some of the boys did it: sheer guts and determination again.

At that time we seldom heard birds whistling: the old crow was about the only one. We had quite a lot of birds around us at odd times before the monsoon set in but they were rare just then. We missed them.

I was coming good in the tucker line on a very liquid diet but although it cleared up the diarrhoea at the same time it was not actually strengthening. It had been a year since Neil had written to me. His letter had made me smile a few times when things had not been too bright. I thought 'Good on you, Neil, I still miss you but we will make it up, with interest'.

The lice caught up with me; in the seams of my clothes. We had absolutely nothing with which to get rid of them, not even the facilities for boiling. They drove hell out of me at night crawling around on my skin and during the day the rash itched like mad. Just another penance for the crime I had not done.

A further casualty list was released to the end of June. It took the number of deaths well over the 700 mark. If other camps had deaths at the same rate as at Neike (12 in 9 days out of 1100 men) during the month, then by 31 July we expected that there would be over 1000 dead, *1 man in 7 in 11 weeks*. [We thought that bad—little did we know.] Among the twelve of our boys, who had died, were some from sheer exhaustion or who literally had worked themselves to death for those men and mates who were weaker; strong men like Leo Sykes and Schofield. ←
Thank God I was at Neike, there was no way that I would be a burden on anyone.

Billy Reeves, who had died of blackwater fever, which was an extreme form of MT malaria, was the only new name I knew from Curly Hardman's camp. I hoped that *he* was still reasonably fit.

The hospital staff (non-combatants, who the Japanese favoured) were paid: privates $8 a month, the WO2, $36. We hoped soon to be paid a dollar or two. We were just workers, the proletariat.

At the end of July the sun came out. It was a beautiful day although hard on my eyes. I played and swam in the river like a five-year-old. It was cold, however, at night. Our blood must have been thin and the mere thought of Katoomba made me shiver. I saw the MO again and was marked down from A to B (of A, B and C categories of sickness). There were many a helluva lot sicker than me, for I did not feel too bad. I had learnt endurance.

Some more canteen stuff arrived. It was an experience to see it transported right to the 'door' on the back of a bloody big elephant. The Sergeant Major called for volunteers 'six men to unload the elephant'. It made me smile. They were marvellous creatures and I thought they should be all over Australia.

I raked up the fly-catching competition, much to the orderly's sorrow. I was sure that he had spent the original dollar. Three of us shared it and we each got a bit of tobacco.

I was coming good on my food too well. I was finding it hard to satisfy my appetite. We had a 'leggi' system. The cooks would make so much gruel or rice in a big pot and we would line up and get a ladle or less into our mess gear. There would be some left over. Each of us had a number and then took it in number order to receive another ladleful or half a ladle of gruel until the pot was emptied. Next meal the 'leggi' would start at the next number. We were happy when our number came up.

When we did at last get our pay, it was only for the time that we had been at Neike. I supposed that I could say goodbye to the pay for all the work on the road before that; and for travelling pay, which some of the other camps had received. Still I got $1.35. Apart from gula malacca and tobacco everything else from Neike village was horribly expensive: condensed milk, biscuits, sauce and oil. Except for the officers and the few men with money, there was nothing in the canteen of food value. The rich may get sick, the same as the poor, but in Thailand money bought health. I could not have fried rissoles, tinned fish, milk and sugar to supplement the monotonous diet of rice and various flavoured water. There was a considerable difference in the health of those who could.

It seemed that a certain number of the sick would be moved to a hospital in the vicinity of Moulmein and the rest of the camp moved about three camps up the road, by the 10 August. An advance party of around 30 MOs and orderlies moved out but we were told little of what was going on.

We were doing what we could for Curly Avard. Jack Mason, especially was a Samaritan the equal of the original. Nothing was too much for him, even though he was sick himself. We (some of us in C Company) put in 10 or 15 cents each to get Curl some gula malacca and tobacco, for of course he collected no pay. I only hoped that the gula would encourage him to eat as he had lost so much weight. Everyone was suffering from a general itching sensation all over the skin. It was the same old cause—vitamin deficiency —and, I thought, unaccustomed sunlight. Quite apart from the lice we could not stop scratching all day. I thought of Bev Howard [a friend of my parents from Concord West] in the First War and his experiences, naked in the sun and going through the seams of his clothes for 'chats'.

It was quite an eventful day, Dad's birthday, 31 July. It started at midnight when I was woken up by Jock with a dixie of rice and stew. I thought a yak had been knocked off. It was a cold supper but I was starving. It was a terrible thing to have an appetite, to want food and there be no way of satisfying it. I ate pretty well, in quantity anyway, all day. Later I got news that cholera had again broken out in the 2/29th camp. I was set back a bit at roll call too when the CSM impatiently kept calling for Gunner Adams until a hard voice yelled out that he had died two days ago, but that was the way it was. Lying down that night I could just hear a violin being played somewhere, above the general noise of the camp. I could not make it out at all and so it brought to mind the relief of Lucknow (when the bagpipes were heard from miles away). Free people have no real idea of what imprisonment is like. It turned out to be a world-famous violinist who had put together a violin he had brought from Changi. He was playing 'Souvenir' at a concert held in another part of the camp and it sounded beautiful. There was also a famous classical pianist, who had an oilcloth key board upon which he practised until he died. But pains in my stomach for my gluttony during the day closed the 24 hours.

It had been a year before, on 1 August, that I wished to sleep for twelve months. What a morning to wake up to: on the banks of a river in the Burma-Thailand mountains it was cold and raining heavily. I was broke, I had just had breakfast of three-quarters of a pint of gruel and half a pint of 'tea' and I was continuously suffering the effects of diarrhoea. In other words I was not too happy. I did not feel like writing the diary up the way I used to. So much had gone out of life, although I still had a fair amount of imagination left. I could have broken out in tears, it was such a miserable day.

The misery and degradation around me was a reality beyond all my previous experience and imagination. The immediate reward for endeavouring to stay alive was to go out, work and be beaten on the railway, knowing for certain I would be back in the hospital section of the camp before long. The rain was incessant. I was wet, cold and filthy dirty in the mud: my guts ached unceasingly and I would strain at the latrines many times, day and night, to produce a small amount of slimy substance, which I would then collect on a leaf to show the doctor. I was half blind without my glasses and as the result of deficiencies in what little food I could keep down. My eyes were sore yet I persisted and was determined to write up my diary. This was mostly done at night by firelight. There was no isolation from the death and disease immediately around me. The attap huts were divided off into bays by the roof supports, and in each bay we would mutually support each other to eat, stay as clean as we could and combat the flies, which bred in the filth, excreta and up the arseholes of dying men. (The maggots would leave the body immediately the man died.) Fear and despair were contagious and we endeavoured to cheer each other up by yarning away about the good times and our future hopes and dreams. Even so, men around me died every day.

Curly Avard, after a false start, was moved. The first crowd of 75 sick were taken away in open trucks. We never definitely knew what happened to men when they were taken away. Of course there were the usual promises that had followed us all the way along the road, that 'things are better at the next camp'. But I thought that more, eventually, would be done for Curl, although as he said, he would miss his mates. I only hoped that he would pull through; at times I had honestly had my doubts but he had guts.

All in the 'convalescent' ward were paraded before Captain Barbour for reclassification and surprisingly I was put on the hospital list for Burma. I was by no means sorry. I only hoped that it would eventuate, although it was a slight blow to my pride. It had bucked up my self-esteem, battling out the last three months, the equal of any man there. With my professional background, my sedentary occupation, my 'cultured' half-Edinburgh/half-Australian accent, I had always been the object of a lot of good-natured ribbing from my mates. I gave as good as I got.

The Burma party were segregated, 415 of us all together. Some were unable to walk. The rest of the camp moved up the road to various camps that it was judged that each man could make. I sent another note up to Curly Avard with Jack Mason, wishing him well. Native labour arrived in the camp and more were expected next day, which was not good. I had had experience before of being camped with the filthy buggers. I hoped to the Lord that they would not reintroduce cholera, which they had had amongst them to date. I supposed that it was really too much to hope for. Neike camp was closing down.

In a way it was a pity that we broke up the camp just as we were beginning to benefit from all the hard work we had done in getting it shipshape: the good latrines, which had been dug by the sick as the Japanese would not release fit men; the corduroy across the worst patches of mud; the draining of our part of the camp to prevent flooding as at the lower end, not to mention that Waite, the first AIF officer to take over the messing, had just improved our meals 300%. But that was always the way.

Talk about mates I made in the army!! I had a 'youngster' of 41 on my hands. I fed him, washed him and ran around getting leaves to wipe his behind. He was Ted Bourke of Randwick and of the MAC [Motorised Ambulance Company]. But it was just as important to see that the men near you were as clean and careful as yourself or else all the care that you took was useless. But what matter, it was 3 August and Mum's birthday.

Twenty more went up to No. 2 camp, so it looked as if it would take quite a while to shift those of us left at Neike. It seemed that it could only be done as trucks became available. Certainly on *one* hand, the meals improved out of sight after the boys had moved out, some very 'rich' stews appeared (except in our dysentery ward, which was on a light liquid diet), but on the *other* hand that was far outweighed by the really dangerous position we were in from any large increase in sickness in the rest of the camp. There were two deaths from cholera among the natives and we had only one MO and 20 orderlies and hygiene men to combat any outbreak, should it go through the 300 of us waiting to move on. It would have been an impossible job if cholera had swept through.

The gula malacca of which I had been writing was the juice collected from the flower of the coconut palm and boiled. It set like candied honey and was like a combination of honey and treacle: not as sweet as honey and not as strong as treacle. It made a good substitute for sugar.

I came out of the dysentery ward and went on to extra tucker like, for example, a rissole, which I hoped would give me the chance to build up and do my eyes some good. I even volunteered for bamboo parties, a fairly light job, which would be good exercise and help digest the extra makan [food].

We had hardened to it and accepted the life at Neike, otherwise it would have seemed all very unreal. Inside the hut there was a big change from the picturesque tropical setting outside, which made the whole thing so fantastic. We slept on the floor, close up to each other, men dying, screaming and moaning; spewing and bogging going on amongst us; delirious fits and morphine injections by the light of a candle; fires in the hut all night; men at all times walking up and down the central passageway to the latrines; it made it all a corner of hell brought to earth. This was no figure of speech if you were lying next to a man about to die and lying next to him still, after he was dead. It was all an experience the like of which very few men had gone through, even in war time. Death is nothing new in war, it was how they died around you that made such a vivid impression.

The Burma party was cut down by a third. More broken Japanese promises to keep men on the railway. God knew how many, if any, were to reach there, wherever it was and if things would be any better. I was still on the list to go but was not building up any hopes. We were waiting to see if another promise would go: that in three months (at the end of August) we would be going back to Bampong.

My 'hospital history' was recorded in my paybook. This was an excellent idea of Major Hunt's in case hospital lists were lost. It was signed by the MO for pension and treatment purposes before discharge from the army, back home.

News was that those left at Changi had been moved to St. John's Island. It was a far more likely move than to Java, as it followed up rumours prevalent for some time, even before we left, that such a move was on. I hoped that Jack Cressdee and Syd Grounds were still all right. That the conditions in Thailand would have killed Syd I had no doubt. He had had malaria too many times as it was.

Another convoy of sick men left to go up the road, probably to Burma. I definitely would have been on it if I had stayed in the dysentery ward. But it was just as well that I did not go for I had another relapse of malaria that afternoon and had my temperature taken at 103°. What with the fever and the quinine tablets it was the same old feeling of delirium all over again. I hoped that I would get it out of my system before returning to Australia or a colder climate. I was put back in hospital again. After I had been eating like a horse I went right off my food but forced down as much as would go. I was next to a Pommy, who washed himself by always saying 'I must go down to the river this afternoon' or 'I wish it would rain and a man could have a bloody good wash'. But he never did and there were hundreds of them. For myself, I had hardly missed a day since the surrender that I did not have a wash of some sort.

The third department of the hospital was the 'Skins' ward. This included bronchitis, diphtheria, scabies, beri-beri, etc. This last caused legs, from the knees down, to swell up like an elephant's and be quite shapeless. In its worst stages it affected any organ in the body. When it reached the heart, it killed you, as it had a number of the boys already. A lack of vitamin B was the trouble. I had been lucky as it had not affected me to then but a good many had had it to various stages so far.

Monday 9 August and the sun made its best effort to come out and did we soak it up. It was raining again by 5 p.m. but it had been a beautiful day. I managed to borrow a cut-throat razor for the first shave in a fortnight. I had even washed my face and hair with soap and slapped on the old hair oil. There was no doubt about this baby. I got out the old Gibb's Dentrifice, had a good tea and thought that all that should clear up the old malaria.

I wondered about the Burma move. We had been caught every time from the start on anything that the Japanese did. They always looked upon the sick— Japanese, prisoner or coolie—as a millstone around their necks and treated them as such. How would they treat a camp full of sick men, unable to work?

Our stews thickened up at meal times but were too rich for us. We even had thick pea soup and a spoonful of sugar on our morning rice. A few of the boys struck it lucky, catching some fish in the river and there were even eggs for sale. As the officers and the orderlies were the only ones who were decently paid it did not do the rest of us much good.

Next day I put the big cross in the diary. Yes, it was the first day in twelve weeks and two days that it did not rain. We hoped that the monsoon was breaking up and that health and spirits would improve all round. We had two fine days and then the rain was back in its usual form. I thought of living in Alice Springs when I returned. The quinine had got me down worse than previously. I was still off my food and my head felt like a big lump of putty sending me quite deaf. But weak! It made my arm tired soaping up to wash and shelling beans on kitchen duty. I was hard pressed cleaning up outside the hut. Like everyone else too the nerves were a bit on edge, which was not helped by the blasting that was going on just outside the camp. It thundered up the valley and crashed against the wall at the far end. But it was disgraceful to feel like that at 22 years of age. It all made me hard, more cynical than ever, very dubious about anything and, if not actually bitter, getting that way. No joie de vivre, that was a certainty.

Something must have been holding up our move. There was a rumour that instead of going to Burma we were going back to Singapore. Up, down or standing still, I was prepared to drift where the tide carried me. I was surprised by some of the Pommy regulars in the hospital with me. Some had been in the army for 10, 15 or 20 years and they had two stripes, some three. That was apparently as far as they could go. I wondered what they would do when they finally got out. They did not. But out in the fresh air that evening, enjoying a smoke and listening to a mouth organ playing away, it was all blighted by a team of arse-licking hospital orderlies, going their hardest. The bastards, and there were quite a few even then, had not a shred of pride in them and would crawl to the Japs unashamedly. That night I was on night duty, cleaning up the mess men made when they could not get to the latrines. It was dirty work but had to be done.

With the sunshine getting a bit stronger and a bit more of it each day, we truly appreciated what a wonderful thing it was. I went sunbaking in the afternoon and could feel the goodness soaking in. That was followed up by a swim. I just could not leave the water or the log I was sitting on as it was just so beautiful. I thought that I might even get some colour back, as I had lost my Singapore tan.

Nineteen men of I Force reached us. They were a medical unit attached to and looking after the Tamils and others. A lovely job. Like us, they were promised to be back at Changi by 30 August. There were 250 of them all together and the few to reach us told us that a J Force of 40 men had gone to Japan. I wondered if Jack Cressdee had gone. I hoped that Friday the 13th had been no worse for him than for me.

The furphies were around the camp, thick and fast:
- We were going back to Kamburai, where we had been on 26/27 April.
- A bridge was down between Neike and Burma and we could not get through.
- Those sick men who had left us were at Songkuri No. 5 camp.
- We would all be back at Bampong by November.

God knew if there was anything in any of them. I prayed that Curly Avard was all right. The truck up would have knocked him around. He did quite a lot for me in the Great World and I would have liked to have been in a position to pull him through.

The July casualty list was no smaller than the June one. It was a crying shame. Although we were equal in numbers, the Pommies had many more deaths than us. Most of the bastards asked for it and in fact, to a certain extent, their deaths were self-inflicted: not sterilising their mess gear; not keeping flies off their food; plain filth.

On Sunday 15 August it had been eighteen months that we had been prisoners. I had been overhearing two fellows talking about home and they reckoned that, although they talked about it, to them it was something 'mythical', a beautiful dream. On the other hand I looked upon it as just a matter of time; I did not know how long it would be, but as definite as the bamboo around me. I had always looked upon our release and going home as a matter of course. I was sure that this view had seen me through, better and 'happier' than most. The day *must dawn*. It just needed patience to wait. More than half the battle, much more, was in the mind and I was sure that I tried more in that department than a lot of the men, originally healthier and stronger than me. Self-control and the will to keep or get well were two of the most important things then and they were two things that too many lacked.

We started getting some vitamin B tablets, which did quite a lot of good. We were lucky also to be getting brown rice for breakfast and two good meals at lunchtime and teatime. A cup of tea turned up like a bolt from the blue. It was beautiful, thanks to the I Force men in the camp. I had been feeling good. I was on a bamboo party in the morning, a swim before lunch, which freshened me up 100% and a siesta in the afternoon. It rained cats and dogs that evening but I was as happy as the proverbial pig. After three months at last I got some mess gear.

Graham Bridgewater had given me a plate before he left and that night I got half a dixie from one of the boys who had died. With a spoon and a fork, I felt civilised once more and threw away the bamboo section, I had been eating out of for some time.

The days were quiet. I would wake up at 9 a.m., breakfast, delouse the shirt and towel, then check parade. During the morning there would be a bamboo party, which would be used over the worst of the mud patches and the latrines, repairing the huts, making utensils and bedpans, firewood, etc., etc. We had become very proficient in our improvisation as to the use of bamboo. In the evening, after another check parade, I wrote up my diary, yarned with the boys, made up my bed and turned in before dark. There was a strong feeling of lassitude. I was sure that it was a relapse after the madness and nightmare that the last four months had been. Men were still going off at a horrible rate. At No. 2 camp 74 had died in the last nine days, just slipping away quietly, not strong enough to live. Songkuri No. 2 Camp was a British camp, the standard of hygiene was bad, the morale was bad and the conditions were deplorable.

I was sick of the subject but again I wrote of the officers taking the food out of our mouths. That morning, 18 August, for the second time a little sugar arrived with our rations. Again we received a level spoonful at breakfast time, counting out 217 level spoonfuls. The half bucket that was left over was taken to the officer's quarters, where there were only four of them, so that they could have sugar for breakfast *every* morning. It was the same when meat or fish came in and the little Hospital Red Cross food. It was pure greed.

It was obvious that all those ideas about the superiority of the white races were absolutely baloney. Superficially maybe, but at rock bottom, black, white or brindle we were all exactly the same. 1400 Chinese came into the camp and in no time one element amongst us were giving them some of our stew and rice while another were collecting whitebait from the kitchen and selling it to them. They bought tobacco at the canteen for a dollar a hatful and sold them 20 cents worth for a dollar or a rupee. It was a performance no different from the way the Chinese, Thai, Burmese and others had treated us.

And next morning as the rest of the sugar did not turn up, some of the boys were going to ask the Japanese QM not to give us any more. He had definitely said 'one man one big spoonful' and given us sufficient for it. It was childish and 'cutting our nose off to spite our face' but it made us mad to get robbed at a time like that. But we were fortunate that Captain Barbour was a diet specialist and he had the rice cooked four different ways for the patients, according to their needs.

The native coolies were certainly taking over the job, at our sector at least. 4000 were in the camp at Neike, sleeping double-decker in the huts where we were single. They were welcome to that part of the road and the railway. Our boys were working up at No. 2 camp to finish parts of the railway there. At No. 1 camp too the coolies had moved in, in greater numbers, reintroducing cholera to the camp. It had to spread to our men. The appalling level of sickness (70 fit men in the whole 670 of the British in No. 1 camp) meant that more native labour was being recruited and worked to death. Thousands came into the area worked by F.Force men, to complete the railway on time.

Suddenly on the night of the 20 August, 45 of us were notified to be ready to move by truck to Burma at daybreak next day. I was given a cholera needle and I packed in the half-dark. I was leaving Neike at last.

The next 24 hours was a day that I would never forget. Awake, up, breakfast in the dark, up to the road just before daybreak, we waited for half an hour in the rain for the trucks. And then did my troubles start. I was in a six-wheeler, 30-hundredweight open truck, sitting on a leaky petrol drum for the whole trip. It burnt all my nether regions. We were jolted, shaken and thrown around for the five and a quarter hours that it took us to go eighteen miles. It was something terrible. I saw Nos. 1, 2 and 3 camps, which were just dilapidated huts in a sea of mud. Our camp, No. 5 was 1 km from the border and was no better. After getting there we found that there were already 80 in a small hut. There was no room for us to sleep anywhere but on the wet ground or in the passageway by the fires. Curly Avard was there, but very low. I stood beside him all the time until he died that night at a quarter to eleven, very quietly. We made sure that no man ever died alone. I could not do anything for I was lucky even to be in time to have a yarn with him that afternoon and give him a smoke. And so to daybreak, without a wink of sleep.

One of the two earlier Burma parties moved on and they had some wicked dysentery cases among them. More sick men were expected to come into the camp but what with the number already there, sitting up all the previous night, it was worse than any nightmare. No. 5 camp was the furthest F Force marched, 205 miles from Bampong. The camp was a sea of mud. The rain filled the graves of men, who had not been properly buried and bodies rose to the surface in the liquid mud. The British prisoners in the hut were filthy, despondent and lacking in spirit. Their death rate was almost twice that of ours and yet conditions were the same. It was a horrible camp, the worst on the railway and I could not get out of it quickly enough. We had absolutely no idea where our destination was or when we might reach it.

Curly was buried on Sunday, 22 August. I determined to see his people when I got back home and let them know all I could. A man had his watch and I accused him of taking it off him but was assured by another man that Curly had sold it for the money to buy what he could. There was never a battler like him and this was expressed by every MO and orderly he had had. If only Captain Barbour had seen him maybe he could have made the trip into Burma and fought through.

Still very tired next morning, not sleeping much the night before, a wash before lunch brightened me up as much as possible. Coming back from lunch we were told that we would be moving in a quarter of an hour. We were trucked and soon came to the Three Pagodas [a pass marking the border of Thailand and Burma] and I would have liked to have known their story.

10
The Agony of Tanbaya

So: *[from my diary]*
       'Weary eyed and cold and wet, our stomachs out of order,
       Jolted, shaken, thrown around, we crossed the Burma border.'

Of course it was raining. The road was better, though, as a lot of work had been done on it by the Dutch and A Force men, whom we passed on the way. They all looked very healthy to us. The road twisted and turned around some bloody big mountains, which fell sheer and rocky to the roadway. It was real bamboo, tiger country. The dense jungle on either side of the railway track was heavily wooded and thick with vines and undergrowth. That the camps were hacked out of the jungle with perangs, long heavy machete like knives, was remarkable. Late in the afternoon we made our half way staging camp, still very tired: a meal, a 'sleep' and a night of diarrhoea finished me off for the day.

Off again next day, I grabbed the best seat in the truck (the Pommies were too slow) for the old behind was still pretty burnt and sore. I was amazed at the work that had been done on the railway. It had gone ahead, from the Burma end, much more quickly than our section in Thailand and every cubic inch had been dug with a chunkel and carried in a basket by a prisoner or a coolie. Every cutting, embankment and bridge, apart from some blasting, had been done by hand. It made the whole project seem gigantic but God!—so heartless. The monsoon had set in again at the end of August. By then it had been expected that the cuttings, embankments and bridges would have been completed. Yet there remained a lot to be done. The deadline for the railway, in this section by the Burma border was 18 September. That meant that there were three weeks to have it ready to take the sleepers and railway lines. Looking at it, it seemed impossible except that the fanatical driving of the Japanese engineers would make it happen. As we left Songkuri No. 5 camp those going out to work, fit, sick and hospital patients, were told that work on the railway earthworks and bridges had to be accelerated. The Japanese and Korean guards, as well as the engineers directing the work, were particularly savage on the British troops, picking them out for abnormally harsh treatment. Their death rate and sickness rate had been twice as high as that of the Australians and the Japanese seemed determined to break what will and strength they had left as some sort of punishment for not having provided their proportion of workers for the road and the railway throughout the whole project.

[The main work was finished on the evening of the 18 September and the 19th was declared a holiday—the first day's break since the commencement of the work in May. From the 20th the work was on washaways of the embankments. Conditions among the sick in hospital continued to be deplorable to the end.]

On our way we reached the limit of the railway lines from the Burma end fairly quickly but then waited all afternoon to move off again. Fortunately there was no rain but a spectacular ring around the sun. At 7 p.m. we went off in one of the motor trains that travelled on either rail or road. We were out of 'Death Valley' (Three Pagoda Pass), which had never before been lived in nor had any sort of permanent population. From the rail I saw quite a few things that I had not seen for four months like birds, kampongs, cows, flowers and electric light. The very air was different. We reached the 62 km point where there were some fairly large railway yards and the base, I thought, for the whole show in Burma. We waited all night for a steam train.

August 25 and at 7.30 a.m. we reached our destination, Tanbaya, cold and very hungry, four months to the day from Bampong. I had come 245 miles, 187 miles on my feet and 58 miles by truck and train. I was a changed man in that time too. The camp (F Force Hospital) was for the chronically ill to the extent that they were unfit for work. Major Hunt, whom I had last seen on 14 February 1942, telling us in Singapore that for us the war was over, was running things well. With half a chance he would make it the best camp in Burma and Thailand. Certainly he was the man to stir things up. He had picked a good staff too. With the expected improvement in our meals, the monsoon over, the rivers and the flood waters receding we, those of us out of the 7000 men of F Force unable to work, hoped to pick up in mind, body and soul. We certainly prayed hard and it looked at the start as if we had a chance.

Hunt got things organised in running the camp. He was the Boss. Everyone able to, worked at something. I was carrying wood, officers dug drains and paths and things were cleaned up right from the start. Every man had to have a shave and a *bath* (that alone was an achievement) and everyone had to eat *all* of their meal, *every* time. There was no dying of starvation with him as so many had done. Meat one day and fresh green vegetables the next bloated me up. But that night I exploded with diarrhoea and things were very uncomfortable, not to mention unpleasant. As yet there was very little in the way of medicines or ointments. I had scabies breaking out between my legs. I hoped that it would not spread before I could get treatment for it. Some of the boys were covered with it and also had tropical ulcers on their feet and legs. My eyes were still weak and sore and, although I had not been blacking out as much, I was not looking forward to the 'noonday sun', when the rains stopped. I wondered how I could make an eyeshade.

It was good to meet up with some of the boys again. Those from the 2/30th No. 1 camp started to arrive and Bill Evans gave me all the news. Curly Hardman had gone on to No. 2 camp. What with malaria and dysentery, he was not too good. Harry Ritchie and Jack Cox were at Tanbaya and the Bailey brothers were expected. It all helped brighten things up. It had been the first time for months that I was able to sit outside, after tea, somewhat dry and yarn away with 2/30th mates, having a smoke. Conversation was still a bit dismal but the talk, in time, we hoped, would get away from mud and death. To finish their part of the railway on time there was always the very real threat that the 30th men would be ordered to work three to four days on end, 24 hours a day, without a break—presumably until they died on the job. Moving around at Tanbaya though, working in the camp and the food still good, we felt that we were picking up already.

The deaths in F Force (7000 men) were approaching 1 in 5 but this figure was worse in particular instances. No. 11 train, a load of Pommies from Changi, who were pretty unfit even before they left, had lost 500 out of 700 men. They were at No. 2 camp, which, with No. 5 camp were the worst of any on the railway. Apart from the weakness and laziness of the individual Pom, as a body they were even more so. They did hardly anything to better their conditions and themselves in the way of latrines, drains and keeping the place clean. I had been among them in their camp and the bodies were not even buried properly, being exposed in the mud. Unfortunately most of the workforce, AIF and British were centred around No. 2 camp at that stage. I hoped that another epidemic of cholera did not break out. F Force had done it harder than anyone could have possibly deserved. I had no doubt though that the Japanese engineers were not finished with us yet. The AIF were then divided into three groups:

- The 2/29th and others still south of Neike.
- The 2/30th, the 2/26th and others in a large group around Songkurai. The Japanese had mixed Australians in with the British at one stage in an attempt to raise the morale and discipline and lower the deaths and sickness rate among them.
- We, the discards, were at Tanbaya in Burma.

I could have gone on to the camp staff as they were short-handed. It would have meant being better fed and looked after more but I thought that I would stay a patient and take the risk. It may have meant me finishing up on the railway again but our NCOs were putting on parade ground stuff and military discipline. It drove me mad. The work as a patient was not that different anyway, carrying wood all day and cleaning up around the camp and in the wards. I did not mind working and helping, for I was more or less my own boss on the job.

A party had been able to buy eggs, soap and earthenware bowls for the hospital, besides some tobacco. The eggs were for the beri-beri cases, who were just then being fed like thoroughbreds. The rice in Burma was beautiful compared with the poor quality, mouldy stuff we had been getting. It had been the cause of a lot of the dysentery and diarrhoea.

Life at Burma started to get quite civilised again. There was a stream only about 20 yards from the hut with flowers growing in it. We were that hard and callous by then that it all looked out of place.

Although we had started to think that we were to get a new deal we had brought quite a few relics of the old one with us. Apart from the lice, which we were slowly starting to get rid of, we brought dysentery and cholera along too. There were nine deaths in the camp almost that first day and the party to arrive soon after us was isolated and a cholera suspect placed all on his own. We knew that those of us sent up as unfit for work on the railway were in fact sent up more or less to die but we hoped that there would be no new outbreaks of disease in the camp: that the deaths would be confined to those 'lingering' on, unable to recover.

I had another bastard of a night. It was peculiar how diarrhoea affected me for I would be as right as rain for a couple of days and then...bang! As yet there was no blood, may the Lord be praised. I would stay in bed and then a wash would brighten me up a bit. My bed was made up of uneven bamboo slats, two rice bags, gas cape, a piece of thin canvas and my jungle pants. I slept in my shirt with my old Raffles towel for a blanket and my pillow was my wallet, diaries and water bottle covered over with a couple of pairs of pants. We were all skin and bone and I would have weighed about 75 lbs or a bit less. With scabies, bones sticking out and no flesh at all on my behind, lying down was painful and uncomfortable. Sleep was difficult except from sheer exhaustion.

Eight hundred men had arrived at Tanbaya and it was expected to reach 1200. Deaths, deaths, deaths: there were nine more for burning. One party brought six corpses with them. They had died of exposure and rough handling on the way. They were just too weak for the trip. The next party carried two more: every incoming party brought their dead. It was thought that by the time the Japanese in charge of the railway job had finished the line in Thailand, in F Force the number of deaths would have amounted to 50% of those who started. The death rate was accelerating as each day passed. It was frightening. If a man did get through he would not forget, for the rest of his life, that he was lucky to be alive. Luck played a part. If the 2/29th had not been in train 2; if I had not had my glasses broken at Bampong; if I had not gone on to the river camp at Neike; if I had not got malaria on 15 June, it was probable that I would not have been alive to travel to Tanbaya. It was not all finished yet. Although this was a hospital and patients were arriving, none brought medical supplies, containers or anything with them. Very few could be treated for tropical ulcers.

Ulcers, mostly on the legs and feet, were scraped clean of pus and maggots with a spoon. It was agonising, only to be repeated when they filled up again. They started as small sores. When I got some on my leg I went down into the river and let the small fish eat away at the proud flesh. It was just bearable but kept the sores clean and I never got really bad ulcers on my leg. I made a pretty picture though, sitting outside, in the shade of a tree, playing patience in the nude. When a breeze came up it was glorious as the scabies irritated me. We had no ointment or emulsion for the scabs and sunlight and fresh air soothed the skin.

But it was becoming obvious that the hospital camp was not going to be the 'promised land' that we had hoped for. At the end of August, although we'd only seen two fine days since 19 May, it was soon going to be very hot and dry. We thought that our little stream would dry up. There were some filthy bastards who could not be taught or made to stay clean and so we had blowflies everywhere. As our numbers increased to over 1000 men, so our meal ration, per man, did not work out at very much at all. At least it was dished out equitably and was a vast improvement on the hell that we had been through and which the rest of the boys were *still* experiencing. If only we had sufficient:

- Ointments and medicines for dressings and treatments. There was only enough to treat the very worst of the ulcer cases and amputations, there being none to spare for scabies, sores, etc., no bandages, no drugs, no tablets for deficiency diseases like beri-beri, pellagra and loss of eyesight.
- Buckets to feed more than one ward at a time. There were only seven buckets in the whole camp so meals were at all hours. Neither were there enough drums for boiling water.
- Tools to gather wood for the wards and the kitchens. A lot of wood was burnt by the cooks and in the wards at night to ward off mosquitoes.

• Trained nursing orderlies. There were seven fit men on duty at
night. Most of the nursing was done by volunteers from among the
boys; an unpleasant job for which there was little or no pay or credit.
Among ourselves, we looked after each other.

It had been the same all along, only work. There was no help from the Japanese:
they did not care *one* hoot in hell whether we lived or died: except that if we could
not work we were less trouble dead.

The ulcers were wicked. Starting from only a scratch and dirt, it turned from
an infected sore to a large patch of rotten flesh; then gangrene, amputation and
death. And it stank. More and more were getting them and they were brought
about by not being able to cover them up or dress them in the early stages. There
was not a tin of Zambuk [a common patent ointment] in the camp; no sterilised
water for scissors or spoons. Our hospitals were like the scene in *Gone With The
Wind* at the fall of Atlanta. This was especially so at Tanbaya after we had been
shaken up so much on the trip. On Saturday 4 September there had been 17
cremated the day before and 15 on that day up to 5 p.m. There were men crying
and groaning in pain, there was a rupture case near me and dysentery patients, for
whom nothing could be done to give any relief. Curly Avard had been aching in
the stomach for two and a half months. I was not much better myself.

I had never been hit by fever before, anywhere near as bad as that night. It was
possibly dengue fever. I was a chronic malaria case by then, so it could have been
anything. I ached in every muscle in my body, especially the legs, the back and the
head. Back on the quinine, when you had got round to the 300th tablet (with a
little exaggeration) in two and a bit months, they did not make you any brighter.
To make matters worse, the diarrhoea erupted again, more severe than it had yet
been. It was a bastard of a combination with the fever. At that time I was sicker
than I had ever been. [It was only the start.]

Men were still coming up from 'down below'. There were 1400 in the camp
and I hoped that they would keep on being allowed to bring them in, even if it did
make things harder for us. Reports (unofficial of course) were still strong and
consistent of us all going back to Changi ... soon: September, October or November:
when the railway was finished. We just had to wait and live long enough to find
out. More 2/30th boys arrived, Maurrie Ferry, Phil Young and Jack Partridge.

I was still none too bright and was moved into the dysentery ward. As expected
there were men who messed in their blankets, sleeping at my feet and three feet
away there was a man gurgling his last noises in this world. The smell, the filth
and the dirty bastards amongst us made it impossible to get better.

Our 'stews' got weaker and weaker until they got to their worst by being
nonexistent. We were on boiled rice. No vegetables came into the camp at all. The
kitchen staff had been doing a terrific job feeding the camp with the boilers and
gear which would normally have provided for 200 men. They had been going flat
out in shifts, 24 hours a day. The previous night we had got our teatime rice at
10.45 p.m. The meals were terrible still but we had to eat them.

In the last few months I had been paying a considerable number of thanks to
the Lord. Always grateful for small mercies, God, the Devil or Lady Luck had, at
times, been kind. Padre Duckworth had been wonderful in camps down the line.

He was self-sacrificing, understanding, sympathetic and a tower of strength when comfort, understanding and sympathy were looked for. He held services at all times when men gathered in prayer and he nursed, carried and cared for the sick and dying. He buried the dead. He kept hopes alive among the British soldiers who did not have the survival instincts of the Australians. When God walked in the camps of the Burma Railway He did so in the boots of Padre Duckworth.

A party arriving in the camp brought news of a Comforts Issue. In the camp at Neike they had already received 13 packets of cigarettes each. A party left Tanbaya to go there. There were supposed to be barges with milk, beef and stew. I believed it to be Japanese Red Cross stuff and hoped that it was true. It would work miracles down there and it was hoped that transport would be spared to send some really needed medicines to us. It was too late for some as 150 men had been buried in the fortnight since the hospital at Tanbaya had been opened. We had left a godown full of gear and supplies at Bampong, including tinned Comforts stuff, which had been brought from Changi and could not be carried. It was possibly this that was at Neike. Even if nothing came of it, it at least gave us something new to talk about.

By Wednesday 8 September I had picked up a lot. On the Sunday and Monday I had been using the latrines 15 and 20 times a day. I had managed to sleep, though sweating considerably with the fever. My eyes were causing me some concern and writing became a strain. Maurrie Ferry gave me something to do them some good. It may have been distilled water but they were still sore. He was still an optimist, even though coming a wallop last year. He had to come right sometime and we would yet be having pints in Usher's Hotel in Sydney. I was busy that afternoon with needle and cotton making myself a dilly bag to keep the flies off my mess gear. I used the sleeves of my shirt and cut them off for the bag and a wash rag. Bits of cloth were nonexistent. I was lucky to get onto a needle and cotton.

I was told that the line was laid past No. 5 camp. That was 20 km in a fortnight. I was convinced that a Japanese is a man to get a job done in a hurry. My boots though were starting to come to pieces at that time as the stitching had rotted. They had done some solid work in the ten months that I had had them; I had been a wharfie, a gardener, a swaggie, a rail and a road worker.

Major Hunt did his best to get some canteen stuff for us; eggs, bananas, peanuts etc. Other camps but Neike had taken over the Japanese pay in the previous July for the benefit, equally, of everybody. The share of that and possibly some of Lieutenant Colonel Kappe's Malayan money, which was attributed to those of us at Tanbaya, would allow Major Hunt to buy yaks and other food. It would not be enough but it was the only thing that kept us going. The Japs gave us a herd of 20 undersized yaks—for 1400 men.

But the food was by then something really shameful. It was absolutely tasteless and hard to force down. No sooner had I jammed the last spoonful down my throat than I brought it up again in my rice tin. It was horrible the way the Japanese were treating sick men. I would have honestly liked the food given to a pig. Five months before, on 10 April in Singapore, I had written that I was looking forward to the trip, which was however a question mark. The Lord only knew what an answer that query would finally get. Without a doubt every man, who was still alive on Force, was slowly dying. One could not go on having diarrhoea and malaria, expending energy indefinitely, on the food that we were getting. I was back collecting peanut tops and other 'greens' from the jungle around us. They were very good and helped us keep the rice down.

The dysentery ward was terrible to be in. It was just a long lavatory and morgue. The meals were dished up from the same places that men used the bed pans, which were liberally infested with flies and stank. The lazy Pommy bastards made me sick, especially at mealtimes.

From Saturday 11 September I could hardly write. I could hardly see. I had malaria, amoebic dysentery and scabies. I was developing beri-beri and pellagra. My fingers, arms and legs were swelling up. I could push a big indentation in my body with a finger and slowly watch the swelling come back to normal again. I was itching with lice and the scabs around my behind and between my legs. I was a mess and it was to get worse. I would, however, force myself to eat what I could, to wash and bathe the sores on my legs and body, to clean my behind, to get out into the sunshine and move around whenever possible and, most of all, to think of getting back to Changi and home. There was little to sustain us except determination.

I was still able to make daily notes in my diary although unable to write them up. At this stage the creek was drying up, which was unfortunate, not only for water to boil for drinking but for washing too. It was essential that the doctors have water for sterilising their tools. They used wood saws from the railway job for the amputation of legs. When an ulcer reached a stage that it was not going to be checked, the leg was usually amputated while it was thought that the patient had a chance of surviving the trauma. A few did. Most did not. Old nets were used for bandages.

I caught up with China Hall from back in the Ordnance days at Liverpool. I was down with a cough and cold on top of everything else, he was in a bad way as well. Neither of us was too brilliant. We still talked about the good old Ordnance days, though. He always was one of the characters of the unit and incorrigible.

Every so often we would get a pep talk, the food would improve and go off again but I was stuck in the dysentery ward. In the bay I was in, of about twelve of us, there had been four deaths already. It was to reach nine out of ten before we got out. As men died, more came in and they died along side me too. By 20 September, 400 altogether had died in the camp in three weeks. We were fortunate, however, to get on to some towgay shoots and then we started growing some from seed. It was excellent for beri-beri but of course we could not get enough of it. But a lot of problems were made worse by the shortage of workers and those who could move around.

I was certainly feeling none too good. When I vomited up my rice I had to immediately eat it again and make it stay down. We were reduced to simple choices: you either did and lived, or did not and died. Most around me died. The concern in regard to beri-beri, we learnt, was that when it got to your heart it killed you (cardiac beri-beri). As with MT malaria, when it reached the brain you died (cerebral malaria). But a more immediate problem was that we could not grow new skin. We had to cover scabs and sores as best we could. The itching went on interminably. I was running pretty hard and often to the latrines and had to combat blowflies all the time. If they got into an infected sore they laid maggots in it. There was really no way then to clean it up. There were no antiseptics and no disinfectants. By the time a dysentery case was near death the maggots were well inside the colon. We started eating charcoal as a means to try and block ourselves up. We powdered the burnt lumps of wood from the fires and ate it.

By the end of September Brigadier Varley, who was pretty dejected himself, brightened us up with a talk. I was on my feet and went on light duties, in that I could walk. I was not getting much sleep but it meant that I could move around and be useful, cleaning up around the camp. I was getting on to the towgay, beans, peanut tops and stuff from the bush that the Indian doctor at Neike had told us was edible. At one stage I was collecting the fungus off the damp trees to go with the rice. To survive, food of some nutritional value had to be ingested. The quality of the rice had gone off drastically. I thought that I was improving for a while but for my eyes. My blood was rotten it seemed as bumps, lumps and infected tinea would not clear up and the beri-beri and the pellagra were gradually getting worse. We lacked salt, oil and soap but got some coffee and some gula malacca. They were beautiful. Being more active and getting around more, I was for a while eating anything I could get; what appeared to be mushrooms, bamboo shoots, fungus, any variety of vegetable out of the bush. We could not go far, however. I could not walk far anyway but the limits of the camp restricted us to within a few hundred yards of our huts.

What with the charcoal, I had my first black semi-firm stool since last July. Conversation, or more essentially monologues, were cruder than ever. Women were out of sight and out of mind. Men talked about nothing else, in the dysentery ward, but the frequency, the 'formulae', constituency and colour of their stools, the aches in their stomachs and the weakness of their bodies. I had the same thing but did not gloat over it like an appendicitis operation.

While I was on duties around the camp I was even on yak picket once again, seeing that they did not get out of their compound or get sent off [stolen]. It was at this time, 6 October, that the meals fell off like blazes, overnight. There was a scare of some sort up the line, probably an Allied air raid. No trains were coming through. There was a new Japanese Commander, it seemed, but we did not really know what was going on. We had worked out our mushroom patch and salt was hard to buy from the Burmese at the canteen. Not that any of us had any money anyway. The ration party though did get on to 2000 eggs and returned with lots of stories. These were mainly of us moving out. But we were almost out of food. The boys fished for minnows and these went well with the baked hash-like substance from the kitchen. Meanwhile the skin diseases got worse and worse and had everyone scratching like mad.

The meals by then were just foul. These were dry beans with maybe a bit of onion or potato in the rice water. The canteen staff were however getting on to eggs and gula malacca, which was something, if not enough. Then the creek dried right up and the water situation was serious. It meant that there was none for washing.

Just before we were out of water I had been boiling some in a can on the fire in our hut. I stumbled or was jostled and scalded my left leg as I poured the boiling water over it. There was no treatment at all for scalds and it was very sore. I was scared that I would break the skin as a large blister covered the whole area on the calf of my leg, and where I already had two or three sores. I was really scared of getting an ulcer. For days and weeks I was worried and would nurse and cover my leg as best I could. Fortunately the skin stayed intact and the burn healed but I was for ever more to have the scar.

It was bloody hot. Major Hunt gave us some medicine of some sort in the dysentery ward but there was little in the way of medical supplies throughout the camp. We did however get three eggs each and, boiled, they were very nice. What was horrifying was to see the ulcer patients having their ulcers scraped with a spoon. This was so excruciatingly painful that they screamed and wept while it was being done. No one could have stood the agony without reacting to the treatment. One of them attempted suicide. Morale in the camp was falling off as every disease in the book hit us—malaria, septic sores and skin infections, pellagra, beri-beri, dysentery and diarrhoea, diphtheria and even mumps. Major Hunt was already trying to have us moved to where we could be better treated. There seemed to be some dissension, however, among the senior ranks of the Japanese and our forces, probably arising from the demands by the Japanese engineers, and any sort of concession was very unlikely.

I was off duties, I could not do anything and had nothing at hand to occupy my mind. I was in fact sinking lower. I would do anything to avoid a state of stupor. I concentrated my mind on the Law of Contracts, all the picture theatres between the Quay and the Railway in Sydney, Melbourne Cup winners as far back as I could remember, favourite books, the plays of Shakespeare, the records in my collection, all the streets in Wardie in Edinburgh (Fraser Grove, Fraser Crescent, Fraser Avenue...), anything at all to make me think. I kept this up for days and weeks, in fact, encouraging others around me, fighting off torpidity. My hands were sore and swollen fingers made even writing the notes in my diary difficult. I still managed to do so though. There was no treatment for the sores, scabs and scabies and I did not know how my leg would turn out and the conditions in the dysentery ward remained the same, simply horrible. But on Saturday, 16 October I had my first wash in four days.

Next day one of the ulcer cases went missing. He had gone out of his mind and turned up at the next camp up the road. He simply walked off. Meanwhile we prayed for rain. We had to go further afield for water and a new creek was found a kilometre away. It was nice and we were able to wash again. The cookhouse was then moved for the third time, nearer to the creek.

At this time a truck came up from Neike with long awaited supplies. We got seven packets of cigarettes each. What we needed was sulphur to treat the scabies and grease for the sores but we got very little sulphur and no grease or ointment. The amputations went on, as did the deaths. Those of us still going seemed to be in a state of suspended animation . . . neither dead nor alive.

Time mooched on and I put in dreary days and nights, somehow. It was Neil's birthday on 23 October and I put in my worst day ever. I was going off my head with the infected skin, no sleep, pain and discomfort, terrible meals and nothing to do. As well as beri-beri, with swollen legs and fingers, I was suffering with pellagra, another diet-deficiency disease, common to sailors in the the eighteenth century. Sores had broken out on my hands and face. We were not getting any better and so nerves were on edge. Not being workers on the railway it was obvious that the Japanese had sent us up to die. We wondered who would bury the last man.

Padre Duckworth had come up to Tanbaya and was very active. He could buck the boys up and make them more attentive: even to lectures and talks, which he organised. He worked incessantly with and for the men, particularly the worst patients. He and Major Hunt were towers of strength and yet they must have been none too strong themselves.

Our food picked up at times and we got beans, potatoes, yak and rice, three times a day. The beans, as a supplement to the Japanese rice issue and negligible yak issue, were all we had to cure the deficiency diseases rife throughout the camp. When rice polishings could be obtained it was very good for beri-beri. Major Hunt would buy the beans and rice polishings on the black market as he could.

I continued to spend the day bathing my hands, elbows, legs and crotch. It was very hot and the skin would dry up, making the itching worse. I was still eating, though, and was able to write again. The rumour of us moving back to Thailand was persistent but everybody was fed up.

Five bags of rice polishings were good news. Major Hunt claimed that he could clean up 80 to 90% of the beri-beri/pellagra cases and save lives in four weeks if, as it was hoped, the issue continued. I was able to sit down again, gingerly. It was remarkable how quickly the body responded to any improvement in our diet.

Pat O'Rourke got 20 lashes on Monday, 1 November and one week's hard labour. He was implicated in a black-market operation, which had been going on for some weeks. It was degrading that our men adopted the same tactics as the Japanese in order to benefit themselves. We were not keen though on them beating any of the boys up. I was in the money, having sold some of my stuff and it meant that I could buy eggs. We were all very sick and sore. The rumours of a move were stronger and we looked forward to the big day. Deaths in F Force had reached 2500 and many of them were my mates.

As the pellagra got worse I was transferred to the scabies and ulcer ward. God Almighty! Sights, smells, maggots and blowflies. There was no proper treatment, only hot water and that was not too plentiful. In combination with the dysentery I had reached the lowest possible level in the hospital. I ate and looked after myself as much as possible and tried to keep in as good a condition as I could, mentally and physically. It was great news that I was to get some sulphur treatment as more in the way of medical stuff had arrived. The will to survive took great determination, but sometimes, determination alone was not enough. There were fifteen deaths around me in 36 hours. I was slowly cleaning myself up in the effort to keep off my behind all day and night. I slept on my stomach. Not only was my behind sore and scabby but it was important to move around. Syd Cronin and Kevin Hunter of the 2/30th were with me and as always, mates stuck together.

We thought that our move might be on 20 November—to Kanburi and Singapore. I was looking forward to going back to Changi more, much more, than I had looked forward to leaving there last April. I tried keeping on my feet all day while also dressing my hands, elbows and bum. The piles were sticking out, too. However morale was picking up now that we had a hope of getting out.

On 11 November I thought that it would have been a happier day in 1918 for POWs in the last war. That day, again there was a shortage of rice and we went on to half-rations; from two pints a day to one. The 'stews' were none too good either. The beri-beri was up the length of my legs and was a real bastard. God what a place to call home. It was terrible and fantastic enough to be fiction— shitting in mess tins, through the slats and over each other, blowflies, stink, deaths, overcrowding, heat, amputations, ulcers, pellagra and dysentery. That was 11 November in the scabies/ulcer ward.

Virtually neglected by the Japanese, beyond the resources of our own medical personnel to cope with the situation, with men fast losing the will and practicability to live, the isolation from the main body of F. Force, of which we were still part, meant that the conditions of the F. Force hospital at Tanbaya, in Burma, were the worst that I had seen in any camp on the railway from Bampong to the Three Pagoda Pass. It was more than overlooked, I had the impression it was ignored. I was certainly under the impression that we were there to die, until the railway was completed and trains could take the survivors back to Thailand. I was running almost on willpower alone and was determined to survive. I willed myself to live. It *can* be done.

By the 13 November I was in a bad way. The beri-beri had puffed up my legs to the extent that the skin tightened up and I had difficulty walking. I could not do too much at all. No rations came into the camp and the excuse was that a bridge was down. From what we did have though I drew an egg and it was gorgeous and soft. The scabs were drying up again and I was put on sulphur and pig oil treatment in the hope that it would do some good. Water was again scarce and there was to be no washing for five days.

A cholera carrier was isolated and we had another glass rod up our backsides. I could get no sleep, could hardly move and squatted in hourly spells between the bed and the fire all night and most of the day. We were examined by the doctors and I had a multiplicity of things wrong with me:
Dysentery and chronic diarrhoea
Malaria and sore and infected spleen
Pellagra
Beri-beri
Scabies
Haemorrhoids / Fissure
Scalded legs
Partial loss of eyesight
Septic sores
Worms in the bowel [although I did not know it]
Malnutrition / semi starvation
I had been chronically ill, including colds and influenza but mostly
with bacillary and amoebic dysentery and malaria for five months.
I weighed less than 70 lbs [32 kilos].

I was told by the doctor of our ward that I would be better off staying at Tanbaya until I was fit to travel. It was thought that I would not survive the train journey. I would not accept, however, that I be left behind. I went to see Major Hunt and told him that I could walk and was determined to go. He looked me over and OK'd me for the trip. He saved my life. 240 sick men were left at Tanbaya.[It was my belief later that they all died.] To then, 17 November, 600 had already died in the hospital, which was over half of the patients. In some wards the rate was much higher than that. In the ulcer ward where I was, I had been surrounded by a number of men who committed suicide rather than continue to endure the agony. They either refused to accept treatment they could no longer endure or they lost hope. Throughout the camp those that gave up and lost the will to live, died. It was as simple as that.

We received official notification on Friday 19th November 1943 that the move and evacuation of the hospital would commence next day. It was expected that the trip of two to three days on the railway would be no picnic. We were to be 33 to a truck. That day we received the first decent lot of rations for a month or more and we were each to take our own rice, sugar and fish with us. We even got a fresh issue of tobacco.

I was happy about my hands. I was still scabby and they were swollen with beri-beri but I would be travelling light. The sulphur had done little good but I bathed and dressed the sores all day with hot water for the trip. Thinking of my last days in Burma, I was not impressed. Memories haunted me.

Tuesday, 23 November and I was busy. I tore all the scabs off, raced around for treatment, made doovers from rice polishings before breakfast to take with me on the train, went down to the creek for a wash, packed my gear, more dressings and lunch before 3 p.m.; felt pretty sore, resto, poor tea, bad start as we were then searched but got my diaries through in the dark, and then we waited till 11 p.m. to move off. It was still thought that I should not go, that I would not survive the trip, but I crawled up the steps of the truck and once inside the doctors would have had to pull me out.

We were Jonahed from the start. We were 37 to a truck, in the same sort of steel railway trucks in which we had come up from Singapore, cramped up and cold. In half an hour the truck in front of us was off the rails. The Japs got it back on again and progress was very slow. There was the usual wait for an hour at sidings where we were shunted around as they sorted themselves out. The same truck was off the rails again at 4 a.m. We lit fires as we waited and we could see Japs over a bridge as they tried all the rest of the night to get things going again. For some reason we were ordered back into the trucks and made to stay there. It was typical of the Japanese guards. If there was a hard way or an easy way of doing anything they would chose the hard way. If they had to decide whether to let us stay by the fires or put us back in the trucks, they would decide to put us back in the trucks. It seemed to be a principle, to make things as miserable as possible for us. I was sore all night and exhausted from climbing in and out of the truck as it was a big jump to the ground and clamber back every time we stopped for any length of time. The rice-polishings doovers, which I had brought were good. Most of the boys, however, ate their breakfast that night instead of saving it for later.

Next morning we were still there. The truck was dumped over the side of the track and we made slow progress again, cold, hungry and sore and even more cramped up with one truck less. We were back in Thailand. We passed No. 2 camp and Neike and at one stage had done 50 miles in 39 hours. We were issued some rice and gula malacca for two meals but most of it was sour. Then there was another long wait. We were glad of that as it was preferable to rest at night while we were stationary, rather than being tossed around in the truck while trying to go to sleep. In fact I slept for three hours for the first time in two days. The jolting, stopping and starting of the train was not doing any of us any good. Getting knocked around in the cramped truck broke out sores and ulcers and there was absolutely nothing that could be done. The pus and weeping sores simply seeped into our clothes. We were really walking skeletons. Men, who normally weighed 11 to 12 stone (160 lbs) were about 6 to 7 stone (90 lbs). I was about 67 lbs [30 kilos]. There was no flesh at all covering my legs, hips or ribs. Hip bones stuck out at odd angles and it was painful to be knocked against anything solid, such as the steel sides of the truck as we jolted along the track or if the truck came off the rails. Those with recent amputations were in a particularly bad way as wounds reopened. I and other dysentery cases hung backwards out of the doors of the truck, held on to by mates to prevent being thrown to the ground as the train moved along. But we knew that there was nothing in the world worse than where we had just come from and we were determined to see it through. We were so mentally keyed up to reach Kanburi that we put up with whatever we had to; pain, diseased bodies and hunger. In fact the trip was made with little recognition of the areas through which we passed, as our minds were totally concentrated on our destination.

After breakfast on the second day we made slightly faster time, getting up to what seemed 8 mph. There were problems with the bridges. We were held up at one isolated spot when a section of one of the bridges was on fire. Back we went to Konkoita for the day and had a couple of meals there. The bridge was repaired in twelve hours, which was typical. We were on our way but were again delayed as we waited for more carriages to be added. I sold Ron's pencil at one stop as I needed the money to buy eggs and food. We were always hungry, even immediately after being fed. Bridges twice more delayed us and trucks would frequently go off the rails. If they could not be got back on again they were simply dumped over the side. It was hardly surprising that the rails and sleepers had moved as the embankments and rock base for the line had been laid in drenching rain and on a sea of mud. Deliberate sabotage, when we could get away with it, did not help.

Progress continued slowly. As much as anything we were trying the railway out, as certainly we were about the first to go all the way down the just completed line from the Burma side. If a train went over a bridge and was lost, they only lost prisoners. A truck was again off the rails in the early hours of the next morning but we slept in shifts as we travelled, only so many at one time being able to lie down. I even got in a few hours. On the morning of Sunday, 28 November we were again given some cooked rice for breakfast but nothing else all day. We went through Tarsau and reached Kanburi at 11.30 p.m. We had been in the train from

Tuesday night to Sunday night, five days to travel about 250 miles. But we were at our immediate 'Journey's End' and I had survived the trip. We were given some milk and sweet rice and then bedded down, on the ground, in the open, though rain was expected. Next morning I was so starving that when I saw some maggot-infested fish on the ground I scraped away the rotten part and ate the rest in the mud. It was something I was never to forget.

We were broken up into small parties at Kanburi and we were back in the same spot where we had been on the way up. In a lucky break I got some soap and cigarettes but we were very cold, wet and depressed. From what we were told we looked to be in Singapore soon. That Monday though we got an excellent meal at teatime, pork stew, egg, fish and tea. Kanburi was a large camp and seemed to be the base for that end of the railway. Next day, under cold leaden skies, there was nothing to do but shiver and smoke. I went on sick parade. The sores were cleaning up well, having bathed them as well as I could after the train trip, but they were in need of treatment.

On Wednesday, 1 December the sun broke through and everyone was happier. We had moved to a good camp with a roof. The MO Rogers was a battler for his patients and was able to give us proper attention. Eggs were cooked for us and the additional food and medical treatment continued to do us good. The drawback was that water was scarce and we could not swim in the river. It was obvious that those who had stayed at Kanburi and on the lower part of the line had fared much better than the rest of us. They had not been so hard hit with cholera, the officers were working and there had been fewer deaths.

I was picking up, the bowels were getting back to normal and I had the best night's sleep since leaving Changi. I could even sleep on my hips. We were getting eggs, fried, boiled and in an omelette. There was still no swimming though and I had not washed since leaving Burma. That had been over a week ago.

On Friday, 3 December a party of 500 left with Lieutenant Colonel Kappe by boat from Bangkok. We were told that they were going to Singapore but in fact we did not know where they would end up. The railway traffic was heavy on the main Malaya/Thailand line but we were really still too stunned and sick from all that had happened to us to be aware of what was going on around us.

It may have been that the eggs were too good but three fights broke out in the camp. They could not have been from our lot. Two Thai pieces [girls] were around and it was plain that life at Kanburi was in another world. It was, however, quite cold again. Rations had dropped suddenly as nothing was coming in and the numbers in the camp had increased. It had been too good a start to last indefinitely. But I hoped to still be at Kanburi over Christmas. It would have given me time to recover for the train trip to Singapore. I had been there a week, was getting better but had a long, long way to go. I would have been about 70 pounds in weight and was gaining with the extra food.

The Japanese guards were celebrating and in a dangerous mood. They could go berserk so quickly but we would try to keep away from them. Time was going slowly when we were not working but I felt that I could put up with plenty of 'nothing to do'. And then there was another egg issue and our food came good again. It was always unpredictable. I felt that I was continuing to pick up and I was eating as well as and as much as possible. The meals were mainly eggs, vegetables and some meat, while those of us with beri-beri got some vitamin B tablets, which was what we really needed. There were still some deaths amongst us but they were decreasing at the hospital.

It was cold, freezing, in the mornings. I felt the cold and had little or no resistance to chills and flu. But we continued to eat well, with a variety we had not previously seen as prisoners: chips, onions, eggs, fried rice and coffee. It was more than I could possibly eat and digest and I had to learn to take it all very slowly.. That morning, 9 December, H Force moved back to Singapore and it was thought that we would probably be next. We did move from the better part of the camp back to our old spot, in the open and not nearly so good. In doing so I met up with most of the 2/29th boys again. They had done it tough and, in that I survived, I was lucky that I had been moved on at Neike. It was thought that there had been 3000 deaths in all of the 7000 of F Force and it was expected that it would reach 50% as the full effects took place over a period of time.

By our second week we had special meals for Sundays. I was glad that I had made the effort to eat for fried hash at tiffin was the first change from liquid stew for months. We still took things very slowly though, but I did get to go on my first swim parade. I had my first wash.

Next day I was not feeling too good. The diarrhoea and the pains in the stomach came back again after one solid meal. Water was more precious than gold and there was none for drinking. We were in tents and I was cold all the time. I went on sick parade for my eyes and was told to go to the hospital for attention. My stomach was still sore and out of order and it was obvious that it was going to take a long time to recover properly. I learnt then that Tich Martin had just died of pneumonia. I was very sorry to hear it as I had not got to see him at Kanburi. Tich, Curly Avard and I had been close mates at the Great World, in Singapore and on the railway; both were gone.

By Wednesday, there were 1800 men in the hospital at Kanburi. Many of the rest of the POWs, including F Force, were being moved to Japan and Singapore. While waiting for the doctor I met up with more of the boys and it was apparent that our Burma mob were the unlucky ones of F Force. None of the other working camps had experienced the same degradation and neglect that we had suffered at Tanbaya in Burma.

That day, 15 December, I missed seeing the MO at the hospital but I was doubtful if anything could be done for me as my sight was failing. I could hardly write.

11
Return to Changi, Thank God

On Thursday, 16th December I was put with a crowd to immediately return to Singapore. I very quickly packed up my gear and diaries and was ready for the trip back. I had got hold of a scrap of paper to make scribbled notes each day, as best I could, on the train. We were soon off again in the same old rice trucks from Bampong. The first thing I did on the way was to sell off a pair of pants for 2.50 ticals and was as happy as anything with money to spend on fruit and cakes for the trip. We were in wooden trucks this time and it was a lot cooler. Although we were 25 to a truck it promised to be a better train trip than when coming up to Thailand and we made fast time.

Next day we lost a man overboard but he was alive anyway and would follow us up. We were told that we would get one meal a day if we were lucky as they intended pushing us through as quickly as possible. I had bought:

Bananas	.15
Cakes	.50
Eggs	1.50
Fruit	.35
Bread	.30
	2.80

With another .30 ticals, which I had been given, I spent my Thai currency while it was still good. I even accounted for it on the way.

The tucker bag was full and so was I, but was sorry for it very soon with stomach ache. At the same time we had our first death in the truck with a second on the way. But it was good to see the coastline.

After three days on the way, by Saturday, 18 December, we were still in Thailand but nearing the border. It rained. Water was not plentiful as we passed through the green rice fields again and the boy we had been carrying, died. The hardest part however was to sleep, which we did less or more, rather than more or less. We could not all lie down as there was not enough room. Some simply had to lie down because they were too weak to sit up but it meant that the rest of us in the truck had to sit on the hard floor with our legs cramped up and get what sleep we could. Again we had to travel without treatment for sores and tropical ulcers. The Thai uniforms of the railway guards, which we saw at the stations as we passed through, impressed us as much as ever. I was sure that they were modelled from film magazines.

We made the border on Sunday at Padang Beser early in the morning. We were out of Thailand, thank Christ. I never wanted to see the place again. We were into the Malayan jungle and the heat. At Alor Star, we had our third meal in four days. That day too we had the third death, which was not too bad a rate as we knew it. We were still making good time and in fact twelve hours ahead of the trip up. Travelling through rubber instead of bamboo and rice paddy fields, we reached Ipoh at the close of the day. Passing through Kuala Lumpur, Gemas and Kluang, we found it was much the same as the journey north. We learnt that food was scarce for the locals and prices were high. We noticed that horses and Japanese troops were going north. We presumed that the troops would be going to Burma but wondered about the horses. I was feeling better as, not having any money to spend, the enforced light diet was all that my stomach could take. I had my last egg for tea but still could not see properly. I could make out the Japanese names on the railway stations but we were impatient to see our destination.

Tuesday, 21 December and we reached Singapore. It was 1 a.m. and we were put onto trucks and wondered where we would be taken to. Changi at 3 a.m. We showered, were given a cup of tea and slept. I had made it! Asked how I survived I could only answer that it was willpower and that I had not contracted cholera. Everything else I overcame by a determination to live.

It was good to smell old Singapore. It was home from home. After the sick parade and into the hospital for my eyes, I received everything that I wanted: bath, soap, scrubbing brush, clean shorts, bed, mattress, sheet and a pillow. After a wonderful tea I joined up with Curly again, back at our old corner of the Selarang Square too, happy as the proverbial mudlark, once more. Too happy to sleep.

We were a ten-day wonder to the staff at Changi, who were very attentive. They did everything possible for us. We were down for a month's rest and it was beautiful to be clean again. The dirt had been ground into our skin but in clean quarters we would pick up, if given half a chance. The food was not as good as at Kanburi but tastily cooked and served. We were, however, getting proper treatment.

I had my eyes tested and because of the eye strain was given some glasses to try. There was one boy in the ward who was delirious with fever, which gave the staff there an idea of what F Force had gone through. We were to suffer the effects for some time. Syd Grounds and Jack Cressdee were still there and were working on an aerodrome. They were shocked when they saw us and could not do enough for us, for which we were very grateful as we got very restless and nervy.

Christmas Eve brought the Christmas spirit, with carols and visiting. I received presents of cigarettes and clogs, the weather was good and I felt that I was home for Christmas.

On Christmas Day we wrote out letter cards for home and it was a really happy day. We had a three-course dinner, which was excellent and like a pig I ate some of Jack's too. I had not eaten so much in one day as a POW. There was music and although I could not get to the church service, the only thing that dampened the day was a trial blackout, which the Japs put on at night.

The holidays had fallen at a good time of the week, as we thought of home. It was Sunday, Boxing Day, and I was sure that we were not forgotten. A Red Cross ship would have been very opportune but was not to be. We had a breakdown in the camp power instead.

The water and lights were off next day as the hospital made the best of it. Colonel Bye and the doctors worked very hard, though we felt that we were guineapigs sometimes. There were still deaths among the seriously ill but for myself and most others, reaction set in and we slept easily. I was back to 6½ stone (91 lbs) again and would continue to pick up I hoped. There was a strong feeling amongst us of lassitude, laziness and an inability to concentrate on anything, yet interest was being restored in life and hope. Our ten days were up but the attention we received was still good. The food was back to normal again, tasty but insufficient and we felt it needed the 'leggis' to fill us up. But still I was doing well to date.

F Force, those of us still alive, seemed to be disposed of: 250 were in Burma, 600 in Thailand (some possibly sent on to Japan). The remainder were at Changi.

At the latest count 50% of the British troops had died and 28% of the Australians. This clearly showed the difference between the two, as the conditions were identical. These figures were to be added to with the inclusion of the Dutch troops and later deaths. Overall about half of F Force died on the railway. Then there were the maimed, those with lifelong illnesses as a result of the treatment there and the further effects upon the minds and bodies of those who survived. Some of the MOs at Changi were against mixing us in with the general patients and troops at Changi but this view did not prevail. The irony of it all was that, if the railway was not blasted away with Allied bombing, it probably would be washed away before the year was out.

It was again Curly's birthday on the 30th and he, too, was picking up slowly. He would not have wanted his wife, Beatrice, to know him then. The medical equipment at the hospital was ageing but, with improvisation and ingenuity, X-rays, blood transfusions and dentistry were still carried out.

The year closed, one which no one would wish to be repeated:
Quiet, early in the year and mail.
Then Thailand and a march of 185 miles.
Illness: eyes, malaria, dysentery.
Work, slavery, beatings, starvation, rain and drought.
Burma: beri-beri, pellagra, scabies.
Changi: quiet again, not the same laddie. Wiser and more self reliant
if not as healthy.
1943 was over if not forgotten. We looked forward to the New Year.
[I continued to make notes of daily events as from the new year of 1944 but it was not until April that I was able to and had the incentive to resume my diary.]

Blessed be to God in this year of Grace 1944....
(From a somewhat famous diary)

New Year's Day was a bit of a flop. It was a cook's holiday but they deserved it. I was still as happy as a mudlark and I meant it too in a lettercard home. That Christmas had been the happiest of my life as simple comforts meant so much after what I had been through in Burma. A bed, mattress, sheet and pillow were such a novelty after two years of not having them since the hospital at Katong. Unfortunately, as far as happiness went, I could not say the same for Curly Hardman as he was still quite a bit depressed.

I weighed in at 104 lbs and so was put on double the normal rations. This meant six to eight doovers a day! The trouble still was that I was run-down, anaemic and pitifully weak. I could not say enough however in praise of the doctors at Changi. Colonel Billy Bye and all the doctors did a wonderful job on us in regard to both our physical and emotional needs. Those of us who had made it thus far were certainly lucky.

A week later I was on the scales at 111 lbs. That was an added 7 lbs in a week, which had been the rate of weight recovery so far. Attention was still being showered upon us but, as would be expected and as we wanted, actually, the ten-day wonder bit was passing off. As we were under observation we were not allowed to leave the hospital building but I went to a football match anyway and paid the penalty. For five days I was in a high fever and given quinine, which left me pretty weak and I lost four pounds in one night.

Our messages were recorded for broadcast home. Curly was still far from well. He was in the dysentery ward but was picking up. He had lost three stone [19 kilos] in weight over the period in Thailand and was suffering the same mental complaint as me—an inability to concentrate on anything and think clearly (if at all). It did us both good though to be yarning away again. Dacks of the Engineers had called me over to see him during the week, apparently as right as rain, but he collapsed and died that night. That was the way it was and was happening all the time.

After a few days I started to feel much better in regard to the relapse of malaria but reaction to the last couple of week's 'high tension' and nerves set in. I was sleeping all day and all night and did not want to do anything else. It was an oppressive feeling of lethargy, which had crept over me; not laziness, just like a clock about to stop. I had had the feeling before when the body was completely drained of energy and vitality. I was eating as well as could be hoped for but the meals were falling off as there was a scarcity of foodstuff in Singapore generally. The hospital (AGH, Selarang) was still able to buy a great deal of our rations from the proportion of the officers' pay, which was deducted for that purpose, but the future did not look too bright at all. A dollar ($1 Thailand pay) came to light to supplement the 5 cents a day hospital pay, which we received. It was needed too at the prices that tobacco and other items were going up to. But I still felt too dull and dopey to worry about anything.

By the end of January it was Curly's turn for another dose of malaria and it hit him hard, worse than any case I had known. He was crying when I saw him one night, as he was so sore and dispirited. I had taken him some of my food as I was doing well myself. I had put on another 8 lbs, despite being on quinine and atebrin for ten days.

Once again I was getting around and attended an AIF concert, *Dick Whittington*. It had very original music and scenery and the rest was fair.

In and around Changi, apart from the hospitals, the British, American, Dutch, Eurasians and Australians were all in the same area, 8000 of them, of whom 1000 were officers. It made for variety. There was quite a range of entertainment and activities going on and an Educational Centre had been formed, which provided 'anything for anyone'. We had lectures, courses, clubs and the library: concert parties (3), gramophone recitals (Beethoven to the Boswell Sisters) and football matches, besides cards, draughts and chess. Recreation and education played an important part with the men who had remained at Changi, and also in rehabilitating those on the working parties, who had returned.

At the beginning of February we heard rumours that we were to get letters soon and also of a Red Cross ship (a fabled vessel like the *Flying Dutchman*). That week, though, I was extraordinarily lucky as I received a pair of glasses. I had a pair of dark glasses but these were proper spectacles, which had been the property of somebody lately deceased. They were very near the correct prescription too. My eyes, the sockets rather, had for months been very sore but thanks to Marmite and an improving general condition, were coming good. We were still being fed in the AGH like a prize Wodehouse pig and I had never been so full before, even if it was only rice and beans, seven times a day. Little and often was the rule.

Hay Fever by Noel Coward was the event of the week and was an excellent play. The props and acting (especially Julia Bliss) were very good. There was a little theatre going too and J.J Porter's Orchestra was the best small unit I had *ever* heard live. Super hot, it was certainly great to hear a bit of swing and get the old foot tapping again.

I was due to go out of hospital on Saturday, 5 February but got another relapse of malaria instead. I was on the quinine early but it was the seventh dose of malaria in about seven months. I must have been up to my 500th quinine tablet, or so it seemed, and they still made my head dense and my ears ring. The cure was quite as bad as the fever itself.

The sores had cleaned up and I had a clear skin again for the first time for months. Burma! Thank Christ I got out of that place. Fearful as it was, we had accepted and taken things for granted up there, but then, in February 1944 in the AGH, we saw it all relative to normal standards. I shuddered to think of the Hell I had been through—that ulcer, scabies, dysentery ward! I expected that only 10% of the patients left there would ever get out.

I was discharged from the AGH on Friday, 11 February, not feeling too good, off my food but progressing. It had taken some two and a half months to get reasonably well again. I was back with the 2/29th boys and away from the hospital complex and atmosphere. All of F Force were more or less convalescent and getting a good rest. It did not stop the fittest, though, from having to start work on the aerodrome nearby.

It was good to receive a lot of letters, which had apparently been mounting up over the last eight months. These were from Neil, Ron and Hetty; Auntie Effie and Grandma from Edinburgh and a big pile from Jessie. I thought, 'Heaven protect me from that redhead, she is after me!'. I was one of the luckiest in the whole of Changi as I had received 31 letters up to then, 18 February 1944. With the scarcity of paper some had been handy for cigarette papers and even, of necessity, for toilet paper. Splitting paper edgeways was quite an art. It was amazing how, with patience and deft fingers, note paper could be split so that two cigarette papers could be obtained from one small piece of a letter. I had got on to a small notebook early in 1943 and had saved it all through Thailand and Burma for a 1944 diary. Writing paper at Changi was by then non-existent. The library, however, had a very wide range of reading matter, was excellent and well looked after. Singapore must have been scoured of books and every opportunity was taken to acquire more and add to the library.

I had been discharged from the AGH at 123 lbs, 2 lbs heavier than in 'civvy street'. It was all fat around the stomach though. I felt comparatively well and it indicated what a marvellous job the hospital staff had done in rehabilitating the scarecrows, who had survived the Burma Railway.

The concerts were diverting to say the least and when the female impersonators were on, more than just good; the shows were middling to really entertaining. There was no doubt but that the producers were doing wonders with the restricted material and talent available. At that time too, I joined a yacht club, which called itself 'Yachtsmen in Irons'. It was a clever pun to my way of thinking. There were some good sea stories in the Yacht Club library and I was determined still to have *Virginia* at Watsons or Double Bay. When Ron and I had gone sailing in his VJ off Dobroyd Point I had enjoyed it although study prevented me from being a sailor.

We were kept busy at all times. I was mess-orderlying and as prolific a reader as ever. Curly Hardman was down with another relapse of malaria and then I got the same thing. At the end of February my blood test showed BTT+ and I was put on to the liquid quinine. There was no stuff more vile, including rum and gin, and so, as usual for the first few days, I was not worth a dud half cent. Later that week some Red Cross stuff actually put in an appearance: Camel cigarettes, chocolate, sugar, bully beef, cheese, butter, prunes, coffee, etc. It made a tasty change and the event of the year was a salmon rissole. Medical supplies were as important as food, if not more so, and I did not know if the Japanese allowed any in. Clothing too was needed. Two years was a long time for the seat of one's pants to last.

I was in the Malaria Centre once more for a week, then put on fourteen days 'no duty' to rest up a bit. Our pay was still 5 cents a day when in hospital so, apart from other considerations, we could not afford to be sick. Prices were increasing, skyrocketing in fact; the poorest native tobacco went from 25c to 60c per ounce in February. It was as well that I was going without.

Work and camp duties occupied everybody who was not on the sick list. A large ground-levelling project, adjacent to the camp, took 1000 men a day. This was for the Japanese Air Force in making a new aerodrome at Changi. The conditions were certainly different from the work up country: hours were fair, there was no bashing at all and yet those who had stayed in Singapore all the time thought it hard! [Never was there the cruelty and inhumanity at Changi that was the normal pattern in Thailand, Burma and Borneo.] The trailer parties for water and wood were still going on in the camp as was the work in the gardens. These were coming along beautifully, although hardly adequate as we had to rely on them substantially. Gardens were everywhere and we were digging for our existence, not 'for Victory' (as the civilians back home were urged to do).

We were always aware that we were in the army, Black Jack saw to that. There was no way that we would be allowed to get slack. The punishments for transgressions were solid, £5 and 28 days being very light and common punishments. Some stealing was going on but not as much as would be expected. The discipline did us no harm, even if we thought the 'disciplinary actions' to be too tough.

I received $3 back Thai pay, which brought me up to date. This was thanks to Lieutenant Archdale, was unexpected, and was very welcome. I passed $1.50 on to Curly in the way of tobacco but he, in his turn and 'due date' (relapses were as regular as clockwork) was back in hospital with malaria. Fever was very widespread amongst those of us who had been away. Fifty to sixty a day, out of our group of 1000 men, would come down with it. F Force deaths were still occurring though falling off somewhat. I prayed 'God help those still sick at Kanburi'. It was bad enough at Changi, 'spine-bashing' between bouts of malaria. It was amazing though how quickly time passed, yet how slow the mornings and afternoons sometimes seemed. By March we could not get over the fact that it had been three months since Christmas. In that time we had got used to being dosed regularly with a grass extract. This was the juice from the lalang grass, which was prolific around the camp and was crushed and processed at the Grass Factory. It made up for the deficiency of certain vitamins in our diet, which had caused a number of complaints, including partial blindness. It was amazingly effective, if not actually pleasant to take, and was another example of Changi ingenuity and improvisation.

The whole Changi camp was quite an enterprise. Apart from the gardens there was a poultry farm (where unfortunately cholera broke out among the fowls, drastically reducing the hospital egg supply) and a piggery, which supplied pork all round one day. The salination plant was effective, as was the factory making artificial limbs. Skills of many men were utilised, from bookbinding to operating the clandestine wireless sets, in ensuring that the best was done to cope with the inadequacies and deprivations we went through as prisoners to the Japanese.

At the end of March we were still in and around Selarang Barracks. Curly Hardman and the 2/30th were moved over the road and a bit further away. The old Curl! The situation, physically, medically and emotionally was hitting him harder than most of us. I was sure that he would come good again though, a thing that I had despaired of at Kanburi in December last. Our quarters were being rearranged and Japanese guards came into the camp for the first time since September 1942. We were taken over by a new Japanese general who made a few changes, including the promise to increase the ration scale. Notwithstanding *that,* another decrease of two oz of rice a day came into effect immediately.

On the 1st April 1944 we admitted to being all fools.

We were allowed down to Changi Beach at times and I had my first swim for twelve months or more, my second or third in over two years. Swimming was good therapy and we started again to feel that we were part of the human race. Sleeping out on the Padang, under the stars, was beautifully fresh, even if rather cold in the morning. It was good to start to feel alive again. It was the first week of April, Sunday the 2nd, that I wrote up the diary from notes kept since the 1 January. I had not been inclined to do it before, due to the feeling of lethargy and an inability to concentrate on anything. This was symptomatic of the shocking physical condition I was in when brought down from Thailand and the slow but steady rate of recovery since then.

The dice were rolling again and small games of pontoon, poker and euchre were being organised. As always, these were stopped only to start up again. Curly and I could not keep out of it long. I started again on light duties and acknowledged that I had been given an excellent spin over the three months or more...It was to the great credit of Colonel Billy Bye and the AGH staff, together with the cooperation, understanding and organisation of Black Jack Galleghan, that the remnants of F Force again came good in mind and body. The whole program of rest and rehabilitation had been well done. There was almost a compassion in Black Jack that we had not previously known.

Curly was back in the AGH with his fifth relapse of malaria since coming back to Singapore, although it did not hit him so hard. We hoped that it was a sign that the regular recurrences would gradually get less and less severe. The hospital was getting short of quinine and atebrin, with such an increase in consumption over the previous four months.

The new Japanese general certainly made some changes around the camp, concentrating us still closer together and introducing quite a bit of Japanese drill, which we were to observe. To his way of thinking, Changi was the worst POW camp he had known. It may have been that he had not come up against Australians before and certainly not one as difficult as Black Jack Galleghan. But we were not unduly worried.

Although I was working around the camp, there was still a lot of time to fill in. I taught some of the boys to play chess and got in quite a few good games. I was still an avid patience player and, with reading and a bit of a yarn, could always find something to do. I had met up with Bob Logan, from Glasgow again, in the BGH [British General Hospital]. He was paralysed down one side. It gave me a shock when I saw him so and I was really sorry, as Gertie, my cousin, would have known him fairly well.

The light duties were a bit solid when I started work on the aerodrome job. Three hours on the drome in the blinding sun and I was back in the malaria centre with a slide that came up BT+−. But Christ it was hot. The relapse though was comparatively light. It was my ninth dose of malaria altogether and I wondered what would be done to rid it from our systems.

Curly and I were separated for a while when an exchange of men was carried out with a working party at Sime Road, Singapore. He went with them and I gave him $1, which was all I had. I would no doubt have gone too if I had not been in the Malaria Centre when the move took place. It was all luck, whatever happened to us, and we were content to drift with the tide. We did not push things too much. I thought though that I would follow Curly into town if the opportunity came up. It was obvious that there was to be a lot of work done on the drome; work and I were not on speaking terms. I had lost over a stone in weight in the last few weeks of April 1944 and would have been about 100 lbs. It was bloody disgraceful the way we went up and down. I wondered what weight and height Neil would go at that time.

Our rations did improve and a special effort at some variety was made on Sundays. The quinine treatment, though, was cut down from ten days at 30 grams to five days at 20 grams per day. It was enough to get us back on our feet and I went back to the lines on Monday, 24 April.

The rest of that week was rather eventful:

• News came through that at Sime Road there were eighty or so Italian POW's; ex-submarine crews, who wished to be on the right side at the showdown by declaring themselves for King Victor Emmanuel.

• A warning notice was given that next month all of us at Changi and Sime Road camps would be moved into and around the Changi Gaol:

the officers to be separated from the ORs and we would be under direct Japanese administration through our warrant officers. We would be pretty congested there as there were about 10 000 of us but it was something that we had been expecting for quite a long time. We were glad and hoped that there were some disadvantageous circumstances to the Japanese that necessitated the move. The civilian internees, who had been in the area, were to move into Singapore.

• The rest of F Force arrived from Thailand, only 700 strong. This made, we thought, only 2500 of us alive out of the 7000 who had gone up there. We were still steadily diminishing in numbers but not in the hundreds every week as had been the case earlier in the year. Those who came back that week were in exceptionally good condition, fitter than we were, who had come down at Christmas. They had recovered well in the three months at Kanburi. Not many of the Burma crowd, which we had left, made it. Of the ward that I had been in, among the 76 of us who came out, 50 had died. A memorial had been built to those who had died on the railway and road job, which was estimated to be 80 000 in all. [In actual fact the figure would have been much higher but among the native workers it was never known just how many died.]

Letters came in again in May 1944 and I received one from Neil dated 6 July 1943 and another from Mum dated 13 September 1943 in reply to my card of 2 July 1942, nearly two years before. There were more letters from Jessie Scott too, and the boys reckoned that I was well and truly hooked. More letters were to come but it had made 39 that I had received to then. Pay came in too and we had got an increase of 9 cents a day. We needed it as poor local tobacco was $1.55 an ounce and coconuts were 80 cents each. Together that was over a week's wages. I swapped some tobacco for five Australian pennies, which I thought may be worth holding on to. We were happy too that 4000 books and records arrived in the camp from an American Red Cross consignment. These brought us more up to date in regard to the Top 40. Glen Miller's 'I got a Gal from Kalamazoo' got played over and over and over. At the end of the week, to cap everything off, our rations improved slightly, ex reserves.

Colic and diarrhoea were pretty widespread and I was feeling far from good, with a malaria attack coming on, when I went to a Mother's Day service at church. I suffered for it but it was a special day. By the Tuesday the malaria got me properly and did it hit me hard! It was the cruelest bout that I had experienced. Not getting on to it early I had to wait another 48 hours to get a positive slide. I knew then what Curly had gone through at times. By the end of the week I was in Cell No. 3 B 40, in gaol, the malaria and 'no duty' men having been moved.

Changi Gaol was probably the most modern gaol in the world. If we had to be in gaol it was the place to be as it was not too bad at first. We were one or two to a cell, with plenty of room as yet. In fact, to that time, apart from the hospital, I was more comfortable than I had been in any of the camps since being a POW. I had brought my mattress and a pillow with me, although did not keep them long. Curly was there in the gaol too, looking better but still a bit despondent.

Singapore and Malaya were in the grip of rampant inflation. Prices of everything had risen enormously over the last few months. Javanese tobacco had gone from 30 cents to $1.99 and it was the same with pens, watches and other advertised items in town. It was apparent that Singapore was going to have a job straightening out the money problems when the time came to restore economic stability. The Japanese Singapore dollar was probably equivalent to 4 cents of the old money.

Other news at the time was:
  • That Bill Bailey had died. He was one of the real personalities of the 2/30th, the eldest of the three brothers in the unit...Bill, Mick and Gerry.
  • More of the other scattered work forces were expected back at Changi. It would be good to see us back together again, what was left of us anyway.

And still the letters came in. I would have received over 70 by then and yet some of the boys had none at all: most had received about fifteen. I learnt of Mum's accident when falling off a bus in the dark and blamed myself. With a badly gashed leg, I certainly hoped that she would not have a permanent limp. I was sorry to learn that Alan Stewart had been killed while flying in the Middle East and I wondered about Ron invading my paddock and carting off an eligible Croydon girl. I hoped that they would not get married before I got back. Neil made me laugh, ending his letter 'Don't do anything I wouldn't do'. Would he smoke native weed, pawpaw and tea-leaves in newspaper...would he eat three-quarters of a pint of plain rice gruel and call it breakfast...would he eat half of a rotten fish with the maggots still wriggling in the guts...would he scoop a handful of rice out of a pool of mud and thank Christ for the meal...would he pull a car chassis with a two-ton load like a bloody draught horse...would he bore holes 25 feet deep by hand in the middle of the day, 1 degree north of the equator...would he march 185 miles in the jungle, for the most part on two meals a day...would he take a bloody belting from a maniac for not being able to lift a 20-foot log on to his shoulders and have malaria at the same time...would he sleep peacefully among the bugs, lice, cockroaches and rats...would he dream on his birthday of just ordinary civilised things like bread and butter, beaches and the bush, music and moonlight, women and 'what have you' as if they were schemes for Utopia? *'Yes, Neil, you would, but may you never have to do some of the things that I have done'.*

June 2, my birthday and I was a pretty sick laddie. I was delirious on the Monday and a slide had proved MT + BT malaria. BT [benign tertia] was bad enough, MT [malignant tertia] was worse and both together was insufferable. Once again it was the worst go I had ever had and fifteen quinine tablets on the first day made me even sicker still. I did not eat for three days. I had been brought over to the AGH on a trailer on the Tuesday but by the Friday, having got over the initial fever, I felt quite a lot better.

Bloody fever, bloody bug
Always in a bloody fug
MT BT, bloody mug

Bloody, bloody, bloody.
Bloody aches 'n' bloody pain
Bloody shivers here again
A bloody bloke is fair insane
Bloody, bloody, bloody.
Bloody cold 'n' bloody heat
Bloody quinine, take it neat
A bloody man can't even eat
Bloody, bloody, bloody.

A few more verses to the great Australian epic. They just summed up the malaria and how I felt on my twenty-third birthday. Still, in hospital I read my letters over and over, wrote up my diary, read *Pygmalion* again and made the best of it. A man died a couple of beds away from me. He had drawn his tea, finished it, was rolling a smoke when he went out like a light. I went on eating and had a smoke myself. Life was certainly cheap. We had no idea who the next one would be. It could have been any one of us.

Pay was again increased to 45 cents per day for the full-time workers. There was nothing for those on 'no duties' or for the patients in hospital except that some pay was always made up for by contributions from others. Any increase in pay only went on the increased prices. However, I was discharged from hospital in the middle of June, having completed a course of three days of quinine, seven days of atebrin and five days of plasmaquinine, whatever that was. I hoped that it had all got rid of the malaria for a bit. Selarang Barracks was by then deserted and the hospital had been brought to the gaol. I was then outside the cell blocks. We had grown quite attached to the Selarang Barracks, the square and the surroundings.

I was doing a bit of hygiene work after getting out of hospital. This was for a couple of hours a day, voluntarily occupying myself and quite enjoying it. It was very easy work and two hours a day was about my limit. It did not last, however, as I was under observation for jaundice. I was yellowish in the face but it may have been the effect of the atebrin. While the atebrin lasted it was used as a follow-up treatment after the quinine and was very effective in suppressing the fever and getting the temperature down.

Of general interest at the time was that:
* At a camp at Kranji things were not that good: it was the usual practice of feed the workers but not the sick. It was a callous rule and seemed to be basic to the Japanese military philosophy.
* Incoming personal radio messages of a very recent date (as late as 12 June) were being received. Bill Garland received one and was allowed to reply. Very few came in.
* Roy Poy came good with 30 cents for a couple of cigars. I was always pretty open-handed myself when in the chips and there was always one of us on top of things to help us through the bleak periods. The two-up game had been a tail-better's nightmare and Curly and I were broke.

• Blackout exercises were enforced for a couple of nights. I would have loved to have seen our planes overhead, even though at Changi, we were sitting in rather a hot spot.

During the last week of June the camp was put into shape, firstly for an inspection by the Japanese general in command POWs, Singapore, and then by the General i/c the whole Southern Regions (including New Guinea and Sumatra). In the middle of the latter inspection one of the Indian guards apparently thought that he had had enough, so up with his rifle and shot himself. Maybe he was an advanced disciple of Ghandiism and had some grudge against the general.

But the main event of the week was the arrival into the camp of about 60 POWs, Australian, Dutch and British, who were the very few survivors of a shipload of 750 men from Sumatra. They were attacked by a submarine, sinking most of the convoy. They were in a pretty bad way when they were brought to Changi...broken arms and legs, fractured spines, burns and other damage, caused by the explosion of the torpedo and the pressure of the water as their boat went down. Those in the holds had no chance of survival whatsoever. At River Valley Road camp there were some from H and D Forces, from Thailand. They had firstly been shipped from Bangkok to Saigon, with the intention of sending them on to Japan or Korea. This apparently proved impossible. They were then returned to Thailand and brought to Singapore by train. It was typical that they then were going on and off, on and off the boat again to complete their journey.

July 1 and I was attached to the 2/30th Battalion. Both Curly and I were graded 3B2 (very light duties) and we had the job of keeping the lines clean and boiling water for sterilising utensils. We both felt the benefit, in body and mind, of the light work and being useful. It was a slow process picking up again on the dreadful diet. Beri-beri and dysentery were increasing and, on the rations we were on, it was just a matter of time before we all had beri-beri once more. There was just insufficient vitamin content in the food to avoid it.

In fairness I had to admit that the 2/30th was a better run show than the 2/29th. We actually sat at tables outside and it was the first time for 18 months that I had my meals in a near civilised fashion. Knives and forks though were a thing of the dim dark past.

Mail again came in and I received another dozen letters. About the only thing that I could think that the Japanese did in the way of anything humane was to process the letters that were cleared and forwarded from some neutral port. The service was certainly slow but they did arrive eventually. In July 1944 I received a letter from Neil dated November 1942. The enclosed photo was amusing as Mum had obviously put on weight; and had the hair gone greyer? There were also a couple of letters from Auntie Louie in London. But as for Jess! Had she fallen for me? I wondered what the redhead was after and thought to tell Neil to let her know that I had caught the pox off a Chinese prostitute, that I was a cholera carrier and had leprosy. I hoped that she meant well, but she was coming on a bit strong.

Some of the boys were very good at making a tinder box. They would char a piece of fabric and strike a spark so that it would smoulder and light a cigarette. It was really a surprise when we got an issue of matches that week, being three to a box. They were quite a novelty for they had been like cigarette papers, saucers, forks, bread, Bing Crosby and blondes—gone and almost forgotten. F Force was a memory that still invaded our dreams and conversation, rearing its ugly head. Ugghh! For those of us who came through it, nothing will never have a profounder influence on our lives than those terrible and ghastly two months in Burma. Jock has told me that after they lit the fire in Burma in August, it never went out until February, burning bodies every day.

I tried myself out physically and very much doubted if I would be able to throw a cricket ball 40 yards. It took all my energy and time to carry six gallons of water a distance of 80 yards.

Since coming into the 30th, these had been the most contented days since being a prisoner. Out of a smoke and the food rather terrible, yet I made up for it by being left in peace, Curly for company, an excellent ratio between work and play, good books to read and a nightly yarn with the boys when the day's work was done. It made me just contented to bear my lot and appreciate the lines of Omar Khayyam:

> Here with Loaf of Bread beneath the Bough,
> A Book of Verse, a Flask of Wine and Thou
> Beside me sitting in the Wilderness.
> Then Wilderness is paradise enow.

The truest words ever put into print. And as for Curly (or Keth as it would be) I could not have had a better friend at the time, rough diamond though he was. He had been as profound an influence on me growing up as had been John Broinowski, my old boss, and I appreciated it. We looked forward to some good times coming. Generally:

- Brown-outs were in force and necessary we hoped. There were even permanent aircraft spotters on top of the gaol towers.
- I had gone a whole month without a relapse of malaria. It was still pretty widespread but I touched wood.
- After reading a book called Microbe Hunters I had a look at microbes over at the medical laboratory. It was very interesting but pretty ghastly to see the things that were rampaging around inside us.
- Black Jack Galleghan and Colonel Holmes, who had been in charge of us since Percival and the senior Generals had gone to Japan, were sacked and the Japs put Lieutenant Colonel Newey of the Singapore Volunteers as Officer i/c in dealing with them. It was rather an unpopular move but Galleghan and Holmes remained as the senior officers of the troops. It could only be assumed that Black Jack was too abrasive for the Japanese to deal with.

I made a bet with Curly at the end of July 1944 (to the extent of a lunch at Usher's or the Carlton for four of us) that we would still be prisoners on Christmas Day. He had five months for everything to be cleaned up. Maybe, I hoped so, he believed it but I could not see the war ever finishing.

There had been one piece of information in a letter, which was circulated around the camp, that convalescent camps had been built in Darwin, Burdekin and other outlandish places where we would be quarantined for 90 days, followed by 60 days leave with an interstate rail pass. It sounded right and I thought that

I would be paying visits to Kyogle (Peter and Auntie Laura), Brisbane and Melbourne (the 29th boys) as well as Sydney. We learnt too that the monies from the Red Cross and Comforts Fund POW Appeals would run to about 12 shillings a week, besides the 16s.10d. that our deferred pay was supposed to be up to. I hoped that it was so as I looked forward to furnishing a small flat at Double Bay for Neil and me to live in and *Virginia* on the harbour.

One of the boys was making a cigarette or cards box out of aluminium and a black wood, with an enlargement of the RSL badge and various reminders of the Far East set in it. It was marvellous how deft some were with their fingers in making things of very intricate design and workmanship.

It was mid-August and I wrote out a card for home. It was our fourth (and a radio message) in two and a half years. I addressed to Neil: 'Dear Neil, Pleased to be receiving your letters. Self keeping well but missing you too. Give best wishes to Ron, Love Mum & Dad, Doug'. I felt that I would like to beat it home. I was broke again. Pay was 25c, 10c and 5c a day, less 2c on full duties, paid monthly. At the price of cigars, and a smoker like Curl, it did not last long. But I thought at the time that 45c pay was what came into the camp. We would not have known what came in but knew that a lot was deducted for the hospital and to buy food. Not that we complained. Our rations were still the same and predominantly rice.

The concert parties were going well and they intended putting out a song album of Changi compositions after it was all over. We thought it should be good and an interesting souvenir.

Repatriation, through the Red Cross, had been brought up again. It was a disgrace that it had never come to fruition as there were so many men who were of no use to the Japanese and could be sent home. We felt that they would have been, under a civilised administration.

As far as we knew the air-raid alert that week was the first genuine alarm. The Japanese Camp Commandant apologised for the non-arrival of the planes but he was not half as sorry as we were. What did arrive was three and a half tons of tobacco, which brightened things up a bit. We expected that we would have to work and pay for it though. It worked out at three-quarters of a pound each but was a long time getting to us. The drome party was still going out every day, rain or heat. It was not a bad job. Although started a year previously, aeroplanes had been using it for two months or more. We were still levelling off the whole of the Changi area and when we finished it would be one of the biggest airfields in the world. The same remarkable difference continued between the work parties in Singapore and those away from the main Japanese military administration. Work at Changi was almost unionised. There was nothing like the severity and barbarism which was experienced in Burma, Thailand or Borneo.

When not working on the airfield we were always occupied in the camp—darning socks, sewing and patching clothes and duties around the camp. Our clothing was in a pretty bad way and my pants had ten patches in the front and four in the back. I even made a jockstrap for myself. At the time too I dug and tended a garden where I planted beans, potatoes, tomatoes and eggfruit. This was mainly for our team of Curly Hardman, Mick and Gerry Bailey and myself. The idea was that we would have something extra at Christmas. Each day we would get a tropical storm and the rain would pelt down. It was actually cold but I and many others would look after our little gardens just the same.

August 25 and the week included the first anniversary of the worst 24 hours of my life. Never would I forget No. 5 camp on the Thai/Burma border, the night Curly Avard died; when I could not lie down or rather, when I did (in the mud under the bamboo platform of the hut) a Pommy shit on me, men were dead and dying amongst us, ulcers stank and there we were 200 of us in a hut 30 yards long. Outside it was still pouring with rain, bodies were exposed where the surface mud had washed away and the latrine slats broke from under me and I went down to my thighs. The only water available was suicide to drink for the cholera germs and blowflies were over everything. No one could understand the ghastliness of a place like that unless they had been through the same thing. For all that we took it as a matter of course at the time.

[Fifty years later, in 1993, I still see the scene with clarity. I see in my mind exactly where I was that night lying in the mud, some ten feet from the opening at the end of the hut, the slime pouring down on me from a dysentery patient and part of a body, half-buried and visible from where I lay.]

We at Changi though, were feeling much better. Malaria was being beaten and there were only 160 men in the malaria ward at the hospital that week. We received another batch of needles and I was glad to be over the worst of it. I did not want to get malaria any more: eleven times in eleven and a half months was plenty for me. And yet we called ourselves Malayan Millionaires. I had worked out that I had £400 in my pay book at least. At the Changi Education Centre lectures were given on 'Are You Ready for Civvy Street?' to teach those who wished to learn how to spend their money wisely. I did not think that it was taken seriously enough.

A lot of time was spent planning and thinking about our future in a world and after a war which had been won. I still intended to have the hull of *Virginia* professionally built and Curly thought about building a 45-foot wishbone ketch to sail around the world. It was not a matter of saying how wonderful it would be *if* we did but rather *when* we would carry out all our plans and dreams. It was also on my mind that, with all my deferred pay, I might be able to buy a junior partnership with Lawford Richardson and John Broinowski in the chartered accountants' practice. I would forego all the holidays, boats and flats if the opportunity was offered. I wondered, too, if the Repatriation Department would finance a BEc at University for me. The plans, dreams and aspirations kept us going when time seemed to mooch so slowly.

We were all putting on weight and filling out. I weighed 124 lbs and had a 31½ inch chest, so was back to normal. We had almost settled down to the life and outlook that we had before going up north. We would never be quite the same again but sport and even a few fights occurred amongst us. Baseball was popular and we looked and felt a lot healthier. We started to enjoy things once more. The concerts were good and getting better and there were some really good comedians and musicians in the camp, including the best jazz trombone player that I had ever heard, a Yank by the name of Hap Kelly. Our garden started producing and the tomatoes were the first crop. They were beautiful, though very small. My main job in the camp had been water boiling for some time but we were broke again three days after pay day ($14 between us), after paying back our debts, buying a bit of tobacco and investing in the poker and two-up games.

It turned out that the tobacco that came into the camp was for free and we started to get four issues a week of an ounce each time. It was poor tobacco but acceptable, as it was the first issue we had received for over twelve months. Curly was down again with some obscure fever, which did not show up in a slide. It was still bad though: worse than malaria. Appendix trouble was common too. Due to the large quantities of dirt and grit that we ate with the rice, prawns, etc., it was thought that eventually 80% of us would have had our appendixes removed. Anything that went through the camp went through the lot of us.

Les Gallard died in the last week of September. He had been very ill with dysentery and other complaints for a year and had managed to hold out that long. It was another bloody disgraceful F Force death. There were many others too, for whom it was just a matter of time. Colds were very prevalent but there was nothing we could do about them but get wet and stay wet most of the day. As we did not wear shirts we felt the cold although, in fact, the temperature did not drop that much. Without much body fat we just felt cold. At the canteen, coconuts were a $1 each, which was indicative of the high prices generally. They were away beyond the reach of most of us. In fact I was nearly always broke or in debt, as there was no way I could restrain Curly's extravagant tastes while he had money burning a hole in his pocket.

The work on the Changi aerodrome continued on three shifts a day; 8 a.m. (daybreak) to 2 p.m.; 2 p.m. to 8 p.m. (sundown); and 8 a.m. to 5.30 p.m. The first two were without a break all day but for tea and a bit of gruel, the day shift having lunch on the job. Naturally there was no shade of any sort, so the heat was unbearable during the afternoon. It was all military stuff that we were doing, the airfield itself, a road off it for the dispersal of planes and camouflage pits for the planes to hide under. The Japanese engineers were forcing the pace a little. As always it was being carried out by hand with shovel and chunkel, filling and emptying skips of dirt. The 'light duty' job was on the long wide road off the 'drome, while the 'fit' men dug the pits and levelled the airfield. It seemed like thousands of us were involved, including the local natives, shifting tons of dirt. Actually in October it was the first real days of work that I had done since June 1943, sixteen months previously. Each day the work parties were allocated to:

- The gardens, where quite a few acres were under cultivation and were our only source of vegetables.
- The aerodrome, which was near the camp and gaol.
- The railway station and the wharves in Singapore, where 200 men were sent at 8 a.m. each day, not getting back until 7 p.m. This was the heaviest job of all.
- Work in the camp, digging pits and bore holes, camp maintenance and trailer parties.

At least we got one day off a week.

Outside of Changi camp, work was going on at Blakang Mati and Pula Bukim, as well as at a number of other places in Singapore but we had no contact with them at all: not even at the hospital.

Sodomy, for the first time in Changi that I knew of, came to light. Two men were locked up in the gaol. I learnt, too, that some Pommies were at it at one camp in Thailand. It was inevitable, I supposed; really it was only surprising that such a long time had elapsed without homosexuality getting any real publicity. It was a pretty low act and an offence in the army. Nothing was that private among us considering how jammed up we always were in all the camps that we had been in. Havelock Ellis would have been in his element at Changi, studying repressed sexual impulses, etc., and Sigmund Freud would have had a word a yard long for that feeling, hardly sexual but certainly not platonic, that overpowers a man in desiring feminine company. It seemed something basic to a man's way of life—and God knew, I had never been in love. What a wasted three years. To be 23 years of age and full of hope; although wine, women and song were not really uppermost in our minds.

The concerts were banned for a week, due, we were told, to the too frequent singing of God Save the King. It was a ridiculous excuse, used only to cut down on our few pleasures and morale. But it was impossible to make any real sense out of anything that the Japanese did.

The prisoners of war in the Outram Gaol received inhuman treatment; something bloody terrible. Men were put there for punishment for various offences, mainly for attempting to escape or for being outside the wire. Occasionally, just before one of them died, he was sent to the Changi hospital. A 2/12th Field Engineer was sent there in the last week of October. From the waist down he was swollen terrifically with beri-beri and above that he was emaciated with starvation. Totally blind, Christ only knew what internal injuries he had. The hospital staff had no chance of saving him. Two Dutchmen were also in a pitiable way (one having got as far as Mandalay from Thailand) but they both died. We never really knew the full extent of the atrocities, tortures, beltings and starvation that went on at Outram Road, except that it was something out of the fifteenth century Inquisition. Torture was still practised by the fiendish bastards; every Japanese had that streak in him. In the Outram Road Gaol they practised to the full, those animal traits inherent in their character.

By 3 November 1944 I had become very friendly with a Dutchman, whom I had met while working on the dispersal road; Pieter 't Hart, a fighter pilot of the NEI Air Force. He was a bit younger than me but much the same sort of a cove that I was. His English was very good and our friendship just sort of clicked. From that time on he would come across to our part of the camp, sometimes with his mate Lex, and we would yarn away on all sorts of things. He was very much amused by Curly Hardman who had quietened down quite a lot, though I did not think that Piet had ever met anyone quite so outrageous and outspoken as Curly in his life before. We would talk about Java and Soekebomi as much as about Australia and Sydney. He had actually been shot down in a Brewster Buffalo in flames by a Jap Zero but managed to parachute down with badly burnt legs. [We have stayed in contact and have been friends ever since.]

There was a lot of trading going on. Too much was apparently being sold to the local population for a new regulation came out which required that watches, jewellery and rings be handed in. It was surprising that there was much stuff still around. We had never really been allowed to sell personal items to the local people but it had always gone on and nothing was going to stop it.

On the road job I was mixing cement. It was a job that I thought Dad could have on his own. On our Sundays off though, I still read a lot and had finished *Frenchman's Creek* by Daphne du Maurier but it was not to the standard of *Rebecca*. I also read Wilde's *Ballad of Reading Goal*, which was an all-time favourite of mine. *'He did not wear his scarlet coat for blood and wine are red, and blood and wine were on his hands when they found him with the dead, the poor dead woman, whom he loved and murdered in her bed'*. I knew it off by heart.

After sixteen months I was once again marked 'fit'. This was quite a milestone and I was glad that I was again 'one of the boys'. It was all thanks to Dr Billy Bye and his hospital/convalescent program, which had worked wonders for us. Trained at Royal North Shore, I believe, he brought to Changi the medical and administrative skills relevant and necessary for the running of a large hospital. It was as though he gave us individual attention although, of course, the medical staff dealt with us on a day to day basis—taking sick parades and administering the wards. I did not know where Major Hunt went to after Burma or Captain Mills after Konkoita, but these too were outstanding doctors and had greatly influenced my will to live in 1943.

At air-raid practice on the drome they brought up a machine-gun and stood over the boys as they were herded together. I could not see that it had anything to do with air-raid precautions, except to gun down any POW who moved, threateningly or not.

I received a letter and photograph from Mum and then our mail was held up. Somebody stole the sheet off Takahashi's [the Japanese Camp Commandant] bed. So no mail. But we continued to receive our one ounce tobacco issue with a sheet of newspaper to smoke it in each week.

We believed that some A and D Force men had again been sent up-country from the River Valley Road camp. The poor bastards! It was hoped that they had not gone back on the railway. Parties of men continued to be taken away but, as always, we had no idea where they went to.

In early November 1944 we had our own aeroplanes over for the first time in nearly three years. They were B 29s on a reconnaissance flight and, apart from the ack-ack fire, were not molested. It made a big difference to us and even the most pessimistic amongst us had smiles on their faces. An ack-ack shell landed beside the dysentery ward, not three feet from a couple of men, but why no bombs, we thought.

On Monday, 5 November I started work on the aerodrome itself. God, it was big. It must have been 2½ to 3 miles long and 1½ miles wide, in the shape of a cross. It was as flat as a board. On the Wednesday a couple more of our planes were back again and any Japanese aircraft in the vicinity cleared out. We were doubly pleased on the drome when the 'alert' went, for it always meant half an hour's respite for us. On the Thursday I put in the hardest day's work since the Neike camp in Thailand. A bastard of a day but it was not really comparable with the railway job. But I was back in harness.

Directly from my diary:

One thousand days and one thousand nights! Christ, it seems a lifetime with the lifetime of experience that has gone into them, every place and incident being so vivid and real in our memories.

That first march from Tanglin to Changi that I'll never forget, and back again a week later to start working for the Japanese. Labouring on the wharves, the railway stations and the warehouses of Singapore: three months of sweating, thieving and beltings, followed tho by a very easy job in the Great World, hungry until the Red Cross ship came in, but an excellent break.

To Changi once more for Christmas, working in the gardens, our first letters arriving and then F Force. By train like cattle up to Thailand, a march of 170 miles straight, and on the worst (if any) food possible, along a jungle track, and commenced work immediately on the Bangkok-Rangoon railway. Indescribable cruelty in the jungle forcing the pace: cholera, dysentery, malaria, beri-beri, pellagra, typhus, small pox, pneumonia, pleurisy, tropical ulcers and sheer starvation. Burma. Then Thailand, Malaya and Singapore once more, half our number dead, and Changi for Christmas for the second time. Which seemed like heaven after the purgatory I'd been through that it was the happiest Christmas of my life. Relapse after relapse of malaria and then a long slow process recovering my health. Now for the third time I'm working, nothing more nor less than a slave, making this huge aerodrome.

One thousand days and one thousand nights! They have murdered a lot of my mates, permanently maimed and invalided many more and reduced us all to a pitiable state of health. Eleven thousand of us are now in an area approximately half a mile square, denied civilised foodstuff, clothes and medical supplies from outside, the bulk of our rations is just rice, as it always has been.

But notwithstanding all that, the shame, the horror, the hard work that we've been through, the uncertainty of life itself, our spirits are still high and our hopes for the future as strong as ever: and returning from work after dark on our thousand and first night we still marched and whistled all the way home despite the Japanese. For we have by no means been without our lighter moments and a sense of humour has invariably saved us. The camps have always been under our own administration, especially at Changi, and once home our time and lives have been our own. Many are the memories of quiet peaceful evenings after the day's work is done, of books read and concerts seen which, intermingling with the sweat, blood and dirt has made all this bearable. One thousand days and one thousand nights a prisoner of war!

There was always this seeming attitude that we were in the Japanese Army. We got Japanese commands, in Japanese, on parade and on the march to and from the drome. Check parades had been re-introduced a few months previously, when we were lined up and counted, five nights a week. At that time too an accident occurred, either at the Naval base or on the wharves, when Dutch POWs were handling explosives. A blast killed a number of Chinese coolies and Dutchmen on the spot and another two died shortly after they were admitted to the Changi hospital. We were sure that it was against International Law for POWs to work on shells, bombs, mortars and the like but we had done so all along.

There were also admitted to the hospital some very sick men from Pulah Damit. 1200 prisoners and civilian internees from Java were there building a dock, though actually only 300 were working. The rest were down with malaria, beri-beri and other diseases, rice and salt being all they got to eat; no vegetables. On the aerodrome, with us, it was bloody barbarous, the number of children, some not as high as a shovel, who worked there every day.

English-speaking 'Gestapo' men moved amongst us after dark. They got around in only a pair of shorts, like ourselves, and, while unobserved, attempted to listen to groups of men talking. They tried to find us out doing or knowing anything that we were not supposed to know. I did not think that they were too successful and one, I believed, was pushed around a bit one night.

Our planes came over for the third time and, as on former occasions, the ack-ack fire was erratic and the siren too late. Again it was only a reconnaissance raid as no bombs were dropped.

By the end of November we had a celebration of the first anniversary of the formation of the 2/30th Battalion Association. Fortunately some extra rations had come in the day before and, with the money and coffee given by the officers, an excellent show was made. We had cakes and sweet coffee all round and the whole thing had cost $500. The Association was taken seriously in the 2/30th and we determined to keep up the association with each other afterwards.

Mail came in too. I got my first letter from Betty Gibbs, who would have been quite a bit of fluff by then. I would have liked a photo of Ron and Lois but as it was, I only wished it was Mum and Dad writing to me every week, instead of Jess.

To the Chinese, it is a matter of great religious significance when two full moons occur in the one month. This happened in November and the celebrations went on into December. They were dressed in their Sunday best in a house just outside our camp and kicked up a weird and wonderful row. We were approaching our own season of celebration and the boys made toys for the kids interned in Singapore: from dolls to kiddy cars they were a pretty good effort. Money was sent monthly to the women in the Sime Road internment camp but we never saw them. The pantomime season was due to start and had been in rehearsal. *Twinkle Toes*. Gawd struth! and for tough, foul-mouthed prisoners of war. But it was believed to be 'kerazy' and the scenery marvellous. At the time too, I promised Dave Tait a cigarette case when I got home. I hoped that I would remember.

I was on the morning shift on the drome. We got up at 4 a.m., Singapore time, before daybreak and went off to work and back for lunch. The day included a five mile march and six hours of work on only two pints of rice gruel; then a pint of mixed rice hash with what ever came in to mix in with it when we got back. I was knocked up by the end of the week and even looked like a labourer with corns on my hands from all the shovelling. We would try to get away with doing as little as possible, on sheer principle, but it was always a battle.

We witnessed the lowest act amongst us when one of the boys was caught with drugs and medical supplies (morphia, sulphanilamide etc.) in his possession with the intention of selling them. I thought that he was the greatest bastard that I had ever come across. In Burma, when those medicines were scarce and precious, his life had been saved by the same things, and the extra food he received at the expense of the rest of the camp after his leg was amputated. He was prepared to deprive others in the same position of their chances of living in order to fill his own stomach. Others were implicated and it was another example of the lowest instincts of man appearing in times of harsh adversity. It was the same sort of thing that had caused the contempt that we had for the officers, who, as a whole, had misused the trust and responsibilities placed upon them. It was only natural, I supposed, the temptation being so great. If you had $20 and first choice of the rations and were still hungry, would you share your money and go on to an equal basis with a man who had only $3 and was hungrier still. The officers didn't.

We had our fair share of criminals in the camp, petty and otherwise. 'Desperate Dan' was a camp identity. He was virtually the CID squad and had the appearance of a melodrama villain. He was a hard man but did a good job in cleaning up a lot of the crime around the place.

In a card from Jess dated 12 June she included news of the invasion of France. We had been glad that the Second Front had been opened but apparently it had not gone ahead with the speed expected of it as we were then into their winter. Quite a few of us believed that we would still be prisoners at Christmas 1945. We were always aware of the progress of the war as the BBC newscasts were monitored on secret radio sets within the camp. Few knew where they were but we certainly got the news.

On the drome job something or somebody was restraining the Japanese guards and engineers from using sticks, chunkel handles, boots, etc. on us when things went wrong. It was, for them, unnatural and it was obvious that they would have just loved to get at us, as they had in Thailand. Thank God anyway that somebody was holding them back. Our combined prayers to the Almighty and other private gods at last had some effect on the aircraft around the aerodrome. One of their training planes stalled and crashed, killing the pilot. One less!

The concert party pantomime was equal to all the reports and one of their best. Crazy it certainly was. Slim de Grey wrote the music and his 'I've Found the Key to My Castle in the Air' was a lovely slow foxtrot (slightly similar to 'Too Many Parties'). The whole concert group had developed into a very strong and talented team. They really were professionals.

But cold! I had not been warm, day or night, for a fortnight. It was 'winter' and the rainy season. With insufficient clothing and in a weakened physical state, I felt the cold more than at any time since leaving Scotland.

Christmas was not the merriest. I was on sick parade and had not been right for a week or more. Sunday was our day off and was very quiet. Piet brought me round a very good Xmas card, which he had drawn himself. At midnight I went to a Christmas Eve service at church for Mum's sake and on the Monday, Christmas Day, Curly and I were out 'working' on the road. In fact we spent most of the day yarning away under a coconut palm. The food was good all day, too good, and pay and a tobacco issue were welcome. Boxing Day saw most of us down with colic and diarrhoea and it was a bastard of a day working on the drome. On the Wednesday I was back on sick parade and put into the hospital. Epsom Salts, enemas and a fluid diet for a week cleaned me right out and fixed me.

On New Years Day there were a lot of disappointed men, who earlier in the year, had expected us to be out of it all by then. I won my bet with Curly but patience was getting harder to practise with life and routine so terribly monotonous.

And so we began 1945. I wondered what was in the crystal ball for the coming year. It was not even a safe bet that I would be alive at the end of it. But 'tid 'apa'. This was a very common Malayan expression, which we used often. It covered just about any situation but mainly meant, 'what the hell, there's nothing I can do about it'. New Years Day was a quiet holiday. I wondered how the surf was running at Bondi. Curly raised the wind for some tobacco and Changi Aspinall & Co. put in a cigar or two for us. I had given up smoking, which meant that I did not smoke when I did not have it but Curly was incorrigible. I was sure that he could have produced a cigar at a nude party in the middle of the Sahara. He was a good mate and we shared everything. I had even got a mattress, which I cut down to give him half. We had a garden still going and we were then growing Californian spinach.

Mid-January saw our best air-raid to date. Quite a bit of hardware was dropped and the Japanese Fighters even had a go. One of our planes was shot down and two or four of theirs. We did not know the extent of the damage done but three of our fellows were brought to Changi, being wounded in Orchard Road, in the middle of the City. We did not think it right that POWs should be working on the aerodromes, railway stations, wharves, docks and oil dumps, when the air-raids became so frequent. Maybe something was being done about it for work was stopped on the drome for a few days.

Small working parties of 200 or so men were taken away and rumours of a larger party to go were consistent. Curly was back in hospital with malaria and 37 tuberculosis cases were brought in from Kranji, where the conditions were just too damp. I was back in hospital too, to have piles cut out. They had been troubling me for years it seemed, but were just another of those things that I simply put up with.

The canteen in the camp was closed down on Takahashi's orders. He had discovered that the purchases exceeded the camp income and naturally wanted an explanation. It was all pretty amusing and I was not surprised.

The after-effects of the haemorrhoids operation was painful. Every movement of the body seemed to affect the area around the base of the spine. Fortunately I had had a local anaesthetic but there was no morphia, no vaseline, olive oil or proper treatment. Anyway, Captain Taylor, the 2/30th MO, reckoned that Major Nairn, who operated, had fixed me up for good, so it was worth it. I was not able to sit up for a week though. I would never forget what it was like with a great wad of gauze up my backside for days and the pain when it was eventually taken out. I was even frightened to eat for the bloody agony of passing food through me. But I survived. At the same time, three of the boys were in for appendix operations. The hospital surgical section was always very busy and we were extremely lucky to have two such able surgeons as Fagan and Nairn. They had been up and coming surgical specialists before the war and certainly gained a lot of experience at Changi. They had cut and carved up men in all sorts of places, while I was in the ward, from strictures to ingrowing toenails. One 2/19th man died that week, who had cut his throat on Christmas Day but was interrupted halfway through the job, making it worse for everybody. He had been making horrible gurgling noises while I was there and I thought that he was better gone. He was insane. I learnt, too, that Bobby Logan, who knew my cousin Gertie in Glasgow and whom I had met up with a number of times, had died at Kranji. Paralysis had set in, which was hereditary it seemed but it was still a bloody shame. I had lost what little condition I had built up before Christmas and was down to 7 stone 10 lbs and a 25½ inch waist. What with the malnutrition over the last three years, it did not take much to lay you low. I was light-headed and in pain with hunger but still too frightened to eat anything, far less half-cooked rice. But I expected to get over it.

For the last two weeks of January and into February we had been getting air-raids every day. Eighty odd planes, some presumably twice, were sighted on 1 February and we thought that they were probably from India, with the RAF using B29s. Slit trenches were dug in the camp but as so many of the raids had been only reconnaissance patrols, the Japanese were getting careless in regard to the air-raid siren and going for cover. We expected that soon, someone was going to get hurt amongst us. There had been a panic at the River Valley Road camp, with broken arms and collarbones, all for nothing.

I was back in the lines again by 9 February 1945 and had received a cable from Mum dated 11 January, which brought me right up to date. I was glad that Neil was doing so well in the PMG Dept and not in the Army: and Ron too, who I assumed was not yet married. Curly Hardman and I had visions of cruising around the world in a boat, *Beatrice*, which he was planning to build and we wondered if Ron could make the radio transmitter/receiver for the trip. Pieter 't Hart and I still visited each other pretty regularly. I hoped to see him in Australia after the war and take him to Sydney's shows and sports, scenery and sights, swimming, surfing and sailing. He was 21 or 22 years of age at the end of January and was the youngest fighter pilot in the NEI Air Force. He was very lucky to be alive for they lost 75% of their flying personnel and 95% of their planes. I gave those pilots their due, they could have it all on their own, DFCs and VCs and all.

But no one would need to pass disparaging remarks on the POWs after the war was over, as ours had been the toughest job, to survive, in wartime. I considered those eight and a half months in Thailand and Burma with F Force as the most frightful experience for white men, anywhere, at any time during the war, including the much vaunted Siberia.

Our rations were severely cut and there was a clear distinction between 'no duty', 'light duty' and 'heavy duty' workers. The latter were cut from 16 ozs of rice to 12 ozs a day and others proportionately. Not being an outside worker I got a little over half a pint of rice hash at lunchtime, which was our main meal. The cut had seriously affected the hospital and the officers too. Then we were told that it was going to be cut again. Things were getting tough and when a POW said 'tough' he meant 'tough'.

There was an incident down at the aerodrome that week. Two 2/29th boys attacked and robbed a coolie and finished up killing him. At that time it had not had an effect on the camp, but if they were not to be shot, I thought they would be lucky if they saw the outside of a prison in twelve years. They were taken to the Outram Road Gaol, so God help them.

Richardson, a TB patient, died that week too. It had been his twenty-first birthday a fortnight before but he died weighing about 5 stone. It was bloody terrible that the Japanese would not get fresh milk or anything of that nature for the TB cases, which would have given them a chance. It was criminal.

A third of the men (the ORs) were without boots. Rubber sandals were being made in the camp but they were worse to work in than none at all. Wooden clogs were about the only things worn in the camp as any issue of shoes or boots from the 'ordnance' depot went to the officers. God help any of us if we went away on another working party with nothing on our feet. Tropic ulcers down to the bone were sheer hell and the excruciating agony of having them treated and scraped was unbelievable. Curly's boots were useless and he went to work in some Japanese canvas boots that he had got hold of. When my boots gave up I was lucky enough to get another pair from one of the cooks. Someone else wore them, though, while I was not doing outside work. The man was lucky too, who had a pair of decent socks. Mine were beyond darning, just holes with socks around them. Neither socks nor proper boots, or any clothing really had ever been supplied to us by the Japanese. We never saw anything from the stores, which they had captured and taken over at the time of the surrender.

Incoming English-language newspapers were cut out in February. It was surprising that a regular issue of the local paper had been maintained for so long. Apparently the Japanese editors could not invent good news to print. The air-raid that week was the best since the Japanese did Singapore over. An amazing cloud of smoke arose above the city, the like of which I had not seen before. It came from burning oil and petrol dumps and was exactly like a huge cauliflower. It made us happy.

In March the further 10% cut in rations came about. Then there were two more decent air-raids, when five men in the convalescent ward at the hospital were wounded by shrapnel from a small shell, which exploded on the roof. We were made to dig slit trenches beneath the floors of our huts, which would have been death traps in the event of fire.

The good news was that half a dozen goats had been purchased for the TB ward, valued, I had heard, at $20 000 but we really had no idea what they cost. It was expected that in a few months the patients would receive the benefit of them. And then after a lot of 'it is', 'it isn't', a White Cross ship finally docked in Singapore. A party went to Serangoon to stack the stuff and they reported that it was mainly comprised of individual parcels. It was very acceptable but, as on the previous occasion, it was made up of silly stuff like tins of pork loaf, sweet rice, packets of tea, etc. They were Comforts Fund parcels for the troops overseas instead of cans and bags of bully beef, milk, flour and Marmite, which is what we needed. It was a godsend though that some medical supplies came, which was the most important thing of all. It was not very much that finally arrived in the camp as it had to go a long way to include Japanese, Indians and POWs, all over Malaya and Singapore. A little clothing came in and I would have given pounds for a singlet, even. But we thought that now that this relief ship had got through, it might become easier to get some more to us.

I was the 'tchar wallah' [tea-maker] and had my old billy-boiling/mess orderly job back again. I reckoned that I would have nothing but electricity and gas fires in the future after lighting fires with green rubber wood and waterlogged palm fronds for so long.

Colonel Billy Bye had said that, of every one of the men whom he had examined recently, not *one* had a normal heart and respiration. Particular attention was paid to Curly and me when we had been in hospital a short while before and something seemed to be knocking inside us. It was no wonder, as for three years we had been doing a hard day's work on no breakfast at all to talk about. I only hoped that it would not leave us all with a weak heart for the rest of our lives; we wondered what effect the POW conditions might have on us but hoped that good food and convalescence would fix us up.

The drome work was getting tough and the boys, including Curly, were cracking up. The ever-changing shift work had a lot to do with it besides the fact that one of the Japanese engineers was riding the boys pretty solidly. The rain and mud had been consistent too. We went on to two meals a day again and wished that they would let up on us.

In the middle of March 1945 the concerts were discontinued and the concert party dissolved. The Japanese general in command objected to a couple of scenes in the last production, one of a ballet representing the white man's supremacy over the Asiatics and another of us arriving home. So, with a bit of immorality thrown in, from his point of view he had some right. There were those, most of us, who were always defiant, with a lack of any subtlety and this time the concert party had overdone it. We were proud of them, not sorry—the yellow bastards. In fact, that is what they sang on stage 'A tisket a tasket, I've lost my yellow bastard'. But when, in the ballet, they had a white man throwing off his chains and overcoming his Asiatic oppressors, that was too much.

I tasted my first snail and thought it was beautiful. Boiled and then fried, it was a delicacy. We were on a slow starvation scale of rations, being down to 8 ounces of rice, per day for light duty men and 9½ ounces for the heavy duty workers, plus whatever vegetables came in from the garden. The meals did not cover the energy expended, especially for the drome parties and those who went out for wood with the trailers. If it was to keep up for long enough we would be wiped out. We started on seaweed in a big way and although there was not much taste to it, at least it was bulk and something to eat. Some of the boys started on frogs, beheaded, skinned and gutted. I tasted a leg but it was not very nice. We were in a considerably weakened state due to hunger, which brought about frequent attacks of dizziness and black-outs: and a continual feeling of lethargy that could not be overcome. Curly had cracked up and gone back into hospital. It was not as bad as in Thailand and Burma but there, if you lived, you could for the most part get enough to eat from those who were dying. At Changi, however, at that time, March 1945, we simply could not get sufficient to eat at all for what was expected of us.

And then on top of and in spite of it all, the Japanese increased the drome working party strength, necessitating the sending out of 'unfit' men. It was something really pitiful and I collapsed down there myself and had to be brought home. To make us march and work twelve hours a day on the food we were getting was bloody murderous and criminal. I then learnt that another big working party must soon go into Singapore, fit and unfit men. I finished that week fucked, fed up and far from home.

I was back to see Major Nairn, the surgeon, and it was a fissure that had been causing me a lot of trouble and pain. In fact I had been far from the best for the three months since Christmas. I got some injections for the fissure and palm oil too from the Regimental Aid Post to alleviate the pain and, fortunately, was able to take things a bit easier for a while.

Most of the boys in the 2/30th, about 250 of the fittest, moved to Johore as a working party there. It was possible that they would be more comfortably housed and better fed than at Changi. All the 'fit' men, probably about 3000, were down to go to various camps in April 1945 to dig and build Japanese defence positions, trenches, machine-gun posts, tunnels and other works around the island. We, who were left, excluding the hospital, expected to be moved into Changi Gaol. On 28th and 29 March there was a full moon as bright as day. There were a couple of beautiful night raids as our planes flew over: ack-ack and machine-gun fire, bombs, fires and flares lit up the sky. I had to take the boys' words for it as it would have taken the invasion itself to wake me up. It was Easter and a little Red Cross stuff had been allowed in.

12
In Changi Gaol

All of us left in the 'outside' camp moved into the gaol in mid April and into the cells. As luck would have it our mob were put on the fourth floor and the stair climbing was a drag. Duties got heavier and heavier. In addition to the drome, Singapore, garden and trailer parties, a thousand of us on light duties had to dig a deep, wide 'non escape' trench on one side of the camp, which was to be filled in with barbed wire. I had been fainting and blacking out frequently and collapsed again while digging in the trench. I was carried back to camp. I received a further series of injections for the fissure but was far from well: sore, weak, tired, fed up and nerves playing up too. I wished that they would either give us enough to eat or else machine-gun the lot of us. We always expected that this would be their last resort at the end.

Curly was the same and his stomach was still causing him problems. Sleep was the only escape and that was not always easy. I even craved morphine at times. Some, fortunately, were on a supplementary diet in the hospital, as I had been a year previously, as their weight loss made them look like skeletons. They were down to 4, 5 and 6 stone. Food poisoning, from some dehydrated vegetables, brought in months before and held in reserve, went through the gaol and did not help.

We had settled into the gaol, although the stairs drove us mad. What we could not get used to in the cells (three to a cell) was waking up in the dark. There was no way of knowing whether you had been asleep for an hour or five hours: whether it was nearly time to get up or if you had just gone to sleep. It was pitch black and the disorientation, with no outside view, was soul-destroying. In the centre of the cell was a raised platform like a slab, nothing else. One slept on the slab and one on either side, on hard concrete: no lights. At least the door stayed open, not that there was much movement. During the day we all had jobs to do but at night, tired as we were, it got to us. Confinement. There was a pathetic death of a 2/26th boy, suicide or accident we did not know but he was found down in a bore hole of one of the latrines.

Any smoking was of tobacco stalks, not the leaf. It was cheap. We were going through my letters for cigarette papers as Curly's had all been used up. I only wished that everyone had written to me on air-mail paper.

The 2/30th had to continue sending out their quota of light duty men to make up the drome numbers and Curly was wild over the favouritism and unfair treatment exercised by the CSMs [Company Sergeant Majors], who picked those who had to go and those who stayed in camp. It was apparent that the same men, who had previously held the best jobs, like cooks and orderly-room clerks, were the same ones who stayed in the gaol. Curly was the only man in the battalion with the guts to do more than just talk. He finished up getting the CO and CSMs sacked from the job of picking who stayed in camp and who went out. Things then ran a lot better and fairer within the unit. But that was the sort of thing that upset him, physically. The dyspepsia and stomach trouble he had was due, I thought, as much to nerves as to the bad food.

It may have been Curly's agitation or not but 45 of us, mostly gardeners, moved downstairs, out of the cells and were set up comfortably with beds, mattresses, mats on the floor, a chair, stool and an improvised shelf on the wall for our mess gear. It was the nearest to civilisation that we had known since being prisoners. The only drawback was that we were at the foot of the stairs and that it was noisy at six-thirty every morning when the drome party went off to work. It was not much of a complaint. Lofty Ambrose was in charge of us. He had been in the First World War and you knew where you stood with Lofty. He was down from 16 stone of solid muscle to 10 stone and was naturally craving for more food. His system demanded it. The weight loss was particularly hard on the bigger men. I could go from 9 stone to 7, even 6 or 5 but to go from 16 stone to 10 or even 9 or 8 was too much. The rice gruel we were getting every day had been used in peacetime for glue; as paste for making paper bags. It may have been an adhesive paste but it did not stick to us for very long. I was working as a mess orderly for a few days but got the sack, which suited me. So out on the garden party I went, not that I could keep going for long. I was determined to stick it out however.

By the middle of May I had been working as long as I could but I came to a full stop. Curly was annoyed that I had kept it up as long as I did, so I went on sick parade and was interviewed by the medical specialist at the hospital. He was critical too that I had been so pig-headed and foolish as to keep going when obviously I could hardly stand up for long. He put me into hospital for a week's rest. There was nothing actually wrong with me, it seemed, other than malnutrition, over-exertion and loss of weight. Duties and demands upon us by the Japanese were so solid that only a week could be spared. I was not the only one in an advanced weakened state, even if I was a bit worse off than most. The majority of the men in the camp at Changi Gaol were in a pitiful state. There was a good Medical Officer in charge of the ward, a Major Uhr, an X-ray specialist from Brisbane. He was a man you could talk to. While in the hospital the feverishness that I had been getting developed and I was running a high temperature. There was every symptom of malaria but I did not throw a positive slide. A blood culture was taken from my arm with a syringe for lab examination. Apparently I had some disease of the blood for I went on to fifty M & B tablets every two hours. These were early sulphanilamide drugs, brought out by May & Baker and used in the tropics in large doses.

I knew very little of that week: fever and sick from the M & Bs, I could only call to mind Curly carrying me on a stretcher for screening, Billy Bye examining me and going on to eggs, milk and chicken. I *must* have been sick.

The fever broke, thank God, and, after the course of the M & Bs, which was a marvellous discovery and one of the wonder drugs of the time, I started to come good, though could hardly walk. I was weaker than at any time since the surrender. Extra soup, milk (a quart a day) and two eggs a day did me the world of good. I was very fortunate to be one of the few on such a diet, as eggs were expensive and scarce and the milk (Red Cross powdered milk) was forfeited by the men in the lines for use in the hospital. It was a slow job putting on weight and strength. I was still dazed, and with a head like a block of concrete. The severe sickness of that three weeks at the end of May 1945 had come on so suddenly and unexpectedly that at the beginning I did not know that I was sick at all. Curly was in the hospital with malaria at the time too but came across to see me pretty often. However, I was nearly always asleep. I hoped though that he benefited from the stay there, even with the malaria and quinine knocking him around.

I was kept in hospital for more than the planned week, while continuing to improve under intensive care. I was able to throw off the air of gloom and despondency that had come over me and so after a while was a lot happier. In fact I was getting back in the groove and certainly benefited from the special diet that I was on. Through Ernie Parkes of the 2/30th I met Hilton Miles from Haberfield, back home. We did a lot of talking that week about the local lasses, people we both knew, of Uncle Dave Stewart and family and Heather Baines, the H & D milk bar and quite a lot of the local gossip around the district. Although living in Wattle Street he did not know Ron and Lottie. But it was good to talk of home. It was the sort of therapy that was needed in order to avoid becoming introspective and selfish.

It was my birthday on Saturday, 2 June and it was one of those days when everything goes right. For the third birthday running I was far from well but my weight was up to 100 lbs. I had my first shower and shave for three weeks and, what was more, did my washing. Curly had got me a pair of shorts, which I had to take in from a 40-inch waist to 24 but, even if they were underpants really, they were shorts to us. The meals were good with the eggs and milk and the day closed with mates around me, yarning and talking away as if we had not seen each other for weeks. Later in the week I had to go off the extra food I had been getting as a lot of sick men came in from Sumatra. I had my turn and I was grateful.

I worked out that I had over £500 in my pay book at 6s. a day, which was our rate of army pay, plus 2s. overseas service. But Curly was back in hospital with his stomach playing up (duodenal dyspepsia). He was typical of many at Changi. He was so restless and just could not relax as Mick Bailey and I could. It was a pity, although he did twice as much in the team as Mick and I put together.

The drome party had finished at the end of May and it really must have been one of the biggest aerodromes in the world. The 'unfit' like me, in hospital, were out of the gaol at least and the 'fit' had gone into our old camp at the rear of the gaol. There was a big difference. On the established Japanese principle of feeding the workers and bugger the sick, they got twice as much of everything as we did: rations, Red Cross supplies and pay. What Red Cross stuff we did get though, tooth powder, shaving cream, comb, razor, pencil and toilet paper was very acceptable, if not what we really needed.

The rats in the camp (the rodent variety) were getting very numerous, which was bad in the case of typhus and plague. At that time too the air-raids had fallen off and there were only reconnaissance flights overhead. But what upset me more than anything was that my reading glasses had been stolen and, I expected, already sold on the black market in Singapore. It was a pretty low act. I could hardly read and certainly not for long. Writing up my diary, sewing and playing cards was a strain. It was the fourth pair that had either been stolen or broken.

Colonel Bye held a 'skinny' parade. It was a pathetic sight, reminiscent of Tanbaya in Burma, though hardly as bad as that. I was included as I had been slipping back over the last three weeks or so in weight and strength. I then went 6 stone 10 lbs, a waist of 22¾ inches and a chest measurement of 28¾ inches, which was not much for a young bloke of 24 years. I was moved to another ward where they did what they could for me in the way of a little extra food. There was no doubt that Lieutenant Colonel Billy Bye was the busiest and hardest working man in the camp. He was the leading physician there and had taken on his own shoulders a huge responsibility, supervising the whole medical side of the hospital, as well as taking an active part in all the serious cases. He was a marvellous doctor and a marvellous man.

And he had to understand and put up with the Japanese character. The following pamphlet was distributed to the camp at Blakang Mati but was typical of the orders given to all the camps.

```
GENTLEMAN REMARKS !
You British officers and soldiers are obliged to obey
these rules.
1) You are confined to your barracks and gardens and no
allowed out without permit of Japanese Soldiers of Niki
troop.
2) You cannot enter any other barracks or houses without
permission except your own barracks No. 1941.
3) You can take nothing except those which you are permitted
from our Director.
4) You must do everything exactly and punctually as the
excellent Army of the British Empire...that is get up and
go to bed and eat at the decided hours.
5) Your Director is obliged to report to the Japanese
officers on duty about the condition of your troops of the
means of the aid of the watchman.
6) Your Director must order your own guard which controls
your own Army by the aid of the Japanese guards.
7) Smoking is strictly prohibited except at the decided
place.
8) Others you are all bound to the Japanese officers on
duty.
If you break the above orders you shall be shoot to death.
By Order V.Miki
```

Tommy Nixon's idea of a joke at six in the morning was to say to Curly, 'Curl, there are bigger, better and brighter things to come, but you and I will never live to see them'. The cream of the joke was the distinct possibility of it being true.

The Red Cross stuff finished. About 10 lbs of food each, had been spread over twelve weeks. Of the tinned stuff that did come in, much of it was rusted through and the contents spoilt as it was three to four years old.

On 30 June 1945 my 1944/1945 diary ran out of pages. There was no possibility of getting another notebook so I cut up my remaining letters and bound them together so that I could write on the backs of them. I had an indelible pencil, which I kept sharpened as the writing got smaller and smaller to record hopes, dreams and what was going on around me.

A considerable number of men moved away from the goal in a combined working party and dispersal move. The best thought was that they were there to work. The worst thought and apprehension was that, in the event of an Allied invasion, there would be no concentration of prisoners and that consequently the smaller the parties the more easily they could be disposed of. There were probably only the unfit men, the hospital patients and the officers left in and around the gaol. I believed that there were 40 POW camps spread over the island. We, left at Changi, thought that we may be in for a warm and sticky time as, in the vicinity, were the principal Naval and Air Force bases for the South-East Asian region. God help us! It certainly appeared that the Japanese intended making a stand to defend Singapore. If there was to be an allied attack it was expected that it would come from Earl Mountbatten's Burma forces, driving south. Knowing the Japanese character, and realising that they would murder us all before any surrender, we armed ourselves as best we could. I had an army-issue table knife ground down to a point as at least something in the way of self-defence.

I read the concluding lines of Bernard Shaw's St.Joan...'How long oh Lord, how long' . . . How Long, oh Lord, how long.

Into July I was losing weight again, going down to 91 lbs and then 89 lbs. The hospital staff received the heavy-duty ration scale but they did not share it with the patients, even under the lap. We were obsessed with food and it was the commonest subject of conversation. But such was hunger. Though I sympathised with those who could talk of nothing else, it got on my nerves a bit as I had my own empty feelings. But I was lucky enough to get onto book. *Brush up Your French.* I was annoyed that I had not taken advantage of the last three years of learning to read it well for it was something that I would have liked to be able to do. I hoped that I would improve my French before I got out of Singapore, as it looked to be a long time yet. I was reading too much without my glasses but I would have gone mad if I gave it up.

Air-raids were back again but they flew so high that they were out of sight at times. Closer to the ground I had lice through my clothes again and they were hellishly hard to get rid of. But I also got some tobacco for a smoke and, of all things, a letter with a photo from Jessie Scott.

The doctors were more concerned than ever over the physical state of the 6000-odd men in the camp, especially of those in the hospital. Nearly everyone was constantly losing weight and, in most cases, it was simply a matter of life and death: a matter of survival. Approximately 200 had been picked out to receive a little extra food. Just not enough was coming in to sustain life over any length of time. I had been getting weaker every week. Being one of the 200, I was strictly confined to the ward, not that I had any desire to go out anywhere. Receiving the extra food, at the expense of the rest of the patients, I would have been very foolish and wrong to waste it, using up energy unnecessarily. Things were quiet though and even a Korean guard shooting himself in the hospital area failed to cause any commotion. Curly and the boys would visit me when they were well enough themselves and yarning and reading, when we could, filled in the day. I was in fact wasting away with malnutrition and some blood disease. Again I kept my mind active by writing up my diary, reading and studying French, to try and overcome the deterioration of body strength and weight. This was notwithstanding that I was on a supplementary diet in the hospital. It was the same willpower that had sustained me on the Burma railway but this time it seemed that it would have to be maintained for a very long time if I was to win out in the end.

An attempt had been made to curtail the money-lending practices that went on in the camp. This was by way of Promissory Notes to be honoured at home. Rates of exchange were lower than 8 Japanese Singapore dollars to the £1. At the inflated prices a pound should have been worth $120 but the supply and demand fixed the price, often at two to four dollars to the pound. Some had money to lend, most of us had nothing. The risks taken, in most cases, to accumulate any sort of a bank made the money itself that much more valuable. There was the added risk of bad debts, for, apart from the borrower being alive it was questionable if the PNs, IOUs and cheques would be enforceable at law. For all that, many men had made a considerable amount of money in various ways since we had been prisoners, mostly from thieving from the Japanese military installations and selling on the black market. Quite a lot had been lent, principally to the officers, either on notes or gentlemen's agreements, to be honoured at home.

August was the month that the prophets and the optimists had been waiting for for some time past. I hoped that their predictions would come true. We had been seeing a new type of Allied aeroplane overhead: twin-fuselage Lockheed Lightnings. These cheered us up considerably, especially the contempt that they had for the Japanese defenses. It may have been that there were no defenses at all for there was no ack-ack fire nor aircraft put up against them.

On 1st August, after twelve weeks in hospital, much the same, I went back to the gaol on 'no work for a week'. No sooner had I got settled down into more congenial surroundings with my 2/30th mates than I got a fresh relapse of malaria with a positive BT+ slide. I was on quinine again. It was Japanese stuff and vile; 10 grams, twice a day for five days. It was merely a suppressive course. I was thankful though that the fever was not nearly as bad as that experienced last May. The surprise though, that week, came from the 2/30th Battalion Association Insurance Fund, which apparently had become financial enough to pay those who were in hospital for eleven weeks or more. I received $11 over and above my hospital pay, which was very good. It was further evidence of the spirit within the battalion to share whatever went: danger, risk, the good and the bad. The character of the unit was unique in 8th Division of the AIF.

Out on the work parties there had been some unfortunate and disgraceful deaths among our men, while digging the Japanese defence positions. This work was always carried out regardless of any safety measures and, for the second time, a tunnel collapsed while the men were inside.

I did not know much about love but I did often wonder if it was gravity or graft that made the world go round. The Japanese commander in charge of us suggested that the watches held in safe custody be exchanged for two or three bags of rice per day, taken from the supply held in reserve. For all the lack of food, there was enough rice held back to last us until next January and which we were not allowed to touch. The scheme might have been accepted, as the present need was so great, but the offer was later cut down to small amounts of coffee, sugar, etc. (Red Cross stuff) per watch and was not worth it.

I was put on to a three-day sulphur ointment course for general skin complaints arising from the malnutrition and, for only the second time in over three and a half years, I had a hot bath in about four inches of water. It was beautiful so I followed it up with a haircut and shave, cleaned my teeth, did my washing and attacked the bloody lice in the camp disinfector. It was not that often that I was really clean.

What is happening in the world, we asked ourselves. Surely if the war goes on long enough, somebody will eventually do something. We could not even bring ourselves to put any trust in that. When one asked himself 'How long', by the view out of the window it could easily go on until *1955*. I often prayed for a bloody big explosion or something like that to liven things up. I was looking forward to going back to the gaol in the following week for a change and hoped to manage to stay there on 'no duties' for a week or so. But I was certainly getting thin; my waist measurement was down to 22 inches and I weighed 6 stone 6 lbs (90 lbs still). Curly was down with a relapse of MT malaria and was not feeling too good either.

At the canteen, expenditure had been curtailed to only our Japanese pay, per man. It was all very well for the officers to be limited to $20 but we only got $1.50. It was just another example of the officers putting it over us. But then, on Friday night, 10 August, there was a 'ripple' going through the camp, making even the pessimists wonder. Close now, I believed.

13
Marking Time

11 August

It's all over!! Since dawn some wonderful furphies had spread through the camp. 'They've packed it in!'. At first flatly disbelieved; it was too long in coming and we were too sceptical and disillusioned to believe it. Then, 'It might be true'. 'Colonel Dillon is in conference with Murai', 'All Japan wants is to retain their sovereignty', 'They say it is true', 'We've to carry on as usual'. There were no demonstrations of jubilation all that morning, 'It's right all right', 'I can't believe it', 'It's hard to realise', 'It's too big', 'Been too long coming', 'We've been fooled too often'. So it went on but it did seem to be fact, even though there had not been anything to prove it or show it by 12 o'clock. It would not sink in until we actually saw the Union Jack over the gaol, our planes arriving with the staff to take over the administration, a large increase in rations from the reserve stocks and Red Cross dumps in town or something that we could see and grasp.

Of course it shook our nerves up a bit and made the heart palpitate but there was no exuberance, cheering or anything like that; we had been listening to rumours and official news for three and a half years and it would take more than words to convince us of even our freedom. We talked of home and our people a lot that morning for there was sure to be a lot of rejoicing there. I was sorry for the relatives and friends who would shortly hear of boys who had died as prisoners of war: many thousands of them. It made us wild and bitter to think of the way so many of our mates had gone, not to mention the cruelty we, who were still alive, had borne. The hatred we had for the whole Japanese nation would never die. I only hoped that our authorities could get hold of Toyiama and other Japanese and Koreans, who were listed as war criminals. I was not usually vindictive.

That afternoon was very quiet and there was not the slightest difference to any other day; in fact the whole thing was one big query mark. A rather dubious reaction had set in by tea time for it was too big a thing for us to swallow in one gulp, after so long. There had been no changes to our routine that evening and we learnt that the Emperor had agreed to the Potsdam terms but their War Minister had ordered the troops to fight on. So was it the biggest day in our lives or wasn't it?

That night I signed a new will, which I had arranged to be drawn up a short while previously when the future looked so bleak and being in Singapore was by no means a good insurance risk. I left £200 to Neil, £200 to Curly Hardman and the rest to Mum, which should have been more than the other two amounts. I was not morbid, just prepared.

Not many of the boys got to sleep too easily that night and a lot of tobacco was smoked. Next morning the news had it that the Japanese capitulation was being negotiated and that the internees and POWs were to remain quiet for the time being. By midday next day, Sunday 12 August, we had no indication whatsoever from the Japanese commander at Changi of the outcome of two days of negotiation.

Consequently there had been no alteration to our routine at all: work parties again went out that morning, rations were unchanged and Korean and Indian guards were still at their posts.

It was all quiet on the Singapore front. We were getting impatient for something to happen. It was generally expected that the Allied fleet would arrive in Singapore within a couple of days and that then things would speed up. We thought that we would be off within a week but we had no idea where we would be taken to. Ceylon and Geraldton in Western Australia were the favourite destinations. I did not want to go home just then in the deplorable condition that I was in, underweight, unable to eat proper food, fever-ridden and God knows what else. Two months in Ceylon, just getting fit, I thought would be better. But I did want to be home for Neil's twenty-first birthday in October, which I thought we might celebrate, jointly. There were so many wonderful things ahead of us from bread and jam to reunions with those we were close to. It was all quickly approaching reality, even if, until we were right away from barbed-wire and Japanese bayonets, we would not realise our freedom properly. We had a considerable amount of mental adjustment to make after the degrading existence that we had led. Years of anxiety had left their mark.

On the Monday, three days after it was all supposed to be over, we were in a queer state. What with sleepless nights, uncertainty and reaction after the last few days of excitement, a not actually gloomy feeling but more a depressed scepticism had spread widely over the hospital where I was. I was tired, disgusted and fed up with the sounds of 'peace', 'free', 'Japanese', 'signatures', 'negotiations', etc., when nothing was happening. The whole situation was most unclear and, of all things, the brownout siren was sounded as I wrote up my diary that night. We did not know where we stood. I only wished that we had learnt nothing at all until the relieving troops entered the main gate. The phase of uncertainty, wondering if the Japanese general in command, Singapore and South East-Asia would decide to fight on, independently of Tokyo, was most aggravating and could not be over soon enough as far as the general sanity of the camp was concerned: nerves would not stand it. In the state of debility that we were in, we were not a little worked up and some were even off their food, such as it was. It may sound an exaggeration but we were not normal people after so long in confinement, discomfort and semi-starvation. It was raining and cold that afternoon too. Not a minor reason for our impatience in the hospital was that deaths were continuing to be an almost a daily affair, two being buried on Sunday and one that day, Monday 13th. It was pathetic that they died at that stage, even if they had really no chance at all, either there or at home. But there were others who still had a chance if the relieving forces came quickly enough and the Japanese did not stall.

Come Tuesday and we *had* been rather depressed and disappointed, expecting too much too soon. Most of us were prepared then to once more play the waiting game. We were more or less getting back to the state of mind that we had been in for the last month or so; in a partial trance. It made life more bearable as too vivid an imagination would have sent us off our heads. Except for the slight increase in our daily ration and the release of special foods and medicines, taken from stocks held within the camp, the routine continued exactly as it had been before. The influence of habit on the mind was very real. We were settled in our ways and thoughts and so, until a great change took place, we were prepared to go on being POWs. Such was the effect of extreme debility upon those of us in the hospital. It was the wrong way to be but it was more 'soothing'. Some men carried it too far: it had become a complex. In a surprising number of cases, men, living only day by day, had become just dense and selfish. This was especially so with those who had been in hospital for a long time. It was difficult to describe our mental state, our wits dulled by malaria and long suppression. Most of us though, especially the Australians (and the Pommies and the Dutch would admit it) had not got the feeling of mental numbness as badly as was common in the hospital. We would still view things in something like a proper perspective.

It was typical that, after writing the foregoing as to how our hopes were raised and dashed, at four o'clock that Tuesday afternoon, news was brought into our hut that this time it *was* really all over. Excitement overran the camp once again.

Peace or no peace, the troops must smoke. I had been running around, raising the wind and tracking down some tobacco as Curly and I were without a cigarette. I did get onto enough to see us through for a couple of days. I was knocked up getting around too much, for I was still as weak as a kitten. Uncertainty reigned again. The day before it had seemed so definite but time, without incident, bred doubt and that was what got on our nerves. As things apparently stood that day, the Japanese general in command Singapore had as yet received no official notification from Tokyo of any capitulation and so considered himself still at war; in no possible position to surrender his command. Although he must have known it only to be a matter of hours or days, he passed no information on to us at all and neither did he do anything to alleviate our distress in any way by releasing reserve Red Cross supplies or foodstuff, by ceasing the heavy workload upon the working parties or by reuniting the scattered working camps, so that the sick might receive better attention. As we had always thought would happen, the Japanese were squeezing the lemon dry to the very last minute.

It was still raining all day, every day and driving everyone who could under the blanket, cold and hungry. It was not the sort of weather to be cheerful. The time was spent yarning things over between mates. Curly was down with malaria and we were both listed among the more serious cases in the hospital. We expected that we would go home together in an early hospital party and looked forward to being together on the boat, not split up at our happiest period. A wave of pleasure and gratitude came over me for the mere fact of us both being alive: thankful for our own accounts and for our people at home. A little hypocritically, I thanked the Lord sincerely for having got through.

A pathetic and sudden death occurred in the ward that night of a 2/12th man from Hunters Hill. It was quite unexpected and his heart just stopped beating in his sleep. It was such a shame at that stage but there were expected to be many more. We wondered what the combined total of all the British, Australian, American and Dutch deaths among the prisoners in Japanese hands would finally be, not to mention the Chinese and native populations.

Conditions on the Wednesday, 15 August were the same and the senior officers, led by Lieutenant Colonel Dillon (who had taken over from Newey as officer in command administration, in dealing with the Japanese) took the initiative and tried to get in touch with the Japanese authorities to see if anything could be done for us and those at the Outram Road Gaol, while we waited for the formal handing over of Singapore to take place. We hoped that they would be successful. Every day was important as far as we were concerned. Changi camp had always been the principal concentration camp in Malaya and was then classed as a convalescent camp, to be governed, as far as possible, by the medical personnel. Already, I believed, a dispute had taken place between Black Jack Galleghan and Glyn White over the matter of a three-week course of discipline which Black Jack thought the troops needed to become soldiers again. He would never succeed as we, the AIF, would never have put up with it. It was important, though, that we have physical training and physiotherapy when we started to get back our weight and strength but I could not see us back on the drill ground, ever.

That evening some of the boys down near the beach observed what they thought were minesweepers cleaning up the channel. So our stocks rose again.

Patience reasserted itself, for few expected the winding up of things to be much before the end of August and consequently we stopped being disappointed each day while nothing happened. It was dismal weather still, raining every day and just the wrong conditions for what we were going through. By Friday the 17th it seemed as long since the Saturday, when things broke, as the previous three and a half years. I had had only one decent night's sleep in the last week. I was not feeling the best. The green weeds that were boiled up and called stew had little or no goodness in them and passed through me almost completely undigested. While the rations again improved slightly for the fit and light-duty men in the gaol, nothing could really be done for the sick in hospital until the ration scale, imposed by the Japanese, was abolished.

We were surprised when the anti-aircraft guns went off on the Saturday afternoon, warning off a couple of planes which, however, were too far away for us to recognise. Quite spirited it was while it lasted but soon died down. There was a sound like bombs too, but we could not believe that to be the case.

Working parties started winding down in Singapore and that evening, Saturday the 18th, the first of many then expected, arrived back at Changi. Colonel Dillon had managed to see some of the Japanese but nothing, other than the returning parties which may or may not have been connected with the Dillon party, had eventuated as yet. We lived in hope as we waited for the Union Jack to go up and the Flying Fortresses to appear overhead.

The boys were pretty generous, sharing what they had in the expectation of plenty of everything in a short while. Tobacco was short but I thought that, back home, I would give Dad a POW smoke of native tobacco rolled in a page of Gone With The Wind.

Sunday, 19 August and we jumped our first hurdle that day and the war certainly seemed to be all but over. Firstly, those in the Outram Road Gaol, which had been for military prisoners, sentenced by the IJA, were released that afternoon and brought to the hospital at Changi. Surely they must have been the happiest men in the world, some of whom, given ten years or more, had been there since 1942. Others in solitary confinement had not spoken a word but to themselves for eighteen months. They were lucky men, those alive, for so many had been shot only a short while before. These were American airmen, who had been brought down and executed for what were classed as indiscriminate bombing attacks. Secondly, Red Cross parcels were sent out to Changi for daily consumption in the future. The Japanese rice ration was increased to 500 grams (453 g to 1 lb.). This, though, the doctors considered too big a sudden increase and cut it down to 325 grams. So it looked as if I had lost my last pound in weight. I was still 90 lbs.

Other events that day were:

- The handing over by the Japanese general i/c POW camps of the internal administration of the camp to Colonel Dillon and others, while still remaining responsible for the safety and outside liaison of external matters.
- Quite a lot of men came back to Changi from other camps, including Piet 't Hart and Lex Noyon, who had both been away. All together it was expected that we would get up to 14 000 men in Changi, who Dillon intended to separate into their various nationalities to facilitate our removal. Manila, of all places, was rumoured to be the AIF destination. Possibly this was for quarantine purposes, before going home in the summer. We were not really fussy where we went as long as we got away from the Pommies and the Dutch. It was thought the first moves would be made as early as the following week.
- Finally, just before 'lights out', a packet of American cigarettes arrived, per man, completing a momentous day in my young lifetime.

I got another relapse of malaria next day. I was not in the mood to appreciate all the good things that were going on around us. The excitement and nervous strain was continuing to play hell with a lot of the men and the quinine made me pretty much the same. Curly, neither was brilliant. We would have to get malaria just then.

The boys who had been in Singapore working on the tunnels and Japanese defences had been doing it tough. The 2/30th men, doing the same thing in Johore, had worked long hard hours, besides, as usual, not getting enough to eat. Jack Stuart and Darky Nay were over to see me and they had managed to keep their heads above water and stay out of trouble. I was not a little concerned about pneumonia when we finally left the island: the weather was still foul and we felt the cold something wicked.

I learnt that some of our people were dropping Red Cross medical supplies by parachute over various places in the Far East and even in Singapore. We saw nothing of such activity but we did hear our own planes flying over. We were twelve miles from town and the civilian hospital would certainly need supplies as they had had nothing issued to them at all.

Next day I was feeling better as the quinine took hold. There was little sleep the night before as good strong coffee was plentiful as well as Camel and Chesterfield cigarettes. I started playing patience, not having a book to read. It was just as well for I had to rest up my eyes until I got a new pair of glasses. I was going the way of Samuel Pepys. I was surprised that in all the Red Cross stuff there were no playing cards: possibly a censorship restriction to guard against coded messages being sent.

There was a dearth of war news, which was peculiar. I still did not understand how we stood or what our position was. Not the least reason that I wanted things to hurry up was that I had only nine more pages left in my diary and my pencil was going down fast. There had been a colossal amount of food and clothing brought into the camp over the last few days. Obviously the Japanese wanted to fill us out and have us dressed so that our people would not see how poorly and bad we had been. Something like 10 000 parcels had come in. There must have been enough of our own foodstuff on the island to feed a regiment for ten years. It was an absolute criminal disgrace that it should have been withheld from us for five months, when our need had been most acute. I believed however that an offer of eggs on credit at 30 cents each had been declined because of the civilian needs.

I heard a report that Mark Wilson had been released from a gaol in Rangoon. Possibly the authorities at Outram Road Gaol had learnt of this and informed the AIF. Mark had been a good mate of ours in the 2/30th and I had given him up for dead a long time ago. Certainly I gave them no chance against the Burmese jungle. So it looked as if Syd Grounds, Curly Hardman, Mark and myself would be sinking a promised few beers yet. [In fact, however, this was not so and Mark had been executed in May 1943, when captured while attempting to escape.]

I was sleeping next to an ex-wealthy stockbroker by the name of John Green, who had done good work among the men over quite a period. He was one who, with Padre Duckworth and Colonel Bye, it pleased me to have met and and to have felt the respect and admiration that I thought they had so truly earned. Billy Bye, Glyn White and other senior MOs in the hospital were very much concerned over the number of men collapsing in recent weeks: heart seizures from cardiac beri-beri and the like. The last ten days had done a lot of harm, what with the excitement, sudden improvement in diet and lack of sleep. The result was that we were almost put back again to the routine of a fortnight previously and to restart again more slowly. If the rice was solely increased, unduly, it would worsen the camp wide beri-beri: if the Red Cross tinned meat and other food was increased we would all have ulcerated stomachs and if both were increased everyone would have gastroenteritis. These were common already, so the aim was to balance our diet as much as possible, in small amounts, yet maintain a proper intake as far as vitamins, protein and other factors were concerned. Although many were still hungry I thought that most of us were prepared to credit Colonel Bye with knowing best. It was not a hard imposition to put up with for a little longer. Curly and I had been affected in opposite ways by the recent events. I straight away became impatient and excited, got upset and then settled down when nothing happened. Curly was prepared to wait a while at the beginning and then, when things stayed quiet, lost patience and too became upset. It was only natural that we all took things differently.

It was on again! Sure enough in the 2/30th lines they had levelled off a parade ground and erected a flagpole. I had no doubt that the officers and sergeant-majors would start annoying the men as soon as possible. At least the AIF was on its own again, away from the bloody Pommies and Dutchmen, although a non- aggression pact was understood between the Poms and ourselves against the filthy Dutch native troops. It was impossible to cooperate with them when they continued to be so dirty at the latrines, and for example, to raid the garbage heaps at the kitchens and bring back to the hospital ward piles of empty tins and clean them out with their fingers, regardless of flies. It had happened that morning. Many were brought into the hospital with diarrhoea, caused by gluttony and their dirty habits. It made us wild when genuine cases had to be moved out to make way for them. In the hospital we were all mixed up but the AIF had been separated in a camp outside the gaol, where the officers were back with the men.

The new clean clothing that we got was all cheap Japanese stuff and came in all sorts of colours; vests, singlets, shorts, socks and G-strings. I was wearing a blue shirt and white underpants. It felt good to be in clean clothes, especially of a respectable colour after so much khaki in the last four years. Four years! My God. I was an old soldier. But the new clothing brightened up the hospital in more ways than one.

Smoking was still important to us and things brightened up with the issue of ten Chesterfields each. I could not enjoy them yet and thought that maybe it was the quinine. Some of the boys reverted to the native tobacco and cigars to get any satisfaction.

As far as forecasting our immediate future, we were prepared to wait until the end of the month for 'Linger Longer Louis', a not very respectful term for Lord Louis Mountbatten. Time was moving faster, however, as we got more sleep and that something was occurring each day. It was good to yarn and talk to boys who we had not seen for a while.

We had lost track of world events but surely things were progressing and not unduly delayed. I could not see why, with an atom bomb in one hand and a pen in the other, that it should take three weeks to make the Japanese sign. But it seemed that it would.

An official conference was held on Friday, 14 August between Colonel Dillon and General Saito, the Japanese general in command POWs. We were assured that the war was really over and that first we could expect an airdrop of medical supplies, doctors and orderlies (malnutrition experts) at any time from 5 p.m. that day. It was also conveyed that we could lift the brown-out, have our own concerts and gramophones again, make as much noise as we wanted to and have our own bugle calls once more. I looked forward to a good concert. We were also to receive a packet of Japanese or Chinese cigarettes a day, which was most important. At the same time that the belated attention was paid to us, it was aggravating still, to think that a lot of it could have been done much earlier. Better late than never I supposed; most of us were still alive to appreciate it. I even received a blanket that afternoon as my old Japanese cotton one had been in bits for months.

We were still pretty much restricted; food, water (a problem for nearly 14 000 men then at Changi), hospital visiting and working parties. Camp duties continued as regards maintenance and bore-hole digging, while work in the gardens was confined to cropping the vegetables as they ripened. The camp, as a whole I thought, was behaving very well. There was a bit of garden snatching and coconut scrounging but no serious incident had occurred for a fortnight, which was quite remarkable.

Although we did not much recognise one guard from another, there were individuals who had made a practice of making our lives as unbearable as possible. These we could have picked out but they were all taken well away and lost to us. We had too much on our minds to start exerting any vindictiveness. I did not know what would have happened if I or any of the boys had caught up with them, but as long as everybody remained sober I thought that trouble would be avoided. As far as we were concerned, anyway, it was the Chinese who were going to be out to get their own back and heaven protect the Japanese that they got their hands on. I knew that I would not have wanted to be a Japanese in Singapore for the next five years.

I realised that in every hospital ward that I had been in as a POW someone at least had died, except the Eye Ward, at Changi, last May, when I thought it was going to be me. I found out that the fever I had then was akin to malaria (a microbe infection of the bloodstream) but much more virulent and severe. With the inadequate pathological equipment available they were unable to identify the species accurately but it was definitely the worst, in its effect, that they had come across, in me and others. The M&Bs were a drastic cure but effective.

Curly Hardman had been having relapse after relapse of malaria for six weeks, sometimes not throwing a positive slide but mostly of the MT variety. We were treating it casually enough but it was possible that the continuing relapses were storing up serious trouble for us later in a colder climate. In peacetime it had been treated with a great deal of respect but at that time it was nothing to go to the latrine in the rain in the middle of the night with a temperature of 102°.

On 15 August it had been three and a half years as prisoners. A big flag was laid out on the padang on the Saturday with the large letters 'P' and 'W', so that it could be picked out easily from the air for any supply drops by parachute. It was not likely that any airdrops would fall within the camp as it was only a quarter mile square around the gaol, holding 14 000 people. Apparently the POW sign was something that we should have had all along and was then put down for the benefit of any Red Cross officials who may come to the camp.

I had a Yank seaman beside me in hospital, who was one of the plutocrats in the camp. We had found it pretty easy to get along with Americans during the time as prisoners and if I were to go to Manila from Singapore, I was sure that I would have a good time. It had been expressed that the American government wished to return the hospitality given to their troops in Australia. If we were not to go straight home, I hoped that it would turn out that way.

It was good to have the gramophone going again and have a bit of music in the ward. I still liked to hear the old Bing Crosby records. We had a singsong that night too, not that I particularly liked singsongs but I did look forward to a concert that was being organised.

And finally on that day, Saturday, our aircraft came and went like everything else we expected—they didn't.

The shocking weather did not let up. We all had colds or slight flu and with nothing in the way of clothing or medicines to get any warmth or relief from pneumonia; it was a serious threat. Pneumonia had killed many at Kanburi, in Thailand, and we would have to be careful too.

That Sunday I shaved myself for the first time in 1945 (once in 1944 and about three times in 1943). The camp barbers had always been skilled and some had taken great pride in how quickly they could get the whiskers off. One I remembered took about ten seconds and no more than a dozen strokes. He went through a batch of fifty of us in no time. I hoped to get a razor and a blade now that we were getting to be half-civilised. One practice I had always endeavoured to carry out during the last three years had been to 'dress' for tea at night, keeping a change of clothing for the evening. There had been a psychological as well as a cleanliness intent, which most of us, fortunately, had adopted all through. We had been forced to behave like coolies during the day and at least we could maintain our self-respect, among ourselves, at night. This had been an important factor in the matter of morale, which always had been remarkably high. British prestige had certainly fallen off but I felt that they would be appreciated in the future, as never before, by the Chinese.

Sunday night saw a pretty large Thanksgiving church service. I was amazed at the attendance. There were a lot of hypocrites, sanctimoniously thanking God for their deliverance and nice clean clothes, who had not previously expressed any great Christian principles.

Offers came from General Saito of:
 • The leading hotels and private homes for the civilian internees.
 • Alexandria Hospital for the seriously ill POWs and internees.

These were declined for the present as it seemed, from orders from outside, we were to stay where we were and that the medical specialists at Changi could not be spared for detachment to another hospital until relieving doctors took over. The Japs had agreed to supply us with a short-wave radio receiver 'as soon as possible'. Amplifiers had been rigged up at various parts of the camp and so no one wanted to move. We looked forward soon to getting good radio entertainment as well as the news broadcasts. We were certainly amazed when a load of fresh Australian butter came in from the Singapore Cold Stores in town. It must have been there for four years at least. It was quite as fresh as the day it was packed.

Pieter 't Hart was over to see me and came to light with some coffee beans. It was the best present I had received for a very long time for I really did like strong black coffee. I was thinking of presents and what I would buy Curly, Neil, Ron, Mum and Dad, really good things when I got back.

But where was our fleet?

On Tuesday, 28 August, an Allied Liberator (or what we thought was a P24) came over twice, circling very low and dropping leaflets to us. We could easily see them taking photographs and there was a lot of waving from each side. It was certainly a huge plane, a four-engine/twin rudder bomber and the prettiest sight I had ever seen. Three or four loads of leaflets were dropped, in Japanese, Malay, Tamil and English, giving instructions to prisoners, internees and guards.

```
TO ALL ALLIED PRISONERS OF WAR

The Japanese Forces have surrendered unconditionally and
the war is over. We will get supplies to you as soon as is
humanly possible: make arrangements to get you out:
distances involved: some time before we can achieve this.
```

You will help: act as follows:

1. Stay in your camp.

2. Start preparing nominal rolls.

3. List urgent necessities.

4. If starved or underfed for long periods DO NOT eat large quantities of solid food. Those really ill or very weak: fluids, use rice water, boiled best. Gifts of food from local population, cooked. We want you back home, quickly, safe and sound, not wanting to risk your chances from diarrhoea, dysentery and cholera at this stage.

5. Local authorities and/or Allied officers will take charge affairs in a very short time. Be guided by their advice.

It was all sweet music to our ears and it was no wonder that tails were high.

The Japanese had been instructed to give no interference whatsoever to the medical and staff officers, to supplies and to receiving sets, which were expected to be landed. We looked forward to developments and something new each day. Fortunately, we at Singapore were sitting in the front-row seats, so expected things to break very soon. I did not get the strength of the 'distances involved'. Surely it was not too much to expect things to break by the weekend; it was then Tuesday.

Local representatives of the Red Cross carried out an inspection of the whole camp that afternoon, a thing that had never been done before and was a bit late then. Probably their main concern was for the internees, especially the children, and I hoped that they were successful in doing what they could for them.

It was amusing to think that, after waiting three and a half years and praying for the day of our release, we did not know which day it was that, technically, was our last day as prisoners of war. That is, if even then, we were no longer POWs. It was peculiar that the pamphlets, in saying that the war was over, did not inform us of which day it was. Still we were very thankful that the end had come about in this way, from Japan itself, and not, as expected by a direct assault on Malaya, which would have spilt so much blood, good and bad. We had no fear or respect for death but we were sick of it. I knew I was . . . bloody sick of it.

Prewar prices were again in force in Singapore. Whereas a few months before, pork was something like $120 a cattie, it could be bought, I believed, for 40 cents in town, Straits Settlement currency. There was little or no value in the Japanese Singapore dollar. I was using mine up to collect a few signatures.

Many of the camp were on fluid diets. The slight change of diet, together with nervous tension, played up with everybody: gastroenteritis and colic were widespread. I knew that I had not been eating half of the food put in front of me for the last few days. I found it was more comfortable to stay a little hungry. I did though enjoy the coffee. I was up to 95 lbs and putting weight back on again. It was thought this time that we would be evacuated by air to a convalescent centre in Townsville. A nice long holiday on the Reef, on the Army, seemed almost too good to be true. The climate though, in the springtime, was just about right.

The future! There were very few of us at Changi and no doubt the world over, who were not viewing it, if not with actual trepidation, at least with wonder and concern. The readjustment of returning soldiers to civilian ways of life is always considerable and more traumatic than 99% of people at home would realise. It was not a thing to happen overnight. It was a serious factor, which had caused trouble after all wars, with faults on both sides and a personal problem in many homes. I only prayed that when I returned home, we all would show some understanding.

Thursday, 30 August and it was another big day. Liberators were over again at daybreak that morning, this time dropping six officers and orderlies, with supplies. They immediately commandeered a truck and came straight to our camp at Changi. They were members of an Air Division in Ceylon (Red Beret men) and it was wonderful to see them. They virtually took charge of things as an advance guard. They sure had the right attitude to the Japanese, who immediately recognised their authority and it certainly made a big difference to be carrying a cannon around on the hip. They had a busy first day and had not been able to tell us much about the outside world. In a screed issued that night they intimated that they were principally an occupation force and not concerned much with the repatriation of prisoners and internees. They were disgusted with our meal at teatime: pig food they called it and bad pig food at that. We *were*, though, in a better way than they expected. As I had written before, the Japanese were cunning, as a fortnight before we were in rags and by then at least our skinny ribs were covered up with new clothing. But they could give us no probable date of our evacuation, which was what we were interested in most. I certainly had not expected events to take the time it had since 11 August. Our hopes and expectations had been raised so high that day, that it seemed one disappointment after another since then. We were too impatient.

The planes were over again in the afternoon, circling the drome (our efforts there had already proved useful) and again dropping many crates by parachute. I was cursing the loss of my glasses as I could not see all that was going on. That afternoon also, the news was read over the amplifiers at four o'clock. This was quite a change from the old days when it was done in small groups behind closed doors. It seemed that the peace documents were being signed all over the Far East; that the Navy was in Penang and that minesweepers were on their way to Singapore. We were very disappointed that they were unable to pick up the BBC news direct. It would be another marvellous milestone when we could listen to it ourselves again.

That day the pages of my makeshift diary from my letters ran out and I continued with sheets of paper as I could find them.

The end of August and still another sleepless night. I actually spent the hours from 12.30 to 3.30 in the morning writing out the P.O.W. Rubaiyat, an excellent adaptation of Kayham/Fitzgerald to army and war conditions. Without a doubt it was the best literary work that I had come across, which had originated in a POW camp. It was so poetic that the author should have died in Thailand, when the whole tenor of the poem was focused on inevitable death.

Big Douglases and Liberators were daily affairs and better than any tonic to us. Surely, we thought, it won't be long now, when one need not be a racketeer to own a cigarette lighter or an officer to wear a pair of shoes. I did receive a scout hat, a pullover, a white handkerchief and two 'Australia's', all very new and handy. I wondered if I would get my plate, knife and fork home. I wanted to. With my wallets, they were all that I intended to take home with me. [The wallets were too bug ridden to bring home, the plate and the fork got left somewhere but the knife is still in regular use in the kitchen drawer.]

It surprised us that afternoon when, looking down at the guardhouse, we saw that the new Japanese and Korean guards were gone but later it gave us a bigger shock to see them back again. It seemed that there was a difference between Lieutenant Colonel Dillon and Lieutenant Wishart (the newcomer), the former taking them off and the latter putting them back again. He thought that there were none in the camp healthy enough for guard work. The Japanese guards, instead of keeping us in, had to keep their own out. Another mystery was a Lieutenant Colonel who was dropped by parachute on the 28th and had not been heard of since.

Maurrie Ferry, my mate from Liverpool days and an ex sub-editor on the *Sun*, was kept pretty busy as the 'Press' representative and was no doubt accumulating plenty of material for a series of articles in the papers at home. Overseas news was coming through frequently and the reception was very good, especially from Ceylon and India. The short-wave sets that were recently installed were excellent.

August 31 was the Dutchmen's' big day (Queen's Birthday) and the camp was turned over to them. The big news of the day was that two New Zealand pilots were forced down at Kalang Airport, had grabbed a car and came up to visit us at Changi. They were to go out again next day so they would be the first to report personally as to how they found us. Late that night nominal rolls were prepared.

Next day we were allowed down to the beach for a swim but it was too far for most of us in our ward to make it. It was unfortunate for I would have liked to have gone.

The new OC was very critical of the way some of the things were done down at the kitchens and around the camp and was having some changes made. He was a young lieutenant of twenty-three years of age and not frightened to speak his mind either to us or to the Japs. He was very outspoken at a conference the previous day, treating General Saito as a lance-corporal and putting Colonels Holmes, Galleghan and Dillon in their place. He considered them the same as the rest of us, and not healthy enough to carry any administrative job. As I had thought often and as he intimated, we smelt. I was not surprised. Thank God though that a man like Lieutenant Wishart had come in. Habits were ingrained in us after so long and the Japanese domination was not completely abolished from our minds. I could not imagine Holmes or Galleghan commandeering Saito's car and backhanding Japs like they should have been treated. A few of our boys, including me I thought, would have liked to have had a go at them but we were in no position to do so. Lieutenant Wishart also intended getting outside labour, Chinese and Tamils, for our camp kitchens and fatigue duties, which was a good idea.

Newspapers turned up that Saturday, 1 September, too. It was a daily sheet, printed for South-East Asia Command Forces and the edition we got was especially printed for us. They were dropped with canisters of Australian Comforts Fund parcels. A condensed diary of the war in the paper was most interesting and, although we had never been out of touch with outside events by secret radios, even in Thailand receiving the news, we had not really got a clear view of things. From the parcels I received a razor and a blade so I was happy.

The New Zealanders left in their Mosquito bombers and did they go? Coming up the garden valley in front of the gaol, they had to rise to clear the gaol wall and bank to go between the tower and the two main four storey blocks of cells, travelling at a helluva speed. [It was so exciting that I can still see them.] They took no nominal rolls with them for their visit seemed to have been against the rules and was possibly a put up job.

Curly and I finished a great day at our first concert for months.

Sunday: 2 September 1945

'Oh! God at last, today's the last day of the war'.

The surrender ceremony of the Japanese, on board the USS *Missouri*, in Tokyo Bay, was broadcast in the camp that morning; a pen by pen description. At night, after the overseas news, we heard a recording of the opening passages of Truman's speech at the White House and parts of the King's speech to the Far East.

Six years! It had been a long time since Ron and I were listening to the news of the invasion of Poland, that Friday night, and what changes had taken place since then. Not one, though, that I regretted as far as I knew. I worried at times if there was any bad news waiting for me. Doubtless it was the same at home, probably more so, anxious that I was still alive. I was sure, however, that everyone at home had a wonderful time that weekend. Mountbatten promised to get us out just as soon as he could and although Penang was first, surely Singapore would be next. Both the Mountbattens had a good reputation and there seemed to be a more personal atmosphere between the commanders and the men in the services, which was a very good thing. In fact the whole tenor of the war and the armies had changed since the turning of the tide at Port Moresby. We, I supposed, will be looked upon in the 'Old Contemptibles' class, the poor bastards who were in it too early. Martyrs or mules, however, it was nearly over and we had retained our self-respect, richer in the experience.

The planes were over in force, dropping canisters by parachute. These contained mostly Australian Red Cross parcels and were a personal gift from the men at Cocos Islands. It was apparently unofficial and was the probable reason for the planes not landing. They were the first personal Comforts parcels we had seen and it was very good of them.

The main thrill of the day was another two Mosquito bombers, which were put through their paces over the camp. God! If they were bombers what the hell were the latest fighters like? They were the most marvellous kites we had ever seen and the beautiful way they were handled was pretty to watch, with the lovely streamlining of the fuselage, and two engines, set in the wing.

Some guerillas turned up at the gaol that morning too. Australians, British and Chinese, armed like a battleship. They had been operating undercover on the mainland in Malaya, keeping in contact with SEA Command and waiting for things to break out on the West Coast (where we expected the invasion to come from to retake Singapore).Those Commandos could not get enough credit and recognition in my opinion. Boys, who had escaped from this and other camps, also turned up at various points as well. It had been too hard to escape from Changi and very, very few had made it since the first two weeks in February 1942.

This was a fateful day in my life, hoping and praying for things to come, for a new future in a new world.

We were starting to get somewhere. At noon on 3 September the colours were broken and the Union Jack, the Stars and Stripes and the Netherlands flag flew over the gaol. It was really gratifying and made us feel good, just to look at them. It was like a knife cut between what was and what is, placing the frightfulness of the last three and a half years in the past. Many Chinese and British flags were seen in town too, but mostly the Chinese natives were remaining indoors. The Japs still had the old people, who were left, bluffed and they too were waiting for Mountbatten. I heard on the radio that he wanted Government House ready by the 5th. I would have liked to have gone down to Fairy Point to see the fleet come in.

Some more British officers arrived by air, including the missing Lieutenant Colonel, bringing with them radio transmitters. They were then in continual touch with HQ SEAC, which was still in Burma, I thought. I did learn that Gary Cooper and Bob Hope had been in Australia and wondered when it was. Though the flags were flying and the weather had improved with the new era (it had been beautiful the previous night and that day) I had been feeling pretty ill, could not eat and the coffee was the only thing that I really enjoyed. I had a bastard of a night that night. Pain: I thought I would burst. The trouble was the gastroenteritis, caused, among other things, by the change in diet. I just could not take it. So back on to the fluids I went. It had spread throughout the camp, as we had been warned, but there was nothing we could do about it. I had lost my Bondi tan after four months in hospital, I was confined to the camp and not allowed out but it was no time to be woeful.

That night we got some proper medicines for the various things we had wrong with us. We also had picked up on the radio that Mountbatten, the new Supremo, had ordered the Japanese Commander to come and meet the *Sussex*, next day, at a rendezvous off the island. This was to prepare for the reception of the occupation troops without incident or opposition. Next day, when a crowd of the boys returned from a day in town, they told us that they saw the *Sussex* or the *Cleopatra* off Collyer's Quay, although so far no troops had landed. Still, the Navy was there.

We continued to get cigarettes and stuff from the boys on Cocos Island; one of them even sent his half-used tobacco tin. I received an English Comforts bag, which I split with Curly and kept the razor blades to myself. Visits were made to the Sime Road Internment camp by some of our boys and I gave my cigarettes to be taken there and handed around. Some wives came out to Changi, too, by commandeering a car and there were the first-time reunions of couples that had been looked forward to so much. Those coming back to camp also said that they had never seen the native population of Singapore so excited and their enthusiasm was unprecedented. There were smiles from ear to ear. The internees were happy too, as we were (except that soldiers always look for the catch if something nice happens). As was definitely expected, there had been trouble. Many Malays and Sikhs, both mistrusted and hated, were knifed and murdered in other ways, in town. I would hate to have a Chinaman have it in for me. But it seemed best to let them score off their own debts by themselves, before the British crowd took over. I did not know of any incident involving any ex-POWs in retaliatory actions against Korean or Sikh guards or Japanese soldiers.

As it was when the Japanese came on to the island, we were again having trouble with the water supply. Ordered to reduce their numbers to a minimum, the Japanese maintenance crew just walked out of the pumping and power stations and water was restricted everywhere. We could wash only between the hours of six and seven o'clock at night. It was typical of them.

Meanwhile the camp had been wired up with a public-address system and of an evening we had an excellent radio service of local and overseas news as well as gramophone records from within the camp. Listening to a variety program on the radio it was apparent that English jazz drummers *still* had not got past the washboard stage. I was listening to a specially arranged show of old and new songs for released POWs by the BBC, including Benny Goodman's 'Bach Goes to Town', when it was suddenly cut off. God! I swore. But by the end of the week we expected big things. Bloody big things, like the *Queen Mary*.

It was good to see Curly come bursting up to me on the Wednesday morning, feeling like a million dollars. I owed him a lot: material and moral obligations.

We had an order read out: 'Any tins of pineapple issued recently marked "NANIS" or "CHERMIN" are to be returned to the QM store immediately as they contain incendiary explosive'. It was the sort of thing the Japanese or the Chinese would do. Sabotage. Beautiful! We were already blown up in the stomach anyway. We had learnt more of the atrocities which the Japanese had done to white men and women at the Outram Road Gaol too.

Directly from my diary: *'I do really think that this war has ended too early (fortunately for us). The Jap has not received a big enough thrashing. Not sufficiently anyway to bring defeat home to the gullible, thick-headed, child-like, Emperor worshiping masses. This peace is wrong — they haven't the intelligence to appreciate tolerance, humanitarianism and understanding, for a big belt over the face is the only way to make any impression on them. Though no authority, I do think I know the Japanese temperament better than most people and I honestly think that, for our future good, they have been let off too lightly. Sincerely I write this, not through a feeling of vindictiveness but mistrustful that their next generation will remember the defeat of this one. The Germans I do think should get a fair deal but these people are not worthy of it, are not a civilised 20th century race'.* [Time will tell if my thoughts then were right, not for this generation of Japanese but in the future; if latent militarism will resurface, with the same Samurai outlook and aims of expansion as of 1935 to 1945.]

At 3.45 p.m., Indian troops commenced landing in Singapore. They were supposed to have received *no* guarantee of non resistance, so took over on invasion lines, disarming Japs at gunpoint as they came across them and made them sit down on the road, to be picked up later. Another battalion was expected to occupy the Changi area next day. We did pick up an order by radio to Singapore concerning the arrival of a DC4 at the Kalang Airport, next day also, to pick up 40 Americans. They were fortunate as there were only about 60 of them left on the island. When the first Associated Press men came in that evening we were given to understand that our movement would begin in three or four days time. It was expected that it would take a little while to unload all the transports in port and fit them up for the evacuation of the British troops. At the same time it was thought that the AIF would start leaving soon.

Many more reporters and photographers came into the camp, including the first white girl we had seen for many a long day. She was a New Zealand WAAC. Of course she made for the showers and saw us as we really were, not much of us. There was a bit of embarrassment and swearing among the boys. I did not really think that we were ready for nurses and women, as yet, but give us time!

The camp monies, canteen capital, our August pay and other private donations were given to native charities in town. It came to quite a considerable sum but was in Japanese dollars of course, whatever they may have been worth. Of more value were to be the camp chickens and other material items, which were to be distributed similarly when the camp was disbanded. I did hope that the incoming troops would not be antagonistic to the Chinese in Singapore, after they had been so wonderfully good to us. There were many debts that we would have liked to repay.

That night, 6 September, we went back on to Singapore time. There would be no actual change in the daily routine for our schedule had always been ruled by the sunrise and the sunset; the hours they were called made no difference. The Japanese exploited every hour of daylight.

It was good to see the Yanks leave that afternoon and later fly over the camp in a huge Douglas Skymaster. Later we received airmail letters to write home but I was afraid that my first letter was a little disjointed and disappointing. I hoped however that it would be home within a week or ten days. I determined that my next letter home, from a hospital somewhere, would take reams and reams. Meanwhile I awaited a letter from home.

Reporting by the press started as they mixed amongst us. They listened to stories, truth, lies and bullshit, of hardship suffered, especially by the officers! — of the direct beatings and atrocities inflicted by Japanese guards on POWs and of the more widespread and effective suffering caused by the inhuman policy of their High Command in regard to the withholding of food, medical supplies and Red Cross parcels as well as the workloads upon working parties. These could never be exaggerated, for the English language could not adequately describe the extent of all that had occurred. What could be described in plain language was the greed, selfishness, fear and cowardice shown by some officers, particularly English officers, at the expense of the other ranks. I could not remove from my mind the officers at Neike, who stayed inside their tent all the time, fearful of any contact, while the rest of us suffered. That was a story that will never be fully known.

The word brassiere on the BBC? That is progress.

The talk was all of repatriation:
- British personnel were thought to be already embarking from Kranji Hospital.
- 1000 British patients from Changi hospital were chosen for air travel.
- The last of the Americans flew out and their evacuation had been a credit to them.
- It was quiet, unbelievably quiet as far as the Australians were concerned.

The civilian population was wild with excitement and could not do enough for us. Parties into town were organised but the kampongs or villages throughout the island were out of bounds. This was especially so after the occupation forces had come into the Changi area.

We learnt that about a month or six weeks previously, which would have been about the middle of July, plans were laid for a Commando force to come in under fire and get us out (the couple of us who might have still been alive), while the main campaign to retake Malaya and Singapore was in progress. There was a setback and change to the program, seemingly caused by a mistrust of the local population as to the degree of cooperation they might receive. There was a recognised anti-imperial element, particularly in Malaya, and the incoming forces did not know the extent of the opposing local forces, irrespective of the Japanese. It brought about the 'prepared for anything' manner of the eventual entry of the incoming troops, even though the war was over.

Our girlfriend, the New Zealander, Christine North, who had come in with two .45s and a knife on her belt, wearing slacks and a shirt, said that the first hospital ships would be leaving in the following week. However, we knew, in fact, that the RAPWI unit [Repatriation of Allied Prisoners of War and Internees] stood for Retain All Prisoners of War Indefinitely. Shipping we understood was the problem, but it was just that we were keyed-up and ridiculously over-anxious, living by the minute far too much. When it was said that mobile cinemas and concert parties were on their way we knew that we were in for a long wait. I wondered if I would hear some of our Concert Party crowd on the radio and in shows at home: John Frank Woods, Slim de Grey, Jack Geohagen and Syd Piddington. Probably, I thought, for they really were good.

On Saturday 8 September we were addressed over the camp radio by General Christison, C in C, Malaya. He gave an excellent short speech to us, sobering but to the point:

Firstly. Sunday, 9 September at 9.30 a.m. was to have been our D Day. (Thank Christ the atom bomb and the Japanese surrender came first or, without a shadow of doubt, we would have been slaughtered. This order of events was the most important thing in my life for if our forces had attacked a month earlier I would have been, by this date, dead.)

Secondly. He made it clear that his forces were operational troops, whose primary role was not to evacuate POWs, though they did everything they could for us. Ships in Singapore, he said, would start re-watering and oiling to take us away in a day or two.

Now we knew where we stood and were a lot easier in our minds. We had been experiencing a lot of 'firsts for a long time', the Union Jack, white girls (I got Dorothy Cranston to sign a five dollar note for me that day), radios, and the latest that afternoon was a loaf of white bread. I only saw it but even then it was beautiful. The water shortage was again acute, the worst it had ever been, in fact. It was bad when one could not wash. That evening we had a surprise and the band from HMS *Sussex* turned up and played us some 'after dinner' music. It was good of them to come all the way out and it was quite a change for the boys who liked that sort of band music. I was always a jazz fan. What cheered us up even more, was the news that the *Manunda*, from Australia, had docked and that Australian troops would be embarking in a couple of days. That was the news that we had been waiting for. While all this was going on fifteen trucks brought out our rations for Monday, real army rations, not rice and weeds, and we would go on to civilised meals. At last.

Those lucky enough to get into town, lawfully and otherwise, continued to get a right royal time from the fleet and native population. Wally Mason of the 2/30th had a great day looking up a Chinese family who had been good to him during the 'scrounge' days at the Great World back in 1942. And the last thing that night was that we listened to descriptions of marches of the Allied forces through Berlin and Tokyo and learnt that the Japanese were starting to clean up the streets in Singapore, exactly as the British had been made to do after Percival's surrender.

There was a lot that was new to us, apart from the latest aircraft. 'Jeeps' did just the job they were made for: small, fast and terrific acceleration. The left-hand drive made them look strange to us.

The trouble in town was getting serious. It was all very well for the Chinese Communists to sabotage and be a nuisance to the Japanese administration but, naturally I supposed, they did not want to stop their gangsterism, just because the war had ended. They were a menace to the community. Looked upon as bandits by the new military government, it was going to be a big job to bring them under control. Malaya particularly, and Singapore, would not know peace for a good while yet. I expected that it would be the same in Europe as, after all wars, the malcontent element is always the last to settle down after wartime licence.

The RAPWI organisation stated definitely that there would be no priority of nationalities or of officers over the men in the matter of evacuation, but in fact it went by the board. A planeload of British officers and WOs had left that morning. As yet the AIF men in the hospital had not even been classified and listed for embarkation.

Most of the boys in the unit were getting around, near and far and some of the fitter ones had even been up in a plane. Unfortunately Curly and I were not feeling up to it, much as we would have liked to have got about a bit: a bastard of a time to be sick. Gerry Baily and a couple of the 2/30th boys were doing it properly, car and all, until they got caught. By then the cruiser in town was known as the 'Hotel Sussex'. I learnt of another bloody disgraceful piece of work that day too. Major Johnston had the hide to put AWL [absent without leave] in Mark Wilson's records, after he had escaped from No. 1 camp in Thailand. The audacity to cast a slur on him, when he had more courage in escaping (if not more sense) than 99.9% of the rest of us, was incomprehensible.

I did not get on to much news that night for the world and our camp ran on electricity and that had failed: no radio, no news, no lights. I went to sleep early. It was like that for a while; you simply could not get to sleep and then you made up for it day and night.

Monday, 10 September was an extra good day; I even had bread, butter and jam. I took on the mess orderly job to help the ward out and the exercise was good. Ever since leaving Australia in the *Aquitania* I had attracted the mess orderly task at various times. Maybe I was trusted. For entertainment we had an army show, which put on a great act for an hour or so: male and female. The canaries [female singers] were out of the box for good looks too and our 'Judy Garland' would have stamped his foot in jealousy. Pieces of fluff were something it took a while to get used to; it made us feel good, just to see them, which, I imagined was quite an embarrassment for the girls too, hardened as they might have been, being so much with the troops.

It had sunk in by then that we were no longer coolies to the IJA. We could enjoy ourselves. The star turn of the day was an extra good film that night by a mobile talkie unit. Even sitting on an old suitcase, Curly and I, unable to see much or hear it all, we still thoroughly enjoyed *Thousands Cheer*, an all-star MGM line-up. It was just the sort of film for the troops and was really good. Of course the Hollywood/Max Factor beauty of the actresses, the sex appeal and the chorus girls had us right in; we, the veterans of the Bangkok-Moulmein railway, tough, hardened, cynical. We thought that we were past all that. That day made us realise how much we had missed female company and what was in store for us, and them. [Every time that I have since seen *Thousands Cheer* and Lena Horne on late-night television I have experienced the thrill of the first time that I saw it.] The shows bucked us up enormously and, incidentally, it seemed that boogie-woogie was popular at last. The waiting period did not seem so bad after that.

I wrote another letter home that day too, repeating most of my first letter in case it went astray. Just writing it, and the contact, cheered me up. Writing up my diary and then to bed, closed off a perfect (well hardly) day, with, if not 'wine, women and song' then peaches, women and song. For what more could a man ask under the circumstances.

The currency position in town was very serious. When the Military Administration took over the previous week they declared the Japanese notes to be worthless but as yet had not introduced any new money. Consequently most of the civilians found themselves with no money with which to buy essential goods to tide themselves over until free issues of food were organised. There was a mistake or a bungle somewhere, Japanese or British, for people must eat. Many Chinese and Malays came through the camp at Changi, cleaning the place up of food, clothing, tins, anything at all, for the Chinese do like to collect junk. We favoured the Chinese with anything going, rather than the Malays and the Indians.

Now that I had started getting around again, I walked out of the gate and past the empty guardhouse. How gratifying such a simple act was to an ex-prisoner; like a gaolbird jumping through the window. It was wonderful to walk out of the camp, a free man, and look at the barbed-wire from the outside. The exercise connected with the orderly job was doing me good, even if it made me tired at night. I was putting on weight and wanted to spread it all over and not just around the stomach. I intended to get in pretty good shape, better than I had been before joining the army, so aimed to get between 9½ and 10 stone.

That day too, we started on a course of Quinacrine, which was a suppressive and cure for malaria. They were foul-tasting tablets but a guaranteed method to guard against malaria and fever. We thought, if they really worked, it would be a wonderful advance in medical science.

Wednesday, 12 September was a great day for South-East Asia: the formal surrender of the whole southern region by the Japanese to Lord Louis Mountbatten. Planes of all types held a flypast over the island. The ceremony took place in the Town Hall but a parade was held on the big padang in town, which the Japanese working parties had been cleaning up in front of the civilian population for the last few days. Many of the boys went AWL to see it: the march of all the Empire troops, the playing of the national Anthems of the 'big five', Louis' speech, which was very good, and lastly the terrific jeers, catcalls and insults of the Chinese and the natives when the Japs left the dais. We did not hear the naval guns but it must have been the final blow to Japanese ears. Yes, it was all over, even if Asia's troubles were not.

I was busy too. Curl had received an order to stand by to move that day. He packed up all his gear (his and mine could have been wrapped up in a handkerchief) and still, all army movements orders were the same. Cancelled. Later that evening all the AIF in hospital were standing by but it looked as if we MAY get going next day: may, in capital letters and underlined.

I wrote another letter to Neil [I still have it] with a note to Ron. Very much I would have liked to write to Grandma in Scotland but was afraid to until I heard that all was well there. I hoped so. I felt that I had a lot of writing in front of me. It would be a full-time job for the first fortnight after I reached another hospital, as I did not think there was much chance of going straight home. There was so much to write about too, and yet at the same time, so much that would not be mentioned at all. Many of the things of the last three and a half years were dead and buried already, if not in mind and memory. I did not want to go raking up the past; 'dirty washing', war, army life and POW existence. I thought that it would not be understood and would make me seem like a liar. There were a lot of the men with the same view, I was sure.

It was very hard to practise self-restraint as we were like big kids with a box of matches or a bag of lollies. The Australian nurses had come in and were going over well with the boys. They had a uniform of a slouch hat, tunic, long trousers and gaiters. It was good to see them in sensible dress for the tropics.

Pandemonium reigned next day as plans were changed every half hour. What with running around all day on the mess job (I was really running on nervous energy), being on hand in case of a move, backwards and forwards to the boreholes, issues of lollies, cigarettes and matches and many other things, the radio playing swing records all the time, and seeing Curly off, I felt that if I did not get away soon I would crack up again. Curly got away that afternoon, expecting to go home on the *Manunda*. It was a pity that we were split up but I would be catching up with him again. I expected to go on board the hospital ship *Oranje* next day. Maybe all the AIF left would then go home together.

Not the least cause of the upheaval that morning was the visit to the camp by Bill Slim. He too had a great reputation I believed. But many notables were coming to Changi to see us; Lord Louis himself, General Slim of Burma Command, Countess Mountbatten and Blamey, generals and admirals galore. Out of it all we learnt that we were to get three months leave when we got back.

For the fourth night running I saw the 'show within a show' in *Thousands Cheer*. I loved it. Just as I was writing to Ron, they were playing Tommy Dorsey's 'Song of India' over the PA system. How many times had Ron and I played that record back home? It made us all feel that we were becoming civilised human beings again and not beasts of burden. Maybe it was best coming on gradually like that. I wondered if it was to be my last night in Changi. Changi, every Malayan POW's home from home.

14
Journey Home

Friday, 14 September 1945—at last I was on my way back home. That morning started off as usual and then at ten o'clock the transport convoy arrived for those AIF of us still in hospital and things started to move. Packed, farewells and we were off. I wrote my diary right up to that minute, lying in an ambulance, waiting for the rest to catch up. Yes, I left Changi on the broad of my back and looking forward to staying that way for a while yet, catching up on a bit of rest. I had just had my photograph taken on the stretcher before leaving, by whom I did not know. Maybe I would see it one day in an Associated Press publication. Goodbye Changi, the gaol, the hospital, Selarang, the whole area. After Burma and Thailand I had always appreciated it and would ever do so, picnic though it had not been. Changi farewell.

The *Oranje* was the boat for home. The last time that I had seen her was at Circular Quay, in Sydney, and I thought then that her lines were the best I had ever seen. Reaching the Quay in Keppel Harbour, we were showered with kindness by the nurses and staff and then, by sling, hoisted on board to a clean bed, clean sheets and clean pyjamas. It was Selarang, Christmas 1944 all over again. This time did not quite eclipse that return after Thailand but the peace and contentment on board were beautiful. Relaxation was all I asked for, for the next few days.

I was with Bull Trethern and Boonga Atkins, again of Burma association and we even got some pay. I received two good Australian Pounds. I got my peace and quiet all right for I did not feel like moving around much for a while and went onto a light diet. We started the building-up process again, right from scratch. It was the best way, I thought. Friday, 14 September I was on the 'road back'. I was lucky and I knew it.

It was a new phase, a peculiar time of mixed emotions: glad to be alive, looking forward to the family, splitting up and missing mates and army life, uncertainty as to the future, feeling a bit like a duck out of water. I was always asking myself 'What is in front of me, depending on my own resources?' It was all a little disquieting. That was how it affected me anyway. 'The road back' and then I slept.

Even yet we did not know our exact destination, although it seemed certain that we would aim straight for Australia. The *Manunda* may have gone via Labuan. The staff on the *Oranje* was kindness itself, even if, not wishing to trouble them, it was an embarrassment to ask for anything. I was afraid to dirty any of the things around me too, as nearly everything was white or cream. It was so hot, lying at anchor and I was so unused to pyjamas and sheets. Breakfast was beautiful and I wondered if we were not making ourselves slightly ridiculous the way we went into ecstasy over such simple things. I was afraid so, but it could not be helped for everyday things were just wonderful. I had written in my diary that old POW thought: 'I wonder if we are really all dead and this is Hell'. Often in writing up my diary I seemed to switch from the present to the past and it was because such powerful memories and associations could not be forgotten overnight. The present was still too strongly entwined with the past, much as we would have liked to bury all that we had left behind.

My diaries for 1941, 1942 and 1943 were buried at Selarang with other records, and events had moved too fast for me to get them back from 2nd Eschelon. The security there was much more certain, buried many feet deep in the ground, than for me to continue to carry them around and risk discovery in a thorough search. I hoped that they would be all right even if they had been underground for over eighteen months. The later years would not have been much good without the early ones but I was sure they would eventually be sent on to me and they were.

Three o'clock. We've just started moving off. *'God, Australia, here I come'*. The moment for which I had been waiting for a very long time had at last arrived. Speed was all that we asked for and this ship was fast. Eight days, it was thought, and we would be there. There! Home! Sydney and Burwood, the house on the corner and my bed on the verandah. Home. I could not say that I had finished roaming but deep down there is no place like it. No matter what a man says about it, the feeling is always there. And my home had not always been the happiest.

By now I had broken all links with Asia, where I had learnt life the hard way. Of course I was reminded of the day that I had left Europe behind, back in 1935. The water between us and the quay widened but it was a sober farewell, unlike the usual shipside scene of crowds and noise. It was as it should be, under the circumstances, thoughtful and serious: Singapore after a war and the men who had been through it. I thought that the most outstanding feature, over the last few months, was that we were *not* demonstrative, whatever I may have written about it. Feelings were pretty much kept to ourselves. It was something that I hoped would be understood when I made my reunions.

There were a lot of ships in the harbour, many more than usual and they made Singapore look something like her former self. It was a fine day too, which was more cheerful. I only hoped that the voyage would be an easy one and that we did not have the Australian Bight in front of us. I thought it more likely that I would complete the circumnavigation of Australia, started so many years before. I hoped so. I was wondering, too, if we would go north-west, around Sumatra, to miss the minefields before calling at Darwin. The China Sea would be thick with mines. It was good to be at sea, for its own sake, for, ever since I had got over the first seasickness back on 10 April 1931, I had an affectionate feeling for her.

I was a little previous about our getting under way. We were to be anchored in the roadstead, off the island, for another day. It was cooler there and it was a change from land and buildings, having the sea around us. The sun set behind one of the smaller islands and it was a scene I had always found pleasant in the tropics.

Books and magazines were brought around next morning and a radio put at the foot of my bed. The *Oranje* was a hospital ship, which had been given by the Red Cross of the Netherland Indies. The staff were, for the most part, New Zealanders and it made the Red Cross very real to us.

At twelve-thirty we were under way. It was 'Australia, here I come' this time as we swung around, backpedalled and then straight ahead. It was wonderful to see the water slip by and the islands left behind. Although I had travelled a bit in ships and trains, never was I more grateful to make an exit as that time; leaving with no regrets but looking forward to a happier time to come. 'I see a vision splendid of sunlit plains extended . . .' If maybe I would see no plains, the vision was still there.

Sunday, that first day at sea, was quiet, sleeping, reading, yarning with the boys and smoking. I intended to do a fair bit of that and not on Sundays only, but for a few weeks to come. I had quite a list of things to buy from the canteen so I added spending to the list. I expected to beat any letters home so it was no use writing.

If there is one annoying, admitted necessity, on board a ship it is boat drill. So we had boat drill and orders were to carry lifebelts at all times until further notice. That, maybe, was not a bad idea for there were possibly mines drifting in those waters so soon after the war. Lifebelts, I noticed, were improved. They came with whistles and red bulbs for detection and were made of kapok instead of murderous cork.

We received a ration card for buying sweets, chocolate, matches and cigarettes. Rationing was new to us...or maybe it wasn't, when I came to think about it. I *was* hoping to take a fair bit of tobacco home but it seemed that I would not be able to if buying was limited. Not that I was sure that smoking was doing me any good as I got a sort of tight feeling in the chest and was short of breath. I did, though, get a tin of the best pipe tobacco for Dad.

We were heading straight for Australia all right. At sunset that evening, I made it that we were heading south-south-east. In that direction we would not be going through the Sunda Strait and it would cut our time by two or three days. I looked forward to seeing Bali and maybe Timor before sighting either Arnhem Land or Cape York, whichever it was going to be. I still had hopes of seeing what Darwin was like.

That night the boys were entertaining one of the nurses in the ward with quite a few yarns of the past three to four years and, thank God, we could laugh over some of the stories by then. I was sleeping about eleven hours a day so at nine-thirty I did not hear the end of their tales.

I crossed the equator for the fourth time next day, still heading in the same direction at sunrise, if a little south of south-east.

We had received quite a lot from the Red Cross over the last few weeks in the way of personal toilet gear besides lollies, tobacco, matches and cigarettes. We had not been a great burden on them in the past so it was good to receive little gifts in the way of handkerchiefs, razors and tins of cigarettes. I had not received a parcel since I had split up the one I got by parachute but had accumulated a lot of stuff again. What I did want was chocolate, tons and tons of it although I was not allowed too much. I spent a whole 6s.4d. at the canteen. After the Japanese dollar and ten cent notes, the Australian pound felt like a tablecloth. The £2 I got would probably see the trip out. I was disappointed, however, that our army pay had only risen 1s. a day, in 1941, during the whole war. I did think that it would have gone up over the last few years, with, it seemed, the prices of everything else. I wondered how the dependents had got on if their allotment had stayed the same. Still I would have about £650 in my pay book.

There was no doubt about Colonel Billy Bye. Very ill with the change of diet that affected everyone, he still could not have been much fitter than the rest of us: yet he just could not give up attending those of us who were seriously ill. As I was writing he had just come into the ward to see one of the boys with cerebral malaria. Truly, he must be the greatest doctor ever to leave Australia and, of course, he had a huge field in which to show his worth. If ever a man deserved recognition then it was Lieutenant Colonel Bye.

18 September, routine for the day:

6.30 a.m.	Woken for temperature
6.33	Back to sleep
6.35	Woken for wash and shave
6.50	Back to sleep
8.30	Woken for breakfast
8.45	Handout of Red Cross gifts
9.00	Magazines and books to bedside
10.00	Doctors' rounds (re dentist)
10.30	Milk and biscuits
	Read till lunchtime
11.00	Padre's visit
12.30 p.m.	Lunch
1.10	Back to sleep
2.00	Malted milk
	Reading and yarning
3.30	Hot shower
	More reading and yarning
4.00	Malted milk, bread, butter and vegemite
	More reading and yarning
5.00	Funeral at sea. Ship stopped and coffin lowered
	Diary
5.30	Tea
6.30	Chocolate and read an old Women's Weekly
7.45	Malted milk and a smoke
8.00	Diary again
	Received a gift of a chocolate from an orderly
8.30	Yarning with the boys
10.00	Fast asleep

There was no doubt about it, it was a rest cure all right; we could take it. Most days were to be the same and we thought that we would not know ourselves when we hit Sydney.

I was talking to Captain Goran, one of the best of the officers. He looked a lot younger already, as many did. He said that we were going to call at Darwin, then round Thursday Island and down to Sydney. I was really pleased about that, especially if we went inside the reef.

At sunrise we were still heading in the right direction. It was the first thing we checked. Unfortunately our speed was cut down a lot as we had a little corvette travelling with us and we had to get along at her speed. We believed that we would be leaving her at Darwin and then we should be flat out again.

The scene from the rail was beautiful at night. The night, standing there smoking, was really perfect with the moon and its pathway, stretched over the water. It was so cool, I just breathed in the fresh air, finished my cigarette, turned in and slept like a babe. I always did like travel at sea: heaven on earth.

I wrote a letter to Mum [which I also still have] that morning, on the off chance that we may reach Darwin next day. It seemed more likely though that it would be the day after that, Sunday.

On the ship I was lucky enough to be amidships, immediately below the boat deck. Being high up it was beautifully cool. I was in a smaller ward of twelve beds; no portholes but we had all we wanted. The ship was wonderfully fitted out for hospital work. The staff were good sports too. Andy (Percy Anderson) looked after us and the whole staff bought us quite a lot out of their own money, besides getting us stuff from the Red Cross stores. The nurses too, could not do enough either and were far from stand-offish. Even the senior sister did all that she possibly could. It made all the difference when there was a little familiarity between the staff and ourselves. They were already, to us, both nurses and orderlies, 'one of the boys'.

Next day the doctor changed my bed, from inside to a cot and hammock out on the deck. My chest and wind did not seem to be as they should and I was out there where it was much fresher and cooler. I could look over the water all day. The vile stuff I had been smoking for the last few years sure had done my lungs no good at all and I only hoped that it had not done them any serious harm. Some months back it was even thought that I may have had TB. I would find out next day as they were going to X-ray me. I was glad of that as I would have had it done privately, if I had to, before going before the Repatriation doctors. Maybe it was something that would pass away if I gave up smoking, although I had cut it down a lot.

A collection was organised amongst us to buy presents for the sisters and nurses before we left. It was a good idea and would show our appreciation, for they were really good to us.

One remarkable thing on board was the hot freshwater showers. We were told that we were using far too much fresh water and that it may have to be cut down a bit. So we tried but could not resist the long hot showers.

September 21. It was a great day. *We were in Australian waters*. Islands were sighted early in the morning and after I had come up from the X-ray screening room, there she was: beautiful Aussie, if not quite its prettiest at this point. First the air force welcomed us, then we went through the gates in the boom and got three cheers from the crew of a minesweeper as we passed. A torpedo boat crossed our bow by feet to give us a thrill and it certainly was a good-looking craft, kicking up a helluva spray all around us. The planes and the naval craft, with Australia on the skyline were a wonderful sight to us, as could be imagined. We came to a standstill as we picked up the pilot and mail, from a boat that had come out to meet us. We had simply the most marvellous day. Unforgettable.

Approaching the town of Darwin there were dozens of launches, then, amidst the cheering, the foghorns, air-raid sirens and a band playing, we came up to the pier, which was packed. A big 'Welcome Home' sign was prominently displayed. It was emotional (although we would not admit it); it made us feel good and this was a military town. What was Sydney going to be like? At lunchtime most were allowed to go ashore for a few hours. I was confined to the ship and from the deck was talking to an AWAS [Australian Women's Army Service] driver who was down on the dock. She said that she would drive me around, so (although I knew that I should not have), down the gang plank I went, still in my pyjamas, and off to the picnic at the beach with the others. The boys in Darwin were great to talk to and the girls, more AWAS, made us feel at home. Tea, oranges and apples, scones, biscuits and pies were piled high on the tables and the beauty of the day was that it was so informal and non-militarised. Some were wearing shorts and others, like me, pyjamas of all colours, against the khaki of the boys; while some of the AWAS girls were in uniform or in costumes or playsuits. It was terrific to sit in the Australian scrub and us all Aussies. At four o'clock we were brought back by a roundabout way so that we could see the town, which was much larger than I thought it. We saw the main places of interest: Vesty's, the meat company, the Yank HQ, bombed fair and square in the middle, the new Darwin Hotel and shops, not open then, and the post office, where a lot of girls had been killed during a raid, as we learnt. The town had been knocked around a bit but that it contained 90 000 troops was staggering. It was planned to take us to dances, the pictures and fights that evening but we pulled out at five o'clock.

The sister reprimanded me, kindly, when the AWAS driver got me back and I was tired. All the boys had behaved themselves while out, though nearly all, like me, were glad to be back on board. We had tea and then I went straight off to sleep before being woken up to receive three telegrams, possibly in answer to mine that morning. They were from Mum and Dad, Auntie Bella Murrell and Stan and Vi Grimson and made me truly happy. A block of chocolate each came round at nine o'clock and off to sleep again. There was no doubt about Darwin, it was a place I would never forget.

Ten hours sleep that night and I awoke next morning still tired and exhausted. It was said that we would be calling in at Brisbane, which I would be pleased to have a look at, this time, I was sure, from the boat.

The extraordinary weather continued for as yet I had not seen anything like a swell or a wave, thank goodness. I hoped that it would keep up. Of course the boys had to have a flutter. We were listening to the sport that afternoon from Melbourne so there was a sweep on the last race. I had to be in it and it cost me a shilling. I gave up trying to follow the Australian Rules football broadcast but it gave the Melbourne boys a thrill.

A War Crimes Questionnaire was distributed to the Queenslanders. It was to be a personally signed statement of crimes witnessed by all POWs, everywhere. We expected it to carry some weight at subsequent trials.

On deck we had the usual shipboard horse races: 'POW out of Singapore by *Oranje*', sort of thing and quite a lot of money passed hands. It was fun and the evening went very quickly.

98 ÷ 7 = 14 lb. / stone

When I woke on the 23rd, straight across from me were the islands in Torres Strait. We had passed Thursday Island earlier, picked up the pilot, and had come to the stretch I was looking forward to, heading south. We were standing off a bit, although I had seen one good old Australian beach, the best in the world. Between Singapore and Darwin we were cut down to an average of 19 knots but that had been stepped up to 23. She could do 34 and coming to Singapore they said that they had averaged 29 knots. I thought that was pretty good for a boat that size, about 26 000 tons. We did see one stretch of coral and more lighthouses on one strip of coast than I had ever seen. We also saw the start of the Great Dividing Range along that stretch of coast, where it came right down to the sea. Coral sand, which had been blown up the hillside, looked for all the world like snow. It was an unusual sight. I had never seen sand so white as in north Queensland.

My X-ray was satisfactory. It was a relief to know that I did not have TB. I was putting on weight too, not fast but steadily, for I weighed in at 103 lbs, (7 stone 5 lbs). But was I cold! I had put on another jersey and even slept in it, under the blanket. Before turning in we were listening to the news and they were still talking about Japanese treatment of prisoners. The previous night they had reported on the murder of our nurses on the beach in Sumatra. That was the most terrible and horrible crime that they committed. Even we seldom talked about it at Changi as it was so disgusting and personal to us all. This was especially so to some like me, who had known them and been under their care, before they were evacuated from the AGH at Katong, just prior to the surrender. By then too we had learnt what had happened to B Force, who had been taken from Changi to Borneo. When the Australian troops landed at Balikpapan, the Japanese forced the prisoners on the road in a march away from the incoming units. The Japanese shot them, consistently and methodically, as any fell back to the rear. Six men were all that were alive out of the 2500, who had gone to Borneo and later started on the march. That news had not yet been reported.

Waking up to the most superb sunrise, still cold, we passed Cairns, which was just in sight and no more. I was surprised at the ruggedness of the coastline and, especially around Cairns, there were deep inlets in folds of the mountains. Later it became more even, although the range was still right down to the sea.

The prices on board were a bit hard to follow. I paid a halfpenny for a nail file and 2s. for a pretty pack of cards, which I thought rather high, and yet cigarettes were 10d. for 20 Craven A or 1s.4d. for a tin of 50 Woodbines.

It was beautiful basking in the sun of an afternoon. Just to lie back and soak it in was something I could take plenty of. In the months in hospital I had lost my old tan but it was coming back again pretty quickly. This without sunburn too, which was actually a thing I had forgotten altogether for I never had a touch of it in all the five years in the army.

It looked as if I would be going to hospital from the boat. It was to build me up a bit, I supposed, before going on leave. I would have preferred to have done the period away from Sydney and then gone home, but apparently it was not to be that way. It was only weight and strength that I had to put back and, maybe, with the strict civilian rationing, I could do better at Yaralla [113th Australian General Hospital at Concord, in Sydney]. Three weeks there would not be so bad as long as I was home for Neil's twenty-first birthday.

We held our presentation and the nurses and staff were really pleased. I did not know if it had been done for them on other trips but it was an old Australian custom and one of the best. The boys bought the usual things, powder, scent sets, compacts and mirrors and I was not sure what was given to the doctors, Andy and the other orderlies. There were the usual speeches and written appreciation. Actually, I did not know who got the greater pleasure, the nurses or ourselves, for it felt good to take part in such a civilised function. So I thought we were the most pleased, pleasing them.

We could not have been far off the South Pole. We passed Townsville during the night, which had put us in the Antarctic Zone already. At eleven o'clock that morning, I and quite a few others, were in bed, under the blanket and wearing a pullover, too. Travelling south, I could feel it getting colder, like going into an iceworks. We were to reach Brisbane next morning but later it was rumoured that we may not go in after all, due to shipping strikes. They did not want the crew to walk off. That would have mucked things up properly. As it was I stocked up with cigarettes, matches and chocolate as I did not know if I would be able to buy any more. I stocked up with all I could get, in case stuff was really as scarce and rationed at home as we had been told.

The sea lost its glassy surface but it was still very calm. The weather we had been having was quite amazing. Until then the rail had never dipped below the horizon at all, all the way from Singapore. Perfection. Cynics as we were, I would bet that it would rain entering Sydney Harbour on Thursday. If only the good weather would last another two days.

A request list for records to be played came up to us and I picked that lovely favourite of mine, Duke Ellington's 'Sophisticated Lady'. Bull, my mate on board, chose another beautifully slow number, 'Blue Prelude'. I had not come across it before but would look it up. I realised that the long-looked-forward-to session of records with Ron and Neil, might only be a matter of days away. With one or two of Bill and Betty Freeman's records, like 'Paradise' and 'Chloe', it would be some session, winding up of course with a dreamy hour of Duke Ellington. I had had my heart set on it for years for I had missed the kind of music I really liked. Jazz was not really the popular music of the day.

Andy, our favourite orderly, took me around the ship and it was very interesting. The engine room was amazing. It was perfectly clean and airy, with three gleaming rows of a dozen big cylinder heads, painted white and azure blue, with polished copper. We went up forward, over the bridge too and it was as if a gale was blowing up there; there was none of the usual activity between boys and girls in secluded nooks on the boat deck. I would have liked to have seen the ship at night, travelling fast, from about 100 yards off. It would be one of the prettiest scenes possible: the greenish wash of the spray, the white floodlit hull with the red crosses, the band of green lights, the lights from the portholes and decks, and all of it surmounted by the huge, brilliantly lit red cross on the funnel. It was a beautiful ship, at night it was like something out of fairyland; just as Edinburgh Castle is always pictured in my mind. Beauty, in all its variety, was what I had missed most, as I thought about it. I supposed that I was a sort of Sentimental Bloke (at least a Ginger Mick) at heart. That was what I wanted for summer: a little beauty, peace and quietness, stillness, softness. Maybe I would be able to relax at times and be a little introspective, a dreamer. There was something missing; maybe a little bit of that too.

Being ahead of schedule, we stood outside Brisbane for some time that night, not moving up the river until after breakfast next morning. It was Wednesday, 26 September. Although not on the same scale as Darwin, as we only went to the outskirts of the town, we were welcomed and cheered as we made our way past ships and factories. We quickly learnt of a tragic accident when someone waving to us fell through a skylight. Another incident, which brought a lump to the throat, involved a lady who came to see if her boy happened to be on board, or get other news of him, only to learn that he had died in Thailand two years earlier. I was really sorry for her but there was to be a lot more of that, I was afraid.

The wharf at Brisbane was pretty deserted. Ambulances and army officials were there and a band played as we drew in, but it was not the same. At Darwin there had been lots of people and plenty of noise. Sydney, too, we thought would be quiet. Many of the boys had already gone through Sydney in Catalinas by then and the splash made by returning troops was dying down. A notice from Adelaide said that too much was being made of the 'lost Eighth' compared with the men from Europe.

More telegrams arrived for me that morning and, best of all, a letter from Mum, the second or third in nearly four years. There seemed to have been a bit of confusion as to our movements after Darwin but it had never been thought that we would go the other way and call at Melbourne first. The very thought made me shiver.

Certainly history had been updated by the war and I was sure that geography was altered too: the Tropic of Capricorn and the Antarctic Circle were one and the same. I was wearing shirt, shorts, pullover, pyjamas, slippers and a dressing gown and the sun was shining brilliantly.

We were on our way again at one o'clock and, running down the coast, we clapped on a bit of speed. We thought that we would do the 500 miles in 20-24 hours, so looked to be in Sydney next day. Maybe I would see Laura (from Kyogle and Mother's long-time friend), who, I had learnt was an ambulance driver. However, we stopped south of Moreton Bay and remained there until next morning. The idea was to time our arrival in Sydney for early Friday morning.

It set me back a bit next morning when I woke up to see that we were going north. We soon swung round though and we were on our final lap. We were to tie up at Dalgety's wharf, which meant that we would be going under the Bridge. After all the skiting I had done about the harbour, I hoped that the ferries and boats would give us a good and noisy welcome to impress the interstate boys.

I heard 'Lily Marlene' for only the second time from the Brisbane wharf. It was most appealing and catching, surely the best song to come out of the war. I learnt that it was a German song, adopted by the 8th Army, and was then the most popular tune around (as 'In the Mood' had been when I left). The only army song that I could get carried away with was 'Waltzing Matilda'. The old 'Matilda' had echoed in many places. Whenever we sung 'Waltzing Matilda', as we did often marching to work, it was always with the feeling that the Japs could go to Hell.

Looking forward, the surge from the bow fascinated me as I felt the ship lift under my feet. For the first time, that afternoon we struck a bit of a swell. I liked to feel that the ship was alive, prepared to take on anything.

We were issued with our accessories to go with the uniform, when we got it; badges, Australia's, medal ribbons and service stripes. Most of the boys had been fitted out with gear but I did not get them at the time as it seemed that I would not be going on leave. The decorations were so much bullshit as far as I was concerned.

Friday, 28th September 1945. As I thought I would, I woke at five o'clock that morning, showered, shaved, and there it was, North Head. Even to me then the Heads looked cold and inhospitable. My God it was freezing cold. We stopped off Clifton Gardens before going up the harbour at eight o'clock. Everyone was so cold it put a chill on us all: 6 a.m. was an unearthly hour to arrive home. We looked to get cheered up later. The ferries were deserted, too, of course. There had been a lot of additions to the scenery that I had noticed already: the RAAF at North Head, new huts and buildings around the place and the boom across from Middle Harbour. The harbour was ruined as far as its scenic beauty was concerned. Later we moved on, under the Bridge and round to Darling Harbour.

Sure enough, Laura was on the wharf, looking ten years younger. I do not know how it was managed but I went down the gangplank on a stretcher and into the first ambulance. Off we set, with Laura beside me, to the AGH at Yaralla. Many people lined the streets all the way out. We were cheered through the city, and all along Parramatta and Concord Roads. Schoolkids were out to see us as we passed. As I went by I gave a special wave to my old primary school at North Strathfield. I had not stopped waving all the way, for, although in the ambulance, they could see me. In fact I was half out of the ambulance with excitement as Laura held tightly on to me. Being in the first ambulance I led the whole cavalcade. I saw Lottie and Betty at Ashfield and Auntie Bella and the neighbours at Croydon, and then, at Concord, I saw Dad coming through the gate. Off the ambulance, I was carried to the ward.

Then Mum, Dad, Neil and Ron arrived. Neil! I thought he was a stranger; I did not know him at all. He was tall and grown up: what happened to the little brother? I could not get over it. Mum, too, had altered, greyer I thought but Dad and Ron were just the same. God, it was good to see them. Between all five of us, later, I did not know what we talked about, except that I learnt that Grandad had died in 1944. Regulations said that only three could visit the hospital that first day, but as many as wanted could have come. Later Auntie Queenie, Auntie Bella, Auntie Lottie and Uncle Jim came to see me and they all said how pleased they were that I was looking better than they thought that I would. Of course I wore plenty of clothes to try and build myself up. But still I *was* improving.

After tea and everyone had gone I got one of the boys to ring Ron up to ask if he and Neil would come out again. They were there in forty minutes. That was not bad going and we had a great yarn until well after 10 p.m. And then did I sleep.

Next day I had my first real bath since 1941 and it was good. It was so peaceful and was just what I could take. The AGH at Concord was a luxurious hospital. From my experience I could only say that absolutely nothing was too good for the sick and wounded and even more especially so for the boys coming back from Japanese camps. It was really wonderful how the doctors and nurses, the VADs [volunteer nursing staff assistants], and the orderlies in the ward understood how we felt. Civvies, anyone not in uniform, except Neil and Ron of course, took some getting used to.

Having to go to Marrickville that afternoon for another X-ray, I rang up to see if the girl/driver could pick Neil up at Croydon on the way. She did not mind so he came, and we went to Marrickville and then back to the hospital at Concord. Just the two of us was what I was wanting and although again I did not know much about what we talked of, it just felt good to be with him. After tea quite a few more came to see me, including Jimmie Calder. I was glad that Ron went early as I could not talk to him freely, with so many there, and neither of us was too happy about it. The cold that I had was getting worse but I hoped that I would not get influenza out of it. The Sydney weather was bloody terrible. I wished that I was in Townesville or up that way.

[That is where my war diaries ended, on 29 September 1945. I had pleurisy and pneumonia.]

15
Repatriation

As wonderful as the AGH at Concord was, the doctors abided by the inviolate, unwritten rule 'tell the patient nothing'. I knew that I was not well. However, shortly after being there I was allowed out for a brief visit home. I was picked up by Stan and Vi Grimson, who lived in Concord, and home we went to 'Ormiston', 12 Wychbury Avenue. Home. A large Australian flag was prominent and I was welcomed by family and neighbours. Neil lent or gave me a leather jacket, which not only kept me warm but hid how thin I was. I could not say that I felt the best, the strain sometimes showed but I was happy to see the house again. Little, if anything had changed, inside or out.

Neil was a technician in training with the telephone branch of the PMG, having completed his examinations. He received his call-up for enlistment in the army in November 1942 but, as he was in a reserved occupation, that was where he stayed. Dad's work still got him and Mum up at some unearthly hour in the morning for he started at 7.30 a.m., hail or shine, no matter where the job was. It was too soon to consider my plans other than for the immediate future, which was to stay in hospital, recover completely and finally get back health and strength. It was nice, for my mother's sake, to have me home and after an hour or so the Grimsons took me back.

My chest and lungs were a mess. I had been developing a heavy cold, immediately after we had passed Townsville and got further south. It was pneumonia by the time I came through the Heads and up the harbour. Standing on deck, getting colder and colder at six o'clock in the morning did not help.

Pneumonia was more lethal then, although the new wonder drugs that had been developed during the war, were providing a comparatively rapid relief and cure. The X-ray results, after the quick trip home, had apparently shown congestion in the lungs and it was not long afterwards that I was having problems breathing and pain in the chest. The constant coughing and heaving up of the mucky stuff did nothing but make things worse.

It was some weeks before I was out of bed again. If the sister did not actually call out 'anyone for morphine', as I seem to remember at night, it was nevertheless pretty freely available for the asking. There was a dedication about army nursing staff that was at times courageous and always kind, self-sacrificing and noble, if one dare use the words for such down-to-earth types. They were all different: some would coyly pass the face cloth to wash under the sheet while others would give the genitals a thorough scrub.

In time I was over the crisis stage and the high temperature came down. The pain in the chest from the inflammation and infection in my lungs continued to stab through me at uncertain intervals for some months, if not years. I was getting better, though. It was at this time that, when sent down again to Marrickville for tests, I went in short shorts, a sports shirt and an American sailor's cap. The military types were a bit startled and I said that they were the only clothes I possessed. Not long after that I received a summer uniform.

The therapists were always keen to ensure that we were occupied. Once able to be up and out of bed, organised activity sessions were all but compulsory. We were taught to hand-weave rugs, make toys, even knit or do tapestry work, anything we fancied doing, which would occupy our hands and minds. It was a very big Repatriation hospital and there were many men from all theatres of the war alongside me in the workshops. When at last we could go for short walks outside, a couple of us would walk along Concord Road and steal flowers from the front gardens of houses on the way back for the nurses. As it got warmer with the approach of summer, during November, we were allowed a little further afield.

I had not got to Neil's twenty-first birthday party after all. A day or so after the quick visit home, at the beginning of October, he had been transferred from Sydney to Lismore and then to Glen Innes. I was not to see him again until December. It was at Glen Innes, on his twenty-first birthday, that he met Joan.

I too was transferred, in November, from Yaralla to the Lady Gowrie Red Cross Home at Gordon. This was a Red Cross convalescent hospital in the old home of Woolcott Forbes, who was one of Australia's more famous and notorious financiers. The most striking feature of the house was the black marble bathroom. We would luxuriate in the massive round bath in Roman splendour. It was a short walk to the station and on days that I got leave I could visit Betty Gibbs at Mosman and again catch up with Curly Hardman and the legendary Beatrice at Bronte. Ron came out to see me at weekends when he could.

It was in the care of the Red Cross that I really started the long haul back to normality. I was fortunate to be picked to go to Gordon for recuperation as my lungs cleared and the pain of the pleurisy eased. There had been no recurrence of the malaria. At Lady Gowrie I was able to get into the table tennis and other exercises. I put on a bit of weight; we could read and lie in the sun; it was dreamworld. The Red Cross organisation did wonders for the returned servicemen, particularly the wounded and sick and again there seemed to be just that little bit extra sympathy and care for those of us who had been prisoners of the Japanese. During the war the Red Cross had made special appeals for money to go to Prisoners of War. Many a street, all around Australia, was a POW support street and although none of the money came directly to us it had financially strengthened the organisation. They gave generously and wisely for our rest and rehabilitation.

It was a warm summer. Neil came back in December on leave and he and Ron would visit me at Gordon. I do not know how much I talked of POW life but it was probably not very much. I liked Beatrice Hardman. Curly was restless but we had days down at Bronte beach with Beatrice's sisters and we would see her in her cake shop. I was not ready for the Robin Hood Hotel at Charing Cross.

A big thrill was catching up with Betty and Bill Freeman and meeting Judith and Jacqueline. It had been kept for me to be Godfather to Jacqueline, which was nice. They were two beautiful little girls. Living at Neutral Bay, I would get there when I could. Croydon was a bit far and awkward to get to with wartime transport and, while I always looked forward to seeing Mum and Dad, it was not, as yet, as often as I had expected.

After a month or so at the Lady Gowrie Home at Gordon I was sent to the Berida Red Cross Home at Bowral. There I did improve. The supervised diet was continued (Wheatharts and All-Bran) and the matron and staff could not have been nicer. I was lucky. There was fresh country air, tennis and table tennis, walks in town, horse riding, sleep and lots of sleep. I was privileged too. Craigieburn, the up-market guesthouse, was out of bounds but an officer (a barrister) and I were allowed to go and were made welcome. That I took one of the Berida nurses to the Saturday night dance with the guests was quite something. The nurse came from a farm between Robertson and Nowra and I was invited there one day. She and her parents put on a real country tea, with roasted corn on the cob, which was grown on the farm. It was a very happy day.

We rode the horses, which the local riding school provided for us, around Bowral and they would walk and trot until they turned for home. Then they would canter all the way back. I had sore legs inside my thighs at first, but quickly toughened up. I loved it. Petrol rationing was still in force so I did not have many visitors but it was just the break, mentally and physically, that I needed. I was there for about eight weeks, all through summer.

At Bowral, with the fresh air, exercise, social environment, diet and care I finally came as near back to normal as I was ever going to get. No man who was on the Burma Railway would, for the rest of his life, be free of the psychological and physical scars, suffered under those conditions.

On the 31 January I was crazy enough to change my name by Deed Poll from Douglas Ormiston McLaggan to Douglas Ormiston. I told Dad, who was a bit surprised to say the least. Anyway I changed it straight back again and it was never registered anywhere. Mad.

All the time I was being checked up on by visiting medical staff and by February 1946 I had reported back to the AGH at Yaralla for a final examination. They were happy, I was happy and I was sent home.

I had been in touch with Geoff Avard's brothers in that first week in February. They came to see me at Croydon. We talked of the conditions on the Burma Railway and I showed them the pages in my diaries where I had referred to Geoff in the good days (The Great World) and the bad days (on the railway). They appreciated my regard for Geoff, that we had done everything we could for him and that I was alongside him when he died after an epic struggle to survive. Later I went to his home at Canterbury, as I had promised Geoff I would, and his sister and the family appreciated that he died amongst mates who admired his courage.

Neil had gone back to the bush and I took the second bedroom. I set it up with a new burgundy carpet and a new Parker chair; my record player and the telephone; Diana [my nude bedside lamp] and photos. It was everything that I had longed for.

Mum and Dad were understanding. I had caused Mum a lot of anguish and concern, Dad too. We settled down and it worked out well. They had supported the 2/30th Christmas Fund for the children of the men away and felt and kept a strong association with the unit. Dad had taken great pleasure in organising a special day at home for the kids.

Pieter 't Hart, my Dutch pilot mate, from Changi days was sent to Bundaberg in January 1946 as part of a recovery and retraining program for air force personnel. He flew down to Sydney for two weeks of leave in February and we had a happy time going around the bright spots of Sydney . . . everything that we had promised ourselves. He stayed at Croydon for the whole of his leave and was always, and has been ever since, very good company.

I was still in the army on extended leave and went into winter uniform. The 2/30th Battalion never reassembled as far as I knew and I never again went under military discipline. Periodically I would report to a camp at Herne Bay and collect my pay and gear. With six service stripes on my sleeve—1941 1942 1943 1944 1945 1946—I was noticeably among the 'old veterans'. I was 24.

I had stopped the correspondence with Jessie Scott. It was as if she was expecting to come to Australia and marry me so I was sorry if at any time I had given her the wrong idea. I saw Betty Gibbs at times but I stopped that too.

> *When you're away, I'm restless, lonely,*
> *Wretched, bored, dejected; only*
> *Here's the rub, my darling dear,*
> *I feel the same when you are here.*
> -Samuel Hoffenstein

That was as I had written to her, which wasn't nice. I got the impression that she had become just too experienced during the war. I was wrong. Curly and I picked up again though, and I would go out to Bronte and help Beatrice settle him down. I was later to get him a salesman's job on good money, so he was happier later through 1946.

Ron, more than anyone, was closest to me. We talked of sailing, of records, of his job and I met Lois. She was interested in many of the same things and also worked at AWA (in the library, among other things translating German references for the technical staff). We got on well.

Petrol, food and clothing ration cards, shortages of just about everything, few and crowded buses, trains and trams, were the order of the day. A lot had been written of hardships at the various battle fronts but obviously it had never been easy at home.

A 'Ligertwood Enquiry' was held into the circumstances of General Gordon Bennett's escape from Singapore. Although the findings were critical and it was considered that his actions were unjustified, it was accepted that his escape was not to secure his own safety and, in fact, that he did bring back valuable information to Australia. The whole enquiry seemed so unnecessary to those of us who were in his 8th Division and we thought that there must have been more personal motives by other generals (possibly Blamey) to cause Bennett to face a public enquiry. Certainly all of us that I knew, had no criticism of his actions.

What was of more interest at the time was Churchill's call for an enquiry into the Singapore surrender. It was reported that 'Australian accounts reflect on the Indian troops and other credible witnesses disparage the Australians'. Everyone was looking for someone else to blame:

- Scapegoat No.1 was the absence of air cover and the failure to ensure an adequate air force in numbers and fire power to combat the Japanese (Zero) planes.

• Scapegoat No. 2 was the Malayan Command, coupled with the competence and leadership of General Percival.

• Scapegoat No. 3 was the Malayan Civil Administration and the Colonial government's lack of cooperation, particularly in communication with the military authorities.

• Scapegoat No. 4 was the ill-trained troops. Newly arrived reinforcements, as well as those who had been there for several years, were hopelessly untrained.— I could go along with that whole heartedly.

The 100 or so Australians who deserted to the wharves of Singapore before the surrender and escaped in boats from the harbour gave the whole nation a bad name. It certainly happened but it had nothing to do with the course of the war.

As a matter of routine at the time I, with others, had applied for the Burma Star, being another campaign ribbon to add to the four, yet to come. It was reported, however, that it had been decided that Australians, held as prisoners of war by the Japanese in Burma, were not eligible and so that ended the matter. We were more interested in the news that ten Japanese officers had been sentenced to death for their part in the Death Marches in Borneo. From these marches only six survived.

A £70 000 000 Security Loan at 2% p.a. for the rehabilitation of Australian service men and women was soon fully subscribed. Apart from the medical aspect of caring for returning personnel, there was a strong drive to fit men and women back into the mainstream of civilian life, according to their needs.

It was at that time that I was discharged from the AIF on 26 March 1946. I had been in uniform from May 1941: four months in the Universal Trainees, a month in the CMF and then 1605 days in the AIF. There were a few days that I would not want to do over again, but never had I regretted volunteering to go overseas on the draft back in 1941. The opportunity had been there, at Liverpool, to get a commission in the Ordnance Corps but it was too much like being a chartered accountant for me at 20 years of age. I stayed with the boys and stuck it out through the worst that could be thrown at me. I had learnt a lot in life that otherwise would never have come my way. I was still designated a corporal on my Certificate of Discharge but in fact I had lost that rank upon arriving in Malaya and was not paid for it. The accumulated and deferred pay of £650 was a substantial amount at the time and went into the bank. The uniform was hung in the cupboard in the hall at home and an era ended.

At the office, all was fine. My job was waiting for me and they were ready when I was. With thoughts of the examination schedule ahead of me to qualify for the Institute of Chartered Accountants in Australia, plans for sailing and building a boat were dropped. My immediate aim was to complete the exams within a couple of years and this involved ten subjects in all, which was no easy task. We were fortunate that the Institute initiated an extra set of exams in April for ex-servicemen, as well as the regular series in October of each year. The standards were still very high and there was a large failure rate in every subject. I was determined to get through as I had lost so much time. For that reason, in addition to the resumption of studies with the Hemingway and Robertson Institute I took on extra coaching from Keith Yorston's Accountancy College. I was lucky; the months of rehabilitation with the Red Cross had promoted the right mental attitude to work and to study consistently.

And so I got started. I was the last back to the office of those of us who had joined up and I had a lot of catching up to do. The government had introduced a Commonwealth Rehabilitation and Training Scheme (CRTS) for employers of ex-servicemen and John Broinowski had taken advantage of it in respect of those of us, audit clerks, who had returned. It meant that he got our services for nothing as we received the minimum wage of £5 per week. He and Lawford Richardson, however, made it clear to us we could go out and take time off as we felt like it if at any time we felt restricted and tied to the desk. It was a good idea and I do not know that any of us really took advantage of it. The important thing was that the offer was there. The wrench from army life to office routine was pretty severe, but I liked audit work and was quickly setting up accounting systems and managing audits around town.

Leaving the army was the end of an important phase of my life. I was often asked how much I regretted being captured and suffering the deprivations of imprisonment, particularly associated with the cruelty of the Japanese Army. The answer was always, and ever has been, that I had no regrets at all. The experience was of enormous benefit to me. I learnt of the kindness in others, the duty to others and above all the need to work in the common interest. Those in Thailand and Burma who thought that they could go it alone, and could do it on their own, died. Died full stop. Those who shared, supported and worked for the group had a very good chance of surviving, and for the most part, lived. It was as simple as that. I was enormously grateful to have learnt the lesson. However, if there was one single factor why I lived, when all around me men died at Tanbaya in Burma, it was because I forced myself to keep eating whatever I could, either from the jungle or the putrid food from the camp kitchens, even if it meant vomiting it up and re-eating it until some stayed down. It was the will to survive. Most of the chronic dysentery patients could not do it and died with nothing in their stomachs.

When asked also, if I hated or hate the Japanese the answer was *Yes*.

In April 1946, reports on Japanese war crimes were tabled in the Federal Parliament. Mistreatment of General Percival and Lieutenant General Wainwright was included among hundreds of cases and it was established that the slavery conditions carried out in some areas by the Japanese were the worst in military history in any country at any time. The slow death of prisoners by overworking them while withdrawing food and clothing had been a deliberate act by the Japanese Commanders. The Sandakan Death Marches in Borneo were indicative of their widespread intention to remove all prisoners in what were to be the closing stages of the war. Even so, the Japanese war crime trials were to be played down compared with those of the Nazi hierarchy in Germany. There was criticism in this regard but few of us at the receiving end really sought vengeance or retribution.

On May 21 the war crimes trial on the Burma Railway opened in Singapore. It went on record that 'Major Mitzutani, with inhuman sadism, wantonly allowed and deliberately inflicted, misery and suffering, which is impossible for us to realise fully and is difficult even to imagine'. I did not have to imagine it at all and they got the story right when it went on to say 'about half the prisoners failed to survive and many lost limbs'. There have been a number of catastrophes in the twentieth century involving the loss of thousands of lives—on the Western Front in World War I; on the Gallipoli peninsula; from the air over Coventry, Dresden and Hiroshima; on the Eastern Front in Russia in the winter of 1943/44; but never before or since, anywhere, has there been the inhuman infliction of misery, pain and degradation as was imposed upon the prisoners and natives by the Japanese engineers in the eight months of building the railway through the Thailand mountains, and the F. Force hospital associated with it, during the monsoon season of 1943. A quick and sudden death is one thing, be it inflicted from the air or by a gun, but eight months of slowly dying and wasting away, surviving only on will-power, is something quite different.

The Charles Cousins case attracted a lot of attention. He had been a popular 2GB wireless announcer in Sydney before the war and in the army, as Major Cousins, he had been with us in Singapore, before being sent to Japan. He was charged with High Treason for the manner of his broadcasts for the Japanese while a prisoner. With Dovey and Barwick for the Crown and Shand for the defence it was high-powered legal representation. Our impression at the time was, that it had not been hard to persuade him to do the broadcasts, but we could not see that he was doing much harm or any good either, while he was in Singapore.

On 16 September 1946 it was quoted from an official Japanese report that, in regard to the Siam/Burma Railway: 'If anyone is to be called to account for the dreadful death rate the responsibility ought to be placed on the then General Sugiyama, who ordered the construction; on the Minister of War who sanctioned the employment of prisoners and on General Terauchi, who was in charge of the construction'. The time limit was blamed for the deaths of 10 000 allied prisoners, pushed to the utmost to keep the work to schedule. That this coincided with the onset of the wet season, which made working conditions inhuman and almost impossible, made no difference to the individual Japanese guards administering the workloads, punishments and the neglect of the sick, in having the railway completed by the set date in October 1943.

The Cousins hearing lasted 24 days in September. Major Charles Cousins was committed for trial on 14 November 1946. Whether or not the Attorney-General would file an indictment for High Treason, arising from the manner of his broadcasts for the Japanese, as a prisoner of war, was not immediately known.

My first exams came up in October and I completed the Intermediate section of the course, at last, by passing the Auditing paper. At the same time I started on the Final syllabus and passed the paper on the Royal Charter, By-Laws and Ethics of the Profession.

Keth and Beatrice Hardman moved to Lilli Pilli; to a house right on the water at the point. With his boat alongside the jetty it was an ideal spot. At times we would go fishing outside, off the North Cronulla sandbanks or inside the waters of Port Hacking. Dad came down too, at times, and enjoyed it.

In November 1946, a week or so before the date set for the Cousins trial, the State Attorney-General announced that he had decided not to file a bill against him. As a consequence the army stated that he would receive an honourable discharge. A very long drawn-out and expensive process had been brought to a conclusion without any real verdict. Generally, those officers who had liaised heavily with the Japanese as prisoners of war were found not to be guilty of breaches of military duty. The allied officers had been responsible for discipline within the prison camps and for getting men out to work in the numbers required. This had been carried out with varying degrees of zealousness. By the end of 1946 the matter was no longer an issue.

As a break after the exams, late in 1946, while Neil was still at Lismore, I got the train up and spent a few days with him. He had met Joan Hayden there on the day of his twenty-first birthday. The companionship with Neil and Joan was a joy but the train trip was sheer hell. Packed both ways, the passengers stood, sat and slept on the seats, the luggage racks and in the corridors. Railway pies and tea at the railway refreshment rooms at the stations were notorious. For what must have been all of eighteen hours, we were shaken, rattled and rolled. It was quite an experience. When the engine went through a tunnel, smoke poured into the carriages as there were always a number of windows that did not get shut in time or at all: thick, black, gritty smoke. The North Coast Mail was quite a train but it was worth it to see Neil.

In January 1947 it was expected that the Tokyo war crimes trials would take longer than the trial of the Nazi leaders at Nuremberg. They had already gone on for 140 days. Colonel Masoa Kusonose, who was charged with the massacre of 140 Australian soldiers and several civilians at Koropa, New Britain, starved and froze himself to death in barracks at the foot of Mount Fujiyama. He had pledged to submit a statement to the War Crimes Tribunal. His troops were alleged to have tethered Australians with fishing lines, in groups of four to six, and then to have bayoneted and shot them in full view of each other. This was exactly the same as had been done to the 2/29th and 2/19th Australian soldiers when captured during the Muar action in Malaya in January 1942

Evidence of both barbaric cruelty and great bravery was heard at the trials. At one hearing evidence was given that a Wallace Lewis of the AIF had confessed to writing on the wall of a prison latrine 'Chin up, be free by Christmas'. The Japanese threatened to punish all the prisoners unless the culprit came forward. Lewis had falsely confessed to save his mates, thinking probably that he would get a beating at the most. He was tortured to death. From New Britain to northern Japan evidence was heard of many such instances and it came to be realised that this was the Imperial Army's standard practice in dealing with prisoners. It was maintained, in defence, that Japan never ratified the Geneva Convention on the treatment of prisoners of war. It was admitted by the Japanese, however, that they had announced, after the war began, that she would abide by the general outline of this convention.

The Australian Legion of Ex-Servicemen demanded that reparations be claimed against the Japanese and that these reparations be used to assist the POWs. Public attention was drawn to the physical and mental breakdown of many former prisoners of war.

From January 1947 I had been before the War Pensions Assessment Tribunal, which operated under the Australian Soldiers' Repatriation Act. Without being overly generous, the Act was administered with apparent fairness and compensated ex-servicemen and women for injuries and ill-health arising from war service. Without claiming for any specific illnesses, I was adjudged to be more or less permanently suffering from the effects of anxiety state, furunculosis and fissure. I would worry about anything or nothing; I would worry if I had nothing to worry about and lived in a constant state of nervous tension. Any break in the skin or pimple would fester and fill with pus. It was Australian government policy to ensure that the standards of nursing, medical and surgical care provided to those in receipt of repatriation benefits be the best in the country. War Service and Veteran's Affairs were administered by a minister in the Federal Government and were rigorously guarded by the RSL (the Returned Soldiers Sailors and Airmen Imperial League of Australia). This had been a strong lobby and active association since the First World War. As and when I required treatment for skin eruptions I attended the outpatient clinic for tropical skin diseases. The consultant psychiatrist saw that I stayed in a state of mind conducive to constant study and achievement.

It was nice at this time to visit Betty and Bill Freeman, especially as the two little girls were so cute. We would play records, with a keen interest in jazz, and tell tall tales of wartime, during which Bill had been a liaison officer with the US forces in Bougainville. The friendship with Betty had gone back to childhood. It was the warmth and affection of friends that was so important to returning servicemen and women in settling back into competitive life during the postwar period.

Dr. William Bye, after his return, became increasingly deaf. He visited the United States but treatment was ineffective and he died at a relatively young age. Blackjack Galleghan was promoted and knighted. Weary Dunlop, who, like Major Hunt and many other doctors, was in charge of a hospital camp on the Burma Railway and later to be active in the rehabilitation of ex-servicemen and women, was to become the public face of heroism among the prisoners of war to the Japanese. Dr Bye, whose responsibilities and field of influence at Changi were so great, never received the recognition due to him; nor did he get to write from his vast experience in tropic diseases under circumstances unique in medical history. His fame rested in the memory of thousands upon thousands of British, Australian and Dutch patients who had been under his care as a doctor and Head of Changi Hospital. The health and survival of many more thousands was due to the health care programs, the ingenuity and the inventiveness shown under his supervision in Singapore. Such is the fickle fate of fame and fortune as to who enters history. Billy Bye was a great man.

I failed my Bankruptcy Law examination in April 1947. It was a subject with which I was having a great deal of difficulty, but I would sit for it again later in the year. I was not finding it easy to concentrate on my studies. While the determination was there, and due time was devoted to the lessons and progress exercises, there was an inability to absorb the Law subjects to the extent that I would have liked. Law was a difficult subject at any time and the method of study with the Hemingway and Robertson Institute of setting my own pace and submitting the progress exercises from the text books supplied was not working. There was still a tension and anxiety, hung over from the war years, which did not make for a relaxed frame of mind. There was no way however, that I would give up.

The war crimes trials still went on. At Rabaul, evidence was given on cannibalism and the mutilation of Australians. A Japanese General was sentenced to life imprisonment for such atrocities committed by his subordinates. At the 1947 Anzac Day march in Sydney, though, Charles Cousins led the 2/19th A.I.F Battalion at the insistence of the men in his unit. We still failed to see that he had acted wrongly enough to justify the army's harassing him for over twelve months.

In October I passed the Bankruptcy Law and Practice examination. I was happy to have done so and it gave me a great deal of confidence. In fact it was to be a turning point in my studies and I progressed much more quickly from then on. I re-enrolled for additional study with Keith Yorston, who ran the Australian Accountancy College and who had written the definitive text book on Company Law (Yorston, Smyth and Brown). The extra tuition from Mr Brown rejuvenated my whole approach to study. It was all coming good in mind and body. Neil was up in Lismore at the time of the big floods up there, I would go up in the train and we stayed in touch

In Tokyo ex-premier Tojo, at the hearings of the International Military Tribunal, accepted responsibility for Japan's decision to fight and the acts that followed it. He maintained that the Allies provoked Japan into a war of self-defence forcing her to attack Pearl Harbor on 7 December 1941. He accepted 'administrative responsibility' for the treatment of prisoners of war on the Burma-Siam death railway and elsewhere. He remarked that the Japanese conception of prisoners of war was different to the American and European one, as Japan, since ancient times, had deemed it most degrading to be taken a prisoner. Tojo faced charges ranging from murder to having waged aggressive war.

1947 and 1948 were momentous years, events which affected everyone in the world, present and future.

The more formalised study program paid off in my April Law examinations and I passed the Final subjects in Federal Income Tax Law and Practice, Banking and Exchange, Principles of Company Law and Mercantile Law.

Certainly the events of the past and their influence on my mind and attitude were receding. I still attended upon the Repatriation Psychologist at regular if infrequent intervals, but I was determined to concentrate on my studies, forbearing girlfriends, cars and other distractions.

My time was largely spent in work at the office and study at home, at Yorston's Accountancy College and at the Public Library. Neil was at Taree and Kempsey and Ron and I still had our jazz sessions and a growing record collection. Mainly, though, my leisure hours were devoted to study. I passed Auditing and Business Investigations, which was a major paper of the Institute and also Rights and Duties of Executors and Trustees under Wills and Receivers together with Law of Arbitration and Awards. It was a highly satisfactory conclusion to the study year and left only the Final Accounting papers to do. I set myself a goal to sit for the April 1949 examinations and to do this, enrolled with Ron Irish's York Accountancy College for additional study to the Hemingway and Robertson course. It was to be a heavily concentrated program of six months duration.

The International Tribunal found the 25 Japanese leaders on trial in Tokyo guilty of war crimes. Hedeiko Tojo and six others were sentenced to be hanged, including General Doihara, a commander in Singapore in 1944/45, and Seishiro Itagaki, commander in Malaya in 1945. Tojo was duly hanged on 23 December 1948.

April 1949 was an important month for me, sitting for my Final Accounting examinations. They were made up of three papers over three days, two of four hours and one of three hours. The papers covered Advanced Accounting including Partnerships, Executors, Factory and Cost Accounts and had pass mark of 70%. I had been doing trial runs from previous years and had a strong feeling that there would be a question on Consequential Loss/Loss of Profits Insurance. On the first day I read all my exercises on the subject going into town by train and into Paddington by tram, only putting them aside on entering Paddington Town Hall. I turned my exam paper over when told we could start and there, standing out with 35% of the marks for that day, was a major question on accounting for Loss of Profits. I sailed into it and over the next two days my six months of study came good and I was confident of passing. The results came out later and I had obtained first place in Australia for my Final Accounting papers. I was happy to have done so well and to have achieved success in my aim to qualify as a Chartered Accountant (not in practice) as we were then designated. It gave me enormous confidence in myself, not only in the field of business but socially as well. I felt that I could take a leadership position in management and better assist others alongside me in the workplace. I went on to take senior accounting positions, for the most part as a finance director in commerce and industry, having also gained the Australian Institute of Management Medal for the highest marks in the examinations in Advanced Management studies at the Sydney Technical College.

It had been all uphill since November 1943, in Burma. I felt that the long years of recovery and rehabilitation since being on the Burma Railway were behind me, if the ongoing effects were not altogether eliminated. It was a time for looking forward with no regrets or recriminations for the war years. I had my parents, and Neil and Ron, with whom I felt a strong bond of friendship. For what more could I ask? I could never forgive the Japanese for their disregard of simple human values and their cruelty, although I felt richer for the experience. What I had lost in eight years of war and rehabilitation, I felt that it had been made up for in confirming in me an appreciation of the inherent good in people and the essential principles of working in the common interest. It was to last me all my life.

Appendix

The following is a list of mates and others who I met up with in the army and whose names I recorded in my diaries at the time. Many of these men would have had experiences similar to my own.

Name	Unit	Home	Place of Acquaintance
Ted Brown	AAOC (M)	-	Liverpool 5 Company
Jim Flaherty	"	-	"
Don Murty	"	-	F Company
Col Allman	"	-	HQBOD
Jeff Fry	"	-	"
Roy Clarke	"	-	"
Arch Brebant	"	-	Orderly Room
Lietenant Gilbert	"	-	"
W.O. Emery	"	-	"
Jim Carr	"	-	Officers' Mess
Peter Lennon	"	-	Liverpool F Company
Doug Morris	AAOC	-	Depot
George Smith	"	-	"
Cliff Greenwood	"	-	"
Rich Griffiths-Jones	"	-	"
'Mac' McGregor	"	-	Draft
Tony Anthony	"	-	"
Les Pascoe	"	-	"
'China' Hall	"	-	Depot
Wal Davis	"	-	Chilwell School
Jack Cameron	"	-	"
Norm Garland	2/30th	Chatswood, Syd	*Aquitania* 5th Rios
Pat Smythe	"	NSW	"
Norm Waugh	"	NSW	"
Don West	"	Bondi, Syd	"
Les Cook	"	Alexandria, Syd	"
'Eat your Biscuit' Hickey	"	Qld	"
Frank Hopkins	2/29th	Leichhardt, Syd	"
'Con' Edwards	"	Brisbane, Qld	"
Roy Willis	2 Esch	Guildford, Syd	"
'Lofty' Hart	2/3 MT	-	"
'Snowy' Pannowitz	"	-	"
Alan Rainbow	2/30th	Bondi, Syd	"
George Brent	"	NSW	"
'Dicko' Dickenson	"	Redfern, NSW	"
Bob Watson	"	Mackay, Qld	"

Name	Unit	Home	Place of Acquaintance
F.W.Bushby	2/30th	-	*Aquitania* 5th Rios
Ray Simmons (Lt)	"	Como, Syd	"
Geo Winchester (Lt)	"	Chatswood, Syd	"
'Kel' Kelly	2/29th	NSW	"
'Scotty' Anderson	"	Grafton, NSW	"
'Polly' Polyglaise	"	Willoughby, NSW	"
'Hoot' Gibson	"	Parramatta, Syd	"
Rod Mercer	AAOC	Brisbane, Qld	"
Dan Barley	2/26th	Qld	"
'Mac' McLean (Lt)	2/30th	Java NEI	"
'Youngie' Young	2/29th	Pyrmont, Syd	Johore 1 sec 13
Brian Dobson	"	Newcastle, NSW	"
Arthur Reeves	"	Carlton, Syd	"
Alan Ralph	"	Ararat, Vic	"
Dave Holden Vic	"	-	"
Don Trewin (Lt)	"	Tallygaroopna, Vic	13 Platoon
'Bluey' Finn	"	Scotsburn, Vic	Singapore 1 sec 13 pl
'Bluey' Wade	"	Mackay, Qld	"
Burnie Smith	AAOC	Mackay, Qld	Stores
'Silver' Trivethick	2/29th	Vic	Conv Depot AGH Katong
'Bully' Bullen	2/30th	NSW	Great World Singapore
'Snowy' Hutton	"	Annandale, Syd	"
'Curly' Hardman	"	Clovelly, Syd	"
Maurrie Ferry	"	Kensington, Syd	"
Fred Greenwood	"	Clovelly, Syd	"
'Doc' Wilson	"	Rose Bay, Syd	"
Roy Poy	2/29th	Albury, NSW	"
Eric Mark	"	Linton, Vic	"
'Codger' Forewell	"	Brisbane, Qld	"
Ted Stocker	"	Charters Towers, Qld	"
Bill Greenland	"	Newtown, Syd	"
'Curly' Avard	"	Canterbury, Syd	"
'Tich' Martin	2/29th	Parkdale, Mel	"
George Hancock	"	Merino, Vic	"
Dick Trew	"	North Melbourne, Vic	"
Jimmie Foster	"	South Yarra, Mel	"
Bill Rodger	"	Brisbane,Qld	"
Jack Huggins	"	Townsville, Qld	"
Vern Jurgens	"	Merinda, Qld	"
Eric Warrener	"	Ayr, Qld	"
Harry and Vince Thompson	"	Monto, Qld	"
Rex Mason (Lt)	"	Mildura, Vic	"
'Mrs' Gerardy	"	Ipswich, Qld	"
'Sandy' Saunders	"	Jeparit, Vic	"

Name	Unit	Home	Place of Acquaintance
Norm Allen	2/30th	Cooma, NSW	Great World Singapore
Eric 'Padre' Wills	"	Inverell, NSW	"
Taffy Phillips	"	c/- British Australian Society	
Joe Pearce	"	Ashbury, Syd	"
Syd Grounds	"	St Peters, Syd	"
Syd Conin	"	Chatswood, Syd	"
Athol Hyde-Bates	"	W.D. & H.O.Wills	"
Dick Simmons	"	Pymble, Syd	"
Gerry, Mick and Bill Bailey	"	Bellingen, NSW	"
Stan Arneil (Sgt)	"	Marcus Clarke	"
Rex Rowe (Sgt)	"	Clerk, Petty Sessions	"
Tom Corcoran (Sgt)	2/26th	Townsville, Qld	"
Jack Partridge	2/29th	Beaufort, Vic	"
Jimmie Moore	"	Cairns, Qld	"
Cyril Batty	"	Copmanhurst, NSW	"
Phil Young	"	Mt Tamborine, Qld	"
Noel Robins (Sgt)	2/20th	Kings Cross, Syd	Canteen
'Bluey' Gore	2/29th	Mackay, Qld	Transport
'Curly' Wright	2/30th	NSW	Q Store
Clem Everingham	2/30th	NSW	Great World Singapore
'Mac' Mackenzie	"	Narrandera, NSW	"
Clarrie Rettke	"	West Wyalong, NSW	"
Jack Cox	2/29th	NSW	"
Ron Nokes	29 Batt	Birmingham, Eng	"
'Twink' Wintle	6 HHA	Somerset, Eng	"
'Tich' Cotton	RA	North Hants, Eng	"
Harold Wright	55/LRegt	Leicester, Eng	"
Bobbie Logan	155 Field Rgt	Glasgow, Sco	"
Arnie Trustler	2/30th	Bondi, NSW	"
Bob Fordeham	2/29th	NSW	River Valley Road
Harry Griffin	"	North Melbourne	"
George Reeves	"	Auburn, Syd	"
'Curly' Magrath	"	Nth Fitzroy, Mel	"
'Dizzy' Dean	"	Springvale, Vic	"
Bob Wonson	2/20th	Newcastle, NSW	"
Cedric Ewing	"	Chatswood, Syd	"
Dave Anderson	2/29th	Bondi, Syd	"
Steve Allidice (Sgt)	2/30th	Ryde, Syd	"
'Darky' Ryan	"	Redfern, Syd	"
Jack Cresdee	2/29th	Chatswood, Syd	Changi Selarang
'Paddy' O'Toole	"	Richmond, Mel	"
Dave Anderson	"	Bondi, Syd	"
Les Waldran	"	Somerville, Vic	"
'Sparrow' Launder	"	Horsham, Vic	"

Name	Unit	Home	Place of Acquaintance
Jack Haig	2/29th	Coberg, Vic	Changi Selarang
Les Whisker	"	Yarrable, Vic	"
'Yank' Curtis	"	Ravenshoe, Qld	"
Freddie Midina	"	Port Melbourne, Vic	"
Dick Reynolds	"	Mildura, Vic	"
Len Stewart	"	Melbourne Herald	"
Harry Wilson	"	Footscray, Mel	"
Doug Johnson	8 Div Sigs	Ducon Condensers	"
'Mac' McEvoy	"	Ashfield, Syd	"
Jack Clune	2/30th	Taree, NSW	"
George Smith	"	NSW	"
Sammy Dobson	"	Sydney	"
Des Gee	"	Newport, Syd	"
Mark Wilson	"	Tuggerah, NSW	"
'Nugget' Crummy	"	Casino, NSW	"
Harry Abrahams	"	Waterloo, Syd	"
Ernie Parkes	"	Kogarah, Syd	"
Jack Hayden (Sgt)	2/29th	Footscray, Mel	"
Doug Mason	"	Vic	"
'Dunk' Evans	"	Melbourne	"
Reg Wharton	"	Cheltenham, Mel	Garden Party
'Duver' Dunne	"	Port Melbourne, Vic	"
Maurrie Drennan	2/4 MGs	Perth, WA	22/27Bde MIR
Bill Dunne	2/29th	Vic	"
Dave Lloyd (Capt)	"	Hunters Hill, Syd	In transit Sing/Thailand
Timmy Nagle	"	Collingwood, Mel	"
Col McDonald	"	Kew, Mel	"
Cyril Murphy	"	North Fitzroy, Mel	"
Pat Brisling	8 Div HQ	Croydon, Syd	Thailand Road Camp
Jack Lonsdale	2/29th	Cheltenham, Mel	"
'Scobie' Brown	2/30th	Cobar, NSW	Neike
Graham Bridgewater	"	Willoughby, Syd	"
Tommy Nixon	"	Kyogle, NSW	"
Ted Bourke	2/2 MAG	Randwick, Syd	"
Tommy Morrison	AAOC	Bellevue Hill, Syd	"
'Jock' Burse	288 Field Engs RE	Aberdeen, Sco	"
Gordon Mouat	2/29th	Gordonvale, Mel	In transit Thai/Burma
'Boonga' Atkins	2/26th	Innisfail, Qld	Burma, 50km Camp
Bob Parker	RAOC	Motherwell, Sco	"
J.V.Mackie	3 Ind Sigs	Glasgow, Sco	Burma, Tanbaya
Padre Duckworth	Cambridge Regt	Hull, Eng	"
'Snowy' Miles	2/26th	Queenslopes, Bri	Changi Hospital
J.French	2/10th Fld Arty	Brisbane	"
Ernie Kirkeguard	2/29th	Goondiwindi, Qld	Changi Selarang

Name	Unit	Home	Place of Acquaintance
Alf Ainlie	2/29th	Carlton, Mel	Changi Selarang
'Bluey' Haerloch	"	Dalby, Qld	Changi PWD Lines
'Curly' Blomfield	2/30th	Miranda, NSW	Changi Gaol Camp
Jack Stuart	"	Maroubra, Syd	"
Russ Mackie	2/30th	Lismore, NSW	"
Fred Abbotts	"	Dorrigo, NSW	"
Jack Moloney	"	Concord, Syd	"
'Scotty' Wallace	"	Kempsey, NSW	"
Peter Mason	"	Stewarts Creek, NSW	"
Doug Tait	"	Mummulgum, NSW	"
Kevin Maclean	"	Lismore, NSW	"
Ernie Willis	"	Parkes, NSW	"
Ron Harris	"	Lismore, NSW	"
Keith Richardson	"	Lismore, NSW	"
Joe Geoghagen	"	Bomaderry, NSW	"
Guy Hogben	"	Wollongong, NSW	"
Darby Young	"	Wauchope, NSW	"
Eric Stone	"	Paddington, Syd	"
F.Orth	2/1 Fort Engrs	Ashfield, Syd	"
Bill Innes	"	Nth Bondi, Syd	Drome Party
Pieter 't Hart	NEI Air Force	Soekaboemi, Java	"
'Lex' Noyon	NEI	Bandoeng, Java	"
Hilton Miles	2/15 Fld Regt	Haberfield, Syd	Hospital

*

Honour Roll of men I knew. In order of learning of their death.

Name	Unit	Place of Acquaintance	Died
Les Cook	2/30th	Dubbo 5th Rios	Singapore Island
Kel Kelly	"	Aquitania	"
Alan Rainbow	"	"	"
Pete Lennon	2/19th	Liverpool AOC	"
Alan Newman	2/29th	Johore	Changi
Tich O'Shea	"	Changi Concert	Thailand
Clem Everingham	2/30th	Great World/Singapore	"
Billy Keighly	"	"	"
Alex Cameron	2/29th	Selarang/Changi	"
Frank Nokes	2/30th	Great World/Singapore	"
'Goldy' Golding	"	"	"
Dick Lumby	"	Changi/football team	"
Ivan Bancroft	"	Great World/Singapore	"
Jack Carroll	"	Changi/football team	"
Stan Marsh	"	Changi Kitchen	"
Snowy Machin	2/29th	*Aquitania* 5th Rios 2/30th	"
Ben McAllman	"	River Valley Road	"
Lieutenant Downes	2/6 RE	Neike River Thailand	"
Bill Reeves	2/30th	Great World/Singapore	"
'Sailor' Finn	2/29th	2 Working Camp Thailand	"
Leo Styles	"	In transit Singapore/Thailand	"
'Kanga' Gray	"	2 Working Camp Thailand	"
Bill Scholfield	"	"	"
Les Webster	"	Selarang/Changi	"
Tom Corcoran	"	Great World/Singapore	"
Ted Bourke	2/2 MAG	Neike River Thailand	"
'Curly' Avard	2/29th	Great World/Singapore	"
Bob McIntyre	"	Selarang/Changi	"
Wally Bourke	"	5 Camp Thailand	Tanbaya/Burma
'Mul' Mulholland	2/20th	Liverpool/Changi	Thailand
Maxie Cook	2/30th	Great World/Singapore	"
Bobby Bee	"	River Valley Road	"
'Taffy' Hill	8 Div Prov	Neike River Thailand	"
Sid Tucker	2/30th	Great World/Singapore	"
Walter Renison	"	Neike River Thailand	Tanbaya, Burma
Bruce Johnson	"	Selarang/Changi	Thailand
'Pop' Schumaker	2/29th	Great World/Singapore	"
'Podge' Graham	"	Selarang/Changi	Tanbaya, Burma
Steve Porter	"	Great World/Singapore	Thailand
Maurrie Senior	CMP (Brit)	50km Camp Burma	Tanbaya, Burma
Bill Cumberland	2/30th	Great World/Singapore	Thailand
Jim Lark	8 Div Post	Neike River Thailand	Tanbaya, Burma

Name	Unit	Place of Acquaintance	Died
Jack Hayden	2/29th	Selarang/Changi	Tanbaya, Burma
Tom Simpson	"	Great World/Singapore	Thailand
Frank Hopkins	"	Aquitania 5 Rios 2/30th	Tanbaya, Burma
Jim Clarke	6 Fld Co. RAE	Neike River Camp	Thalland
Keith Murchison	2/29th	Selarang/Changi	Tanbaya, Burma
Syd Conen	2/30th	Great World/Singapore	Thailand
Jerry Gardner	2/29th	Selarang/Changi	Tanbaya, Burma
Len Barry	"	Selarang/Changi	Thailand
Alan Ralph	"	Singapore Island	"
Fred Ireland	"	Selarang/Changi	"
Pat Smythe	"	Dubbo 5th Rios 2/30th	"
Vern Jurgens	2/29th	Great World/Singapore	Thailand
'Jacko' Jackson	"	Selarang/Changi	"
Les Thornell	"	"	"
'Tich' Martin	"	Great World/Singapore	"
Harry Griffin	"	Selarang/Changi	"
Harry Frost	"	"	"
Jack Bartlett	2/30th	Great World/Singapore	"
'Scotty' Davison	"	"	"
Mick Walsh	2/29th	Selarang/Changi	"
'Dicko' Dickson	2/10 RAE	Neike River Camp	Changi
'Fatty' Palmer	2/29th	Changi two-up school	"
Frank Tuckey	2/30th	Great World/Singapore	"
Norm Waugh	"	Dubbo 5th Rios 2/30th	Thailand
Jim Dalton	SFV	Neike River Thailand	Tanbaya, Burma
Jim Youngalaui	2/10 RAE	Tanbaya Burma	"
Wally Mason	2/30th	Changi Hospital	Changi
Jim Walsh	"	Great World/Singapore	"
Tim Nagle	2/29th	In transit Sing/Thai	Thailand
'Bluey Boulton'	"	Selarang/Changi	"
Les Marshall	2/30th	River Valley Road	Changi
Bill Bailey	"	"	"
Les Garland	"	Great World/Singapore	"
'Taffy' Phillips	"	"	"
Bobby Logan	55th Fld Rgt	Great World/Singapore	Kranji

*

Index of Names

*